Lois

on the

Loose

THOMAS DUNNE BOOKS / St. Martin's Press ᴍ New York

Lois

on the

Loose

One Woman, One Motorcycle,
20,000 Miles Across the Americas

Lois Pryce

THOMAS DUNNE BOOKS.
An imprint of St. Martin's Press.

www.thomasdunnebooks.com
www.stmartins.com

Book design by Susan Walsh

LIBRARY OF CONGRESS CATALOGING-IN-PUBLICATION DATA

Pryce, Lois.
    Lois on the loose : one woman, one motorcycle, 20,000 miles across the
americas / Lois Pryce.—1st ed.
        p.   cm.
    ISBN-13: 978-0-312-35221-9
    ISBN-10: 0-312-35221-2
    1. Pryce, Lois—Travel—America.   2. Motorcycle touring—America.
3. America—Description and travel.   I. Title.

G465.P79   2007
917.01'54—dc22

                                                                2006051064

First Edition: March 2007

10 9 8 7 6 5 4 3 2 1

To Austin, my real-life superhero

Acknowledgments

My trip was made a whole lot more fun and successful, thanks to the generosity and kindness of many wonderful people, both back home and on the road. I hope I get the opportunity to return all these favours one day.

At Home

Infinite gratitude and love to Austin for his unstinting support during the trip and the writing of this book, Nat Pryce for hours of excellent webmastery, without which this book would never have happened, Mum for providing the predictable parental assistance in Mexico! Gerald Vince for the welding and luggage prep, Richard Baird (RIP) for crate-building assistance, Sarah Crofts for her wise words, Tiffany Coates for advice and tips from the road, Chris Scott for publishing my stories in the *Adventure Motorcycling Handbook* (and for writing it in the first place), Angie and Trundle for last minute tinkering, and to Lisa Hall for her warm welcome home.

On the Road . . . in order of appearance

Mike at Delta Air Cargo in Anchorage for going the extra air-mile, Gordy and Lee Woodley for taking me in off the street, Vito and Heather for their heartwarming hospitality, Grant and Susan Johnson for tea, advice and for creating www.horizonsunlimited.com, which has helped many a globe-trotting biker, Yvonne Regehr for taking me trail riding in BC, Karen and Rob for showing me a good time in Vancouver, Susan Barber for helping me after I fought the law (and the law won), BSA Barb and Rory for a great welcome to America, Eric and Erin Sowle for a week of fun, trail riding and crazy golf, John in Portland for helping with the kickstart, Jerry and Nancy for some good ol' American hospitality, Rick and Erica for a wonderful night in their special houseboat, Kaaren and Toby Boothroyd for Californian luxury and goat-wrangling, Johnny and Lynn for good times in Oakland and for getting this whole book thing rolling, Eli and Rob for providing a corner of England in SF, Pete and Melissa for a great night out and top yarns, Karen and Lola for a wild night on the town (hope you haven't lost your car again), Marc and Darlene for being old friends amongst strangers, Linda and Ted Lazarus for their spectacular hosting in the lap of luxury, Nino, Leo and Helen for motorcycle maintenance and real tea, Christine and Brian for hospitality, a haircut and moral support at the tattoo shop, Joe and Lara for putting up with me for so long, for letting me change tyres in the living room and a million other things, Rachel Delavaud for turning up when she did and being a top travelling companion, Juan Carlos Ibarra for calmness and civility in a strange land, Aiza Gomez for giving me a pair of socks, Edgardo Loo Berroa for kidnapping me in the nicest possible way, Carolina in Bogotá for taking me in at a moment's notice, Ricardo Rocco for livening up the proceedings and for being an all-round good guy, Sjaak for passing on his tips from the road, Willem, Zoila, Jessica, Johan and Maurets in Cuenca who welcomed me into their home on the spur of the moment, Jeffrey Powers for all his help in Cusco getting my bike sorted, Dieter for being a nice Swiss chap, Robb for helping sort out a horrible mess, Frank and Ann likewise and beyond, Ziggy for coming to the rescue, and finally, to all the people who sent me words of encouragement and offers of hospitality while I was on the road, it really made a difference. Oh yes, and another extra thanks to Rachel, as I know how much she enjoys these lists.

The Book

Much gratitude is due to my super-agent, Faye Bender, for her perseverance, professionalism and encouragement, to the unstoppable Jenny Meyer for getting this book published in various corners of the world, to my editor, Peter Joseph, at St. Martin's Press for his heartening enthusiasm, good humour and excellent attention to detail, to Charlie Boston and Simon Radford for their sanity-saving office space and generosity, and to Simon Kennedy for his sage editorial advice.

One

There's a much quoted line from *Zen and the Art of Motorcycle Maintenance* that travelling by car is like watching a movie, but riding a motorcycle is like being in one. As I rode my bike onto a home-bound ferry after a fortnight's holiday in France, I pondered this idea and decided it was wrong. Motorcycling was much, much better.

But sadly, a return ferry journey is never as exciting as the outbound voyage. Rolling off a boat on a motorcycle into a foreign land is one of the most exciting experiences I know. No matter where it is in the world: freewheeling down the ramp, the metallic clank that marks your arrival, and your first glimpse of a strange land. Everything looks different, sounds different, even smells different—you feel different.

Even as a child I was a fully signed-up disciple of Robert Louis Stevenson's famous theory 'It is better to travel hopefully than to arrive.' I was never the one in the backseat shouting, 'Are we nearly there yet?' or if I was, it was in the hope that the answer would be a reassuring no. Family holidays were always a source of thrills and anticipation—until we rolled up to our destination. I didn't actually want to *get* to the holiday cottage in Devon, or the campsite in Cornwall, or wherever we were heading that summer. I wanted to keep moving, to stare out the car window and watch the scenery roll past, to read the town names and road signs, and gaze at the houses and shops, and the people that lived in these mysterious places that I would never know.

The Pride of Portsmouth gave a mournful hoot as she chugged out of the Le Havre docks into a reliably grey English Channel. In just a few hours I would be pounding the familiar tarmac of the M3 back to London. I looked at my watch and noted that at exactly this time tomorrow I would be clocking in at the office again, sitting at my desk, plowing through two weeks' worth of yellow Post-it notes and pointless memos.

How can I hold on to that just-rolled-off-the-ferry feeling? I wondered. How can I make it last? It was time to come up with an answer.

Returning to work after a holiday is rarely a pleasant experience, but it can be made that little bit more bearable if something interesting, or preferably gossip-worthy, has happened in your absence. On this occasion the heart-sinking tedium of once again clocking in at my BBC job was only slightly redeemed by the excitement of an office 'refurb,' or paint job to you and me. Where once there was grey, now there was beige. There was even a celebratory memo about it on my desk—apparently the colour was not beige, but taupe. All part of the 'fresh contemporary feel' that was being 'rolled out across the corporation.' It translated roughly as, 'Forget your bonus, we've spent it on paint. The Management.' Other than that, things seemed pretty much the same; the office plants were still slowly dying, or fake—a description that could be applied to most of the staff too.

This wasn't what I was after; I'd set my hopes on the news of an office affair, a dramatic resignation or at least a good old-fashioned sacking in which the employee in question is escorted off the premises. Why do they do that? I wondered idly, as I trudged up the stairs. Maybe in case the redundant worker freaks out in the lobby and makes a violent lunge at the Investors in People award? The funny thing was, I had arrived to work early. That never happened. I prided myself on typing in my password as the computer clock flicked from 8.59 to 9.00. I've always been suspicious of people who claim to like arriving at work with time to spare. Don't they have a bed to lie in? At this deathly hour the only other living thing in the office was my boss, and he barely fit that description. We greeted each other with our customary bored good mornings and our mutually resentful look that said, 'Oh Christ, do I really have to spend another day with *you*?' Like an unhappy marriage, we were tired of saying good morning every bad morning, tired of looking at each other every day, and tired of travelling to this air-conditioned, jargon-infested institution five days a week. It was a painful ritual but fortunately today he was on the phone, which rendered unnecessary any of that excruciating how-was-your-holiday chitchat.

Since the latest restructuring (a popular hobby of the top bods) he had lost his private office but gained a company car; however, this juggling of status symbols meant that the poor chap was now forced to work amongst his open-plan minions. He was always in the office before anyone else, although this was less to do with professional ambition and more to do with avoiding his wife, his two kids and his endless roll call of home improvements back in the suburbs. Unfortunately, his humbling decampment to the open-plan area, known fondly as the Pigpen, silenced us music-loving, banter-hungry worker ants, resulting in a steep rise in the use of the computer system's instant-messaging facility.

Since relocating to the Pigpen, things had gone from bad to worse for the Boss. His recent fortieth birthday had coincided with his self-conscious arrival at work one day sporting an overgelled spiky hairdo, and his efforts to be 'down with the kids' now included rampant overuse of the word 'street' as an adjective. A brief stint in a punk band in the late seventies gave him, or so he thought, the credentials to talk about 'being on the road', or to suddenly crank up the stereo upon hearing a classic track from his golden era and shout about 'fighting the punk rock wars.' The instant-messaging service would regularly crash under the strain.

This morning I'd caught him on the hop. My premature arrival was not part of his plan and he was clearly in the early throes of a phone call that he'd planned on making alone. The halcyon days of scrapping with skinheads on the Kings Road were a long forgotten memory today—he had some serious grown-up issues to sort out before the onset of the working day. I hid behind my monitor and busied myself with the tedious undressing that we motorcyclists must endure for our fun. Through the rustle of nylon and creak of leather I couldn't help but catch his sotto voce estuary English bristling with consumer rage: 'Is that MFI Basildon branch? My name is Mr. Tyler and I ordered a bathroom suite from you three weeks ago.'

Pause. Sigh.

'Yes, yes, that's right, the Tuscany Moderna in peach coral. Well, yes, it did turn up on Saturday, but the toilet seat is missing.'

I could hear the insincere crackle of MFI Basildon switching to auto-apology mode.

'Well, yes, whatever . . .'

Interrupted by more Essex crackle.

'Frankly, mate, I don't care whose fault it is, I just want you to—'

Loud impatient sigh.

Voice rising with sheer frustration: 'Look! All I want to know is . . . WHEN . . . CAN . . . YOU . . . DELIVER . . . MY . . . TOILET . . . SEAT?'

I was pretending not to listen but wishing one of my Pigpen in-mates were here to share the moment. Strangely, it was at this point that the banality of the situation hit me like a blow in the stomach and suddenly it wasn't funny anymore. It was just utterly depressing. What evil mind invented the open-plan office, where we all sit in neat little rows, breathing recycled air, staring at flickering images while salaciously channel-hopping between our colleagues' private lives? Not to mention the regimented plastic ferns, the sandpaper-grade industrial carpet, the view of the gridlocked A40 flyover, the infernal memos laced with newspeak, the polystyrene cups. And this is the Music Department, a supposedly 'creative' environment! A panicky feeling rose up inside me. 'I've got to get out of here before I turn into one of those people that brings their own mug into work and then writes a complaining e-mail to all staff if anyone else uses it,' I thought. Or maybe I said it out loud.

The Boss was off the phone now and avoiding eye contact.

'How was your holiday?' he said.

'Yeah, great, thanks.' Both of us pretending that I hadn't witnessed him losing his rag over a low-end bathroom fitting.

That about dried up the conversation so I offered him a cup of tea and he produced a mug decorated with a football team's logo from his desk drawer. The mere whiff of a teabag had its usual effect: the door of our Big Boss's office flew open and from behind it appeared our leader, 'SuperBri,' brandishing a mug sporting rival team colours and issuing commands to me regarding artificial sweeteners while he pranced around in front of Mr. Tyler chanting something along the lines of, 'Three nil, three nil . . . you're going down!' I skulked off to the canteen to the sound of my boss's fawning football banter.

Of course, SuperBri didn't know he was called SuperBri. His real name was Brian Simmons, but many years ago in a previous job the following, and now legendary, phone call to an Important Industry Figure had been overheard:

Feet up on the desk, bellowing into the phone: 'Hey, mate! Iiiii-iiiiii'ts . . . SuperBri!'

Pause.

'SuperBri!'

Still upbeat.

'Ha ha! Super Brian.'

Slightly faltering now.

'Brian! Y' know, Brian . . .'

Voice dropping by several decibels.

'Uh, Brian Simmons.'

In sheepish and barely audible tones: 'Brian Simmons from Overtone Records.'

SuperBri had an ego to match his hospitality budget and skin as thick as the BBC's annual report. To further compound his senior executive stereotype he revelled unashamedly in jargon and name-dropping like it was coming into style. No one could beat his verbal diarrhoea and Z-list celebrity shoulder-rubbing reports. Just a simple discussion over a forthcoming project would be littered with classic examples of eighties' business buzzwords including 'pushing the envelope' or 'thinking outside the box' and comments like, 'Actually, I was talking to Mick Fleetwood about this recently . . .' SuperBri never had a meeting at three P.M., he had 'a three o'clock,' but most disarming was his habit of referring to himself in the third person as 'the Master.' 'Learn from the Master, guys, learn from the Master,' he would say after deigning to share one of his Top Marketing Tips with us.

To prevent accusations of not communicating with the lower ranks, he would stroll past the Pigpen at the beginning of each week, pausing briefly to punch the air with his rallying cry of 'Good morning, Marketeers!' We wouldn't see much of him after that until our weekly 'brainstorming' session (for *storming,* read *numbing*), which would inevitably be rounded up by him arriving at the end of the meeting to bang his fist on the table a few times as he offered words of encouragement straight out of *Staff Motivation for Dummies*: 'Good call! Like it. Like it a lot!' This would be followed by his standard battle cry: 'Come *on!* LET'S SELL RECORDS!' before breezing out of the room, his excuses wafting back down the corridor: 'Sorry, guys, can't hang around, I've got a four o'clock with Sue Lawley.'

Through the window, I could see my fellow lemmings moving along the street and across the car park, soon to be sucked in by the revolving glass doors. Exactly eight hours later, the opposite revolution of these doors would spit them all out again to move en masse back to the tube station. It wasn't a complicated process but nonetheless a memo had been issued with the title 'Revolving Doors—Guidelines for Staff.'

As the lemmings began to take their positions, I wondered if they minded any of this at all, or was it just me? Surely I wasn't the only person in this building that craved a totally unrealistic life of nonstop action and adventure, or at least the challenge of tackling a revolving door unaided. Didn't everyone feel like that, or were they just better at hiding it than I was? Did they all stare out the window at aeroplanes, wishing desperately that they were on one, going somewhere, anywhere? Did they too watch motorcycles whizzing by with a pang of envy and imagine what it would be like not to turn off at the same junction every morning, but to keep riding until the road or the land ran out? Mind you, that wouldn't take very long in Britain, and your epic journey would end in a dilapidated seaside resort like Great Yarmouth or Clacton-on-Sea. No, that wasn't the answer to my itchy feet, but I was on the right track. I decided to muse on the problem for a while longer. After all, it was preferable to opening my post, and besides, eBay was down.

I'm pretty sure this was the day I decided to jack it all in and head off on my motorcycle, but it could very well have been another one just like it. There were plenty of days like this and after a while they all blended into each other. I guess that was what kick-started me into action—I wanted every day to be different; I craved the novelty of sleeping in a different place each night, waking up to unfamiliar smells, sounds and languages. Most of all I wanted to be moving along, to always be going somewhere. It's as old as mankind, the urge to roam, but when you get it and succumb to it, for a fleeting moment you kind of feel like you invented it.

. . .

The next day was quite eventful. SuperBri resigned. He'd wangled himself a high-falutin' new job at a rival company. Nobody could believe it. How did he fool them, everyone was saying, although that was after they'd said, 'Hurrah!' or 'Thank God,' or any other joyous exclamation that bubbled forth from their delighted mouths. My boss was happiest of all, and try as he might, he couldn't hide it. You could see the promotion fantasies running wild in his eyes. Punk rock sensibilities—go to hell! An office *and* a car, it was just too much to bear. I imagined the announcement to his wife that night: 'Cancel the plastic toilet seat, we'll get a wooden one, things are gonna be different from now on!' And I think, but I can't swear, that he even went a whole two days without arguing with her on the phone. Of course, SuperBri was full of it. Suddenly he was spending a lot of time in the Pigpen, perching on our desks, reminiscing about the early days, how he'd made the department what it is today, but now he needed to move on, he felt it was the right time to go. No one dared tell him he was way overdue. It seemed his new position was terribly important and high profile. 'It's a big job,' he informed me stoically, his right arm draped round my cringing shoulders, 'but I'm a big-job guy.' 'Dear Brian,' I wrote in his farewell card, 'it's been a pleasure learning from the Master.' Apparently the collection fund for his leaving present had to be topped up with petty cash.

Even with SuperBri out of the picture, the world of taupe and lemmings held little appeal and I started to do a bit of research into this idea of mine—a long-distance motorcycle adventure. The whole thing started out quite vague. I didn't really know where I wanted to go; I just knew I wanted to go somewhere. I made a few tentative enquiries about things like visas and international driving permits. In quiet moments I casually searched the Net for 'motorcycle round the world' or something like that, then I started to dip into technical articles about suitable bikes for different terrains.

'Any bike's subframe is liable to crack with the extra weight of the luggage when travelling on corrugated dirt roads,' it said somewhere. Hmm, I thought . . . mental note: Strengthen subframe. Second mental note: Find out what subframe is. But soon I was calculating savings plans and making lists and scaring myself with U.S. Department of State warnings of civil war, robberies, and terrorism in every country that I fancied visiting. I checked what it said about the UK and it was pretty much the same, so I stopped paying attention after that. By their reckoning I should have been robbed by a bogus taxi driver, bombed by the IRA, pickpocketed, mugged, and date-raped while having a drink in a pub and killed, or at least injured, in a train crash caused by our chaotic rail services. I felt slightly cheated by my humdrum, uneventful life after reading this and wondered if there really was any need to motorcycle across Colombia or the Congo when there was clearly so much action that I was missing out on here, on my very own doorstep.

These planning stages were full of promise and nervous excitement as it gradually dawned on me that I really was going to do this, that in the near future I would be On the Road in a faraway foreign land, that this adventure I had dreamed of for so long was due to be plucked from the depths of the Fantasy file and plonked squarely into Reality. On a research jaunt to a travel bookshop, I was fortunate enough to engage a sales assistant with a discerning nose for motorcycle-related literature. 'You've got to read *Jupiter's Travels* by Ted Simon,' he instructed me as I followed him on a wanderlustful trail to the Travel Writing/Misc. section, 'it's the all-time classic motorcycle travel book, and you must get the *Adventure Motorcycling Handbook,* of course.' 'Are there any motorcycle travel books written by women?' I enquired. It seemed the answer was no. There were a few serious tomes on the joys of motorcycling from a female perspective, but I knew all about that already—that's why I was here.

Back home the bookshelves were creaking and the adventure was brewing. I leafed through action-packed chapters on emergency gearbox repairs in a Siberian swamp or being rescued from certain death by Tuareg nomads in the Sahara. It was all out of my league; big boy's stuff—men who could pull wheelies and fix seized engines with a Swiss army knife. But as I read on, this only made me more determined to have a go. My rational mind told me that if someone else had done it, well, surely that meant I could do it too. After all, I reasoned, what was the worst thing that could happen?

The balance between doing enough research to ensure a successful expedition but not *too* much that I scared myself to death with doom-laden facts and figures turned out to be one of my biggest challenges. In the end I banned myself from reading my collection of motorcycle travel—related material at bedtime, as I got so excited I couldn't sleep. Even poring over maps after 10 P.M. induced hours of feet-twitching insomnia, thus my nighttime reading was eventually restricted to a book on the milder but still useful subject of global weather systems. But sooner or later, I had to decide where in the world I was going.

You imagine that most people can name their dream destination, their 'I've always wanted to go to . . .' hotspot. But my problem was that I've always wanted to go everywhere, so with my map of the world laid out on the floor, the decision-making process went something like this: It's got to be somewhere hot, and I'd like to see those big cacti with the sticking-out arms. OK, Mexico then. Well, why not do the whole continent? North and South America. South America? Ooh yeah, nice and exotic, Carmen Miranda and all that, always did like her hats covered in tropical fruit. And I do want to go somewhere with palm trees. Yes, South America sounds like a good plan.

I considered it hatched.

It was around this time that I was given a significant piece of advice. Naturally, plenty of opinion starts flying around when you decide to do something like this, usually along the lines of 'DON'T!' from people who watch a lot of television. But this pearl of wisdom given to me by a world-traveller friend of mine with thousands of miles under his belt was, *'Make it a mission. Don't just meander here and there. State your goal before you leave, whether it be to motorcycle around the world, or from A to B, or whatever. But this sense of purpose, even though it's self-imposed, is very important in keeping you focused.'*

Now I must admit I scoffed a bit at first as it sounded rather too regimented and organised—all the things I wanted to get away from—but the more I thought about it, the more it made sense. Later that night I laid out my map of the world and sprawled myself over it, peering at the Americas with a newfound sense of purpose. I would start at the top in Alaska, I decided, and ride right down to the bottom, to the very tip of South America, Tierra del Fuego—the Land of Fire—to the most southerly point in the world that can be reached by road, a little Argentine town called Ushuaia. 'Ushuaia.' I said it aloud to myself. I'd never heard of it before, but this little town at the end of the world was to become my sole focus for the foreseeable future. I studied the map for a long time, examining this vast landmass that would become my temporary home. I traced a route down the west coast and discovered that my journey would take me over sixteen thousand miles, across mountains, deserts and jungles and through Nicaragua. Which was a surprise, as I'd always thought it was in Africa.

With my route now inked onto the map, it was time to deal with Conundrum No. 2—the Bike. Up until this point my world of motorcycling had been limited to vintage British road bikes, due to a long-standing love affair with 1950s leather-clad rockers. At the age of thirteen, that magical time when you first realise that the opposite sex might actually have something to offer, I began plastering my bedroom walls with pictures of *Wild One*–era Marlon Brando, Gene Vincent and any other greasy hoodlum that had ever straddled a chunk of throbbing Brit Iron. Although it was many years later that I finally got round to acquiring my motorcycle licence, the obsession with all things noisy, greasy and rockin' had never gone away, and against the advice of experienced and frankly, sensible, motorcycling friends, I cut my biking teeth on a 650cc 1963 BSA. This scheme initially involved more gnashing than cutting of the teeth, but after a series of character-building breakdowns, accidents, electrical failures, oil leaks, snapped chains and the many miles of obligatory pushing associated with British bike ownership, (wo)man finally triumphed over machine and the suitably shiny black and chrome BSA became a trusty friend, providing me with many happy road miles.

However, I realised it wasn't the most practical choice for this expedition of the Americas that was slowly beginning to form in my mind, and I set my research gene into action on the 'What Bike' question. I knew I wanted some sort of off-road model, as I expected (and secretly hoped) to encounter all manner of bone-shaking terrain and dodgy road surfaces, but clocking in at five feet and four inches, I found the seat heights of the popular bikes left my feet dangling in midair. All my research pointed me towards either tall, heavy, rally-style 650s or enormous BMWs with ABS, computerised knickknacks and engines the size of a small car, and a price tag to match.

It was important to me that I should choose a bike that was light enough to pick up by myself, and to wriggle free from, should I ever find myself squashed beneath it. Having once been pinned to a spot of London tarmac by the BSA, watching the petrol tank empty its contents over me, I was keen to avoid a similar plight. On that occasion I was fortunate enough to be rescued by a couple of sturdy pensioners, but, I wondered, would I be so lucky in the middle of the desert? I didn't feel that I could rely on the local nomads as the fourth emergency service. Most important, I wanted a bike that could go anywhere, that would be a friend, not a foe, in a tricky situation, and that I didn't have to worry about scratching the paintwork. *Cheap* and *cheerful* were my watchwords and after much deliberation I decided to fly in the face of perceived wisdom and opted for a 225cc trail bike: the Yamaha XT225 Serow. It was small, light, economical and named after a stocky little mountain deer. What more could I ask for? What I wasn't prepared for were the howls of derision and hoots of laughter from those who considered themselves in the know.

'You're going to do it on a 225 dirt bike?' they would exclaim. 'I pity your arse!'

'Sixteen thousand miles? At fifty miles an hour!' spluttered another.

'Fifty-five,' I corrected him.

Even the man at the air-freight company felt the need to put in his pennies' worth when I requested a quote for flying the bike to Alaska. 'If you don't mind me saying, this is the wrong bike for this type of expedition,' he scrawled on the faxed quote. I threw it in the bin and phoned another freight company.

Meanwhile, back in the Pigpen with no SuperBri, there was a distinct lack of envelope pushing. I decided it was time to remedy that in the most literal fashion, and on the following Monday morning, I gave a white DL envelope (as the stationery department insisted on calling it) a gentle shove over to my boss's desk. He gave me a knowing look, but rather than sit there watching the relief flood over his face, I took a timely walk to the canteen for a celebratory cup of tea, where I observed two identikit media blondes fighting silently, but with thin-lipped determination, over the few pieces of kiwi fruit in the otherwise uninspiring BBC-issue fruit salad. If there'd been any doubt that I'd made the right decision, it was removed at that moment. Back upstairs I was ushered into an office, its walls constructed entirely from glass—another brilliant stab at dehumanisation from Evil Office Design Plc. The other Pigpenners were watching and making silly faces at me.

'So, this is it. You're leaving us,' said the Boss, my resignation letter still in his hand. He was attempting a neutral tone of voice but I'm sure I sensed a touch of glee unwittingly sneaking in.

I nodded in response, trying to look thoughtful and reflective.

'So what are your plans?' he asked with a casual politeness.

I recalled the one and only time I'd opened up to the Boss and told him I was unhappy in my job. His suggestion then was that I should leave to set up a business painting folk art onto watering cans along the English canal system, so I was looking forward to this conversation and hopefully picking up some more career advice.

'I'm going to motorcycle from Alaska to Argentina.'

He gaped at me.

'By yourself?'

'Yes.'

'Well, that's quite something!'

I could tell he didn't believe me.

'Well, as you know, I've had itchy feet for a while,' I said, which meant, 'Well, as you know, I've despised this mind-numbing, soul-sapping job for a while.'

'Well, well, well! Yes, that's quite something! Not the usual back-packing in Thailand for you, though, eh?'

I laughed, for various reasons, but mostly at his MFI-esque concept of adventure.

But he wasn't laughing, he seemed preoccupied by something. Suddenly an air of melancholy enveloped him and he slumped onto a nearby designer sofa, his gelled head in his hands.

'You're doing the right thing, y'know,' he said seriously.

Finally, I'd done something he approved of!

'And you've got to do it now,' he continued, 'before you get married and have kids and all that stuff. God, I wish I'd done some travelling, bit of backpacking, driven across the States or something. Now I'm married, I've got a mortgage and the children . . .' he trailed off miserably before hastily following it up with what everyone says immediately after they've bemoaned the fact that their offspring prevent them from doing what they want.

'Don't get me wrong, I love my kids, wouldn't be without them, but well, y'know . . .'

I spent the next twenty minutes listening to him ponder forty years of what-ifs.

Upon my return to the Pigpen, I dived for the phone and hastily booked a one-way ticket to Alaska.

'I can give you a return for the same price, y'know,' said the travel agent in a broad Liverpudlian tone that gave the unfortunate impression he was offering me a dodgy deal.

'I know,' I explained, 'but I'll be coming back from Buenos Aires and I don't know when.'

'Sounds like you've got a bit of a journey ahead,' he remarked, as he tapped my details into the computer.

Brimming with the excitement of resigning from my job and now booking my flight, I couldn't help but share my plans with this stranger on the other end of the phone. Unfortunately, he didn't share my enthusiasm.

'You're going to ride a motorbike on your own through Central America? Through Honduras, El Salvador and all nutty places like that?'

I answered eagerly in the affirmative.

'You're fookin' mad, lass,' he surmised with a cruel cackle, 'they're all killin' each other over there, they'll 'ave you for brekkie.'

He chuckled merrily at this amusing scenario, completing our transaction with, 'Well, good luck, luv, you're gonna need it.'

I was feeling buoyant enough to dismiss him as a small-minded, scaredy-cat Scouser, although a small part of me wondered if maybe he had a point.

But this was no time to go getting the wobbles. I put the phone down and sent an e-mail to friends, family and colleagues telling them I didn't have a job anymore, but I did have a motorcycle and a seat on a plane bound for Alaska. I really had to go.

'Are you going to have a mobile phone with you?' said my mum when I called her with the news later that day.

'No, but . . .' I paused, as an idea presented itself to me, 'I'll do a Web site, so you can keep track of me.'

'Oh dear,' she replied, 'does that mean I'll have to get a computer?'

It wasn't long after my resignation from the Pigpen that I was bending a friend's ear with an update of my plans when he interrupted my excited ramblings about rabies vaccinations and heavy-duty inner tubes and other fascinating subjects that fill the mind of the budding motorcycle adventuress.

'You know what,' he said, 'you should meet this mate of mine, he's ridden his motorbike round the world twice, he could probably give you some advice. His name's Austin. Actually, funnily enough, he reminds me of you, you're like a female version of him.'

'Well,' I said, intrigued by this cryptic description, 'I'll give him a call.'

Austin came round to visit me soon after on a motorcycle that looked like it had come from, or should be going to, a scrap yard, and burst into my world like a *Boys Own* comic book hero. I had my map of the world laid out on the floor and a mental list of technical, geographical and practical questions for him. But it soon became obvious that my innocent fact-finding mission was veering wildly off course, and the evening degenerated into a pleasing blur of cheap red wine, playing records too loud and yakking until the early hours. We met up again the next week, and the next, always under the chaste premise of serious motorcycle discussion, and soon these 'research meetings' became a regular fixture in my calendar. But it wasn't long before our conversations began straying from the official subject matter and there was no more denying it: Cupid had been secretly paying us regular visits too, and had fired a pair of particularly potent arrows in our direction. I'd always heard wise old married people say about meeting their intended, 'You just know,' but I'd never quite believed it. Now, for the first time ever, I just knew—and the feeling was mutual! I was totally smitten, and totally annoyed.

'This isn't meant to happen!' I protested to my best friend in an emergency phone call. 'I'm not meant to meet the man of my dreams just before I disappear off to the other side of the world on my motorbike!'

I had recently extricated myself from the clutches of a previous long-term liaison, for the sole purpose of being footloose and fancy free along the length of the Pan American Highway. My message to the mothers of America was supposed to be, 'Lock up your sons!' And now this two-wheeled vagabond with a pair of sparkly blue eyes and a naily DR350 had come along and blasted my neatly arranged plans into orbit.

We embarked full throttle on the sort of grand affair they make films about, albeit a Barbara Cartland novel adapted for the screen by Ben Dover. Time stood still and an era of endless fun ensued, whizzing around the countryside on our bikes, lying in fields, chewing blades of grass and making eternal promises. Our nights were spent in fields, under trees or in the back of Austin's Transit van, constantly marvelling at the twist of fate that had thrown us, two perfectly matched halves, together. But throughout all this, the unspoken words hung over us.

'I've still got to go, you know,' I said finally.

'Of course,' he replied. 'You must.'

It was a painful wrench, but we both knew this was just the beginning.

'Fate has dealt us a winning hand,' I proclaimed. 'It's just that the timing's a bit off.'

'We can wait, we've got our whole lives,' Austin said philosophically.

It was true, but with the clock ticking towards my departure date, I had to get busy preparing myself and the Serow for our grand adventure. Somehow, in between conducting the romance of the century and continuing to work out my notice in the Pigpen, the mundane details of vaccinations, spare parts and luggage systems fell into place. It looked as if I would be heading off to Alaska without a hitch, unless you count falling in love, and if so, it was hardly something to complain about.

But there was still one thing, other than Austin, that was keeping me awake at night: Spanish. *Español*. Castellano. Crikey! They even had different names for the same language. And I couldn't speak a word of it. My route took me through the length of Latin America and my knowledge of the lingua franca was pretty much nada. This wasn't to say I hadn't had a go: as part of my trip preparation I had dutifully attended a Spanish evening course taught by an octogenarian, red-blooded Argentine who should have been pensioned off years ago for the safety of his female pupils. But this being twenty-first-century Bridget Jones London, he was up against a fair amount of competition from the male scholars. Most of the class, it soon became clear, had joined up with the single intention of meeting a soul mate, or at the very least, getting a *porción*. The few with more wholesome intentions were easily identified by the fact that they arrived at the first lesson with a shiny new English-Spanish dictionary and completed their homework each week, but these budding bilinguists were very much the minority. Sure enough, as we sat in our draughty, prefab classroom every Wednesday evening chanting, '*Uno, dos, tres* . . . with not even the slightest attempt at a Spanish accent, glances started to be exchanged, books were being shared, eyebrows were raised and as the weeks went by, the more studious of the new pairings began self-consciously arriving at class together, sometimes holding hands in a bold display of togetherness. The less diligent couplings, however, were never seen again and within a few weeks the body count had dropped from thirty of us to just four—a mousey lawyer girl who claimed to have a Spanish boyfriend called Fabio, a middle-aged couple who divided their time between a half-built villa in Málaga and a sun bed in Willesden, and me. All of us at the mercy of a sexually frustrated Argentine pensioner. The couple were only interested in learning words relating to construction. 'Wossa Spanish word for underpinnin'?' the husband kept asking, and the lawyer girl was never seen again after our teacher pointed out that her boyfriend's name meant 'bean grower.' Eventually I decided there was only so much ranting about the Falklands War peppered with sexual innuendos I could take. It was adios, amigos. I would get a phrase book and work out the lingo when I got to Mexico.

With a couple of weeks to go, I jumped into action for the frantic countdown to departure. I became obsessed with making my luggage as light as possible and skimmed down everything I could. One set of clothes would do, two pairs of socks was plenty, three pairs of knickers—turn them inside out and they'd last for six days. In one particularly enthusiastic weight-watching session, I even cut all the irrelevant pages out of my Haynes manual to save a few grams. But still, my luggage seemed to weigh a ton. My flight to Anchorage was booked for April 30 but the bike had a head start of a few days, leaving on the twenty-fifth. On the twenty-fourth my wheel bearings packed in and my clutch cable snapped—you couldn't beat the timing! It was a comical scene that night, as I rounded up my spanner-spinning friends for a spot of last-minute mechanical assistance. We worked in excitable camaraderie by moon and torchlight under a clear, star-studded sky with all the promise that an English spring brings after a long dreary winter, and it occurred to me that this year I wouldn't be around for the usual two-wheeled summer fun. I didn't know where I would be this summer, I realised. Anything, literally anything, could happen—this concept turned my stomach over with an excitement so pure, I could barely contain it. The clunking and clanging of old bearings being bashed out and new bearings being bashed in chimed through the darkness, accompanied by the good-natured sporadic swearing so crucial to a successful motorcycle maintenance session. I'm going to miss all this, I thought ruefully . . . but I'm dying to go.

The rest of London may have been tucked up in bed, but our work had only just started. A round of final checks was made before removing the handlebars, front wheel and forks in an effort to squeeze the bike into the air-freight crate, which was just one cost-cutting cubic metre in volume. With spare parts, tools, luggage, camping gear, fuel cans and maps crammed around this jumble of motorcycle parts that used to be my bike, it took four of us to heave this bulging box of biking paraphernalia into the back of a van. Destination: Heathrow Airport eight o'clock tomorrow morning. I could barely believe it was happening; each significant step— leaving my job, booking the flight, now crating up the bike— brought the reality a little closer, but also the moment I was dreading: bidding adieu to Austin. When the time came, it was even worse than I had imagined. It tore at my heartstrings, but still somewhere deep down, I knew I was doing the right thing.

Significant journeys should always start brutally early in the morning, to convince yourself that you're doing something really special when the dreaded alarm goes off at 3 A.M. Being awake at this hour is wholly unnatural and only acceptable if you're flying somewhere superexciting or you've been up all night. On the morning of April 30 I ticked both boxes—I hadn't slept a wink but I didn't care, I was flying to Anchorage! Anchorage, Alaska! My brother, Nat, was coming out with me for a week's holiday and to provide moral support and assistance with the reassembly of my bike, a process hitherto unknown to either of us but one we had studied assiduously over the last week, even to the extent of drawing up a homemade instruction sheet bearing such technical directives as 'this goes here' and 'do this up tight.' I was glad to have the companionship of Nat; he took my mind off the heartache of leaving Austin, and kept me entertained with novel facts he had discovered about our destination. Having found our seats and typically squabbled over who got the window, he produced some Alaska-related literature from his bag and began instructing me on the correct procedure for dealing with the bear attack that would inevitably greet us as soon as we'd passed through customs.

'It says here that you must make them realise you're a human but also you have to try to make yourself as physically large as possible.'

He showed me a crude line drawing in the book, depicting a man cowering beneath a huge grizzly, his hands raised in the air and a speech bubble coming from his mouth containing the lifesaving statement, 'I AM A HUMAN! YOU ARE A BEAR!'

We sniggered. But it was deadly serious.

'Right,' said Nat authoritatively, 'when we're camping we have to hang our food in a tree—downwind, mind you.' He read on. 'Oh my God! They can smell food in a *tin!* And they like the smell of moisturising lotion.'

I briefly considered the image of a grizzly bear raiding my Nivea cream as Nat turned the page.

'Um, Lois,' he said, slightly awkwardly, 'it's not your, er, y'know, time of the month, is it?'

As with most brothers and sisters, this subject rarely came up for discussion.

'No, why?' I asked, bemused.

'Because it says here that bears can tell when a woman is menstruating and they seek them out for the kill.'

I made a few rough calculations and worked out that if I was to escape a menstrual mauling I had to be out of bear country in just two weeks' time. No chance, there was the whole of Canada to get through.

'I'm not going to have my trip dictated by bloodthirsty bears,' I announced defiantly.

'All together now . . .' said Nat, thrusting his hands into the air as a cue.

'I AM A HUMAN! YOU ARE A BEAR!' we roared in unison, doubling up with laughter.

The air hostess gave us a look.

'Please fasten your seat belts, we are about to take off,' she informed us sniffily.

The plane taxied along the runway for what seemed like ages, picking up speed before that familiar, stomach-knotting roar sent us lunging skyward. From the window I could see the new day's sun emerging, flashing a reflection on the wing and casting its waking glow on a sleepy London. I traced the familiar silvery snake of the Thames, watching it shrink ever smaller as we made the steady climb; and then England was no more, obliterated by a sea of fleecy white clouds.

This was it. Bears, Spanish, heartache—it was too late to worry about any of that now. The adventure was most definitely under way.

Two

Oh Alaska, the Frontier State! What a wonderfully rugged, macho place it is, stuck all the way up there in the faraway frozen north and fairly heaving with that rarest of breeds: Real Men. The male to female ratio is ten to one in Alaska, making it the ideal hunting ground for lonesome ladies looking for love. I wanted to call up all my single friends and tell them to get on the next flight out. But a word of warning to potential husband hunters: Choose carefully. As one local woman put it, the odds are good, but the goods are odd. And there were certainly plenty of mullets on display in the forty-ninth state. Pickup trucks abounded too, their hale 'n' hearty drivers sporting checked shirts, fur-lined boots and other suitably manly outdoor attire. Equally robust-looking dogs, the ultimate Alaskan accessory, accompanied their masters, bouncing along in the back of the truck amongst piles of logs, chain saws and the occasional shotgun, their tongues flopping, panting warm mist into the freezing air and thoroughly enjoying their role as man's best friend. All hunting, all shooting, no-nonsense Alaska. I loved it immediately.

We didn't half feel like a couple of city slickers as we explored the highways and byways of this wild corner of the world. I'd say that my brother and I rather fancied ourselves as outdoor types. This was based, somewhat flimsily, on a childhood of no-frills camping holidays, recreational tree climbing and general 'wholesome activities' (no TV until age ten and then educational programs only). Alaska put us in our place a little bit as it dawned on us that, no, we'd never shot a wild animal, skinned it and cooked it over a campfire, nor did we ever have to use a snowplough to get out the front gate, or any of the other things that Alaskans accept as normal life—like bears breaking into your garden and eating the geraniums, as we read about with much glee in the Anchorage *Daily News*. More accustomed to foraging for our supplies in brightly lit twenty-four-hour supermarkets, we humbly accepted that these folk were in an entirely different league. They were tough 'uns, all right, the real deal; they had to be—they lived half the year in a snowbound, freezing darkness. Inspired by this hardy lifestyle, we got it into our heads that the ideal Alaskan keepsake for Nat to take back home to London would be an enormous pair of antlers. So with my motorcycle still in transit, we hired a pickup truck (in an attempt to fit in with the locals) and headed upstate on our version of a hunting mission.

'You ain't from round here, are ya?' said the voice, guffawing with the throaty gurgle of a dedicated pipe smoker. 'Where you guys from, and whaddya doin' in my store?'

What with the murky light and the ceiling-high stacks of merchandise, I couldn't see who the voice belonged to, but after a while I spotted signs of movement and a wisp of smoke emanating from behind a pile of blunt axe heads, a selection of antique firearms and a few mangy stuffed moose heads, their brown glass eyes looking slightly mournful. And who could blame them? Since their untimely demise they'd been gathering dust in this rambling shack of a junk shop that was crammed to the bursting point with what could be described as 'Alaskabilia,' located on a lonesome stretch of highway where few visitors, let alone paying customers, it seemed, dared to tread.

'London, England,' I responded to the disembodied voice as I tripped over a weighty cast iron cooking pot, causing a disastrous domino effect throughout the store. The pot hit a skillet, which hit a stuffed beaver. The beaver knocked over a fishing pole, setting a few rounds of ammunition rolling across the dirt floor and bouncing off a selection of copper kettles before finally coming to rest against a mountain of used spark plugs.

'Sorry, sorry. Terribly sorry,' I apologised, gathering up an armful of bullets from amongst the chaos.

The proprietor didn't seem to mind, or even notice, for that matter. His days of eye-catching window displays were over, if indeed, they had ever begun.

'London, England, huh?' he grunted, emerging from behind the overburdened counter to reveal a full-on ZZ Top beard tucked into grease-laden dungarees and a mane of long grey hair spilling out from under a grubby baseball cap bearing the slogan NOUVEAU RICHE IS BETTER THAN NO RICHE AT ALL. I begged to differ on this matter but his wild stare and gigantic gnarled hands made me think twice.

'You like my, uh . . . *emporium*?' he growled, acquiring a suitably plummy English accent for the last word and laughing maniacally at his own humour.

'It's brilliant!' Nat and I declared with genuine enthusiasm, surveying the array of rustic clutter and—oh joy, there they were—a selection of antlers in the far corner, poking out from under a mound of rusting hand tools. This place was Wal-Mart for Luddites.

'Alaska ain't what it used to be, y'know,' he announced, taking a step towards us and giving us the chance to inspect the contents of his beard at close range: mostly tobacco and dried spit. 'Oh no, things have changed round here, they want us to be like everyone else now,' he snarled.

'So anyhow,' he continued in more pleasant tones, 'what are you guys doin' in these parts?'

'We'd like to buy some antlers,' I declared boldly.

I'll never forget the look of disgust, the way his entire face changed with that one statement. We should have just run for it then. But no, we stood there and took it, like the lily-livered, limey little townies that we were. Well, that's what he called us anyway.

'So . . . ya want antlers?' he said menacingly, his beard quivering with rage. 'Yeah? Ya say ya want antlers? Ya come over here from London, England, and ya want antlers?'

He started doing a namby-pamby dance around the shop saying, 'I want antlers, I want antlers,' in a sarcastic singsong English accent that I assumed was meant to be an impression of me.

'Don't come in here tellin' me ya want antlers. . . . GO ON! GET OUTTA HERE!' he yelled, his arms flailing towards the door. We ran for the exit as he imparted his final piece of advice.

'If you want antlers you go get 'em, ya hear me?' he shouted after us. 'You get your own goddamn antlers. And you'll be needing one of THESE.'

We glanced over our shoulders to see our beardy Alaskan friend waving a shotgun in the air with wild abandon. 'This is how folks get their antlers round here!' he bellowed.

'And I thought the Americans prided themselves on their customer service,' panted Nat as we pegged it back to the truck.

'Yeah, but Alaskans are different,' I reminded him. I'd been here only long enough to get over my jet lag but this much I'd worked out.

Fortunately, we had the impending arrival and reconstruction of my motorcycle to keep us out of any further antler-related scrapes. Liberating a foreign vehicle from customs isn't meant to be easy, even in the Land of the Free. It's meant to be the sort of task that involves the bashing of one's head against a brick wall while blank-faced bureaucrats toss you from office to office like a Ping-Pong ball and then take a long lunch. I was prepared for this. I would be calm, I would take it in stride, I wouldn't get annoyed or impatient, I would just wait and smile . . . and keep waiting, and keep smiling. And be polite. And call everyone sir and ma'am, like they do round here. So when half an hour after arriving at the office of Delta Air Cargo we found ourselves out in the freight terminal car park, tearing open the familiar crate with all the fervour of a grizzly going in for the kill, I simply couldn't believe my luck.

'Wow! That was smoooooth!' I exclaimed jubilantly as I rummaged through my assortment of motorcycling clobber that I'd packed so carefully just a few days before. It felt strange to see these reminders of home in this new setting, but also comforting, especially when I discovered a pair of unwashed socks stuffed into my crash helmet. Between the two of us, and aided by our homemade instruction manual, the rebuilding of the bike in a quiet corner of the cargo terminal parking lot was an equally smooth affair. It was a glorious day of northern hemisphere sunshine and even the ungainly sprawl of Anchorage airport looked appealing under the vast, cornflower-coloured Alaskan sky. Snow-cloaked mountain ranges dotted with emerald green firs stretched out in every direction and the thought that I would soon be riding across them along the famous AlCan Highway towards Canada and ultimately South America seemed both utterly fantastical and deliriously exciting. Just reading the map gave me a thrill; names like Easy Money Creek and Dalton Cache stirred romantic images of the 1850s gold rush while the Indian and Eskimo names were even more intriguing: Aniyuyaktuvik Creek, for example, which I discovered means 'place where wind has hardened snow so that a snow house can be built.' Who needs fourteen words when one unpronounceable one will do? But my favourite was Lost Temper Creek, named by a 1950s geologist 'because of a camp incident.' I pondered the use of the word *camp* in his report, conjuring up an image of a gay rock hound throwing a tantrum on the banks of a freezing Alaskan river.

I had a feeling that things were going a little too well, and sure enough when I went to start the bike for the obligatory test ride, I was met with nothing more than a doleful *click*. At first I put it down to a flat battery, and we pushed, bumped and jumped the poor

'Some assembly required.' The Serow arrives at Anchorage airport in Alaska.

old Serow around the parking lot, but to no avail. Wondering if the trauma of the transatlantic journey had done something funny to the ignition wiring, I made a few valiant displays of wielding my multimeter, exclaiming, 'I'm so glad I brought this with me,' while I stabbed the probes into various likely looking electrical nooks and crannies. I didn't really know what I was doing, but like the nineteenth-century prospectors before me, I was hoping to strike gold. No such luck, I wouldn't be getting any creek named after me. What an ignominious start to my Pan-American motorcycle trip—hot off the plane and straight into the local Yamaha dealer.

A few days later it was time for Nat to return to London, and I bid him a poignant farewell. It would be many months before we would see each other again. With my bike still out of action, there was nothing else for me to do but hole up in the suitably Alaskan-sounding Eagle River Motel, although I preferred to call it by a more Eskimo-like name: 'place where motorcyclists stay when motorcycle does not start.' Still, I had ninety-nine TV channels to keep me occupied, as Gary the motel manager kept reminding me. It was one of the many things that made America great, he said, and commiserated with me for the measly five that we poor Brits had to make do with. A most kind and helpful chap, he took great interest in my impending adventure and every morning would enquire as to whether my motorcycle would be ready that day, the answer invariably being no. And although well meaning, his standard response of 'Oh darn, what a shame, I bet you never thought your trip of a lifetime would start off like this' became a little wearing after a while.

This delay seemed interminable at the time, but as I would discover over the next few months, once you get on the road you soon forget the days or weeks you spent waiting for a part to arrive or a document to be faxed, or whatever it is that's got you climbing the walls. I watched reruns of Miss Marple to keep the homesickness at bay and reminded myself of something Austin had said that had stuck in my mind: 'Transcontinental motorcycle trips are go, stop, go, stop, the whole way.' Well, yes, fair enough, I thought, but just a little bit of Go would be nice.

The call finally came in: 'Your motorcycle's ready!' and Go I did, like a sprinter off the starting blocks. Gary came out of the motel to take a photo of me finally setting off—capturing the very moment I left Alaska for Argentina, my left arm outstretched above my head, waving a triumphant farewell as I headed into the unknown—Ushuaia, here I come! Then I realised I had to go back to retrieve my camera from him, so it wasn't really a picture of me leaving at all! Significant moments, eh? They're just not all they're cracked up to be.

I bid a fond good-bye to my favourite landmarks: House of Critters (the local pet shop) and The Alaskan Bush Company. The local garden centre? Nope. This is Anchorage's tastefully named downtown strip joint! Out past the city limits on the wide empty highway, flashing signs in orange neon informed me that May was Motorcycle Awareness Month. God bless the Yanks! What other country would come up with such a notion? Back in England, every month is Motorcycle Injure, Abuse and Maim Month. What's more, I felt that this statewide initiative had been implemented solely for my benefit. Well, it had to be, surely? Because no other idiot was riding her motorcycle around Alaska in the beginning of May, freezing her extremities off in the name of fun and adventure, that was for sure.

'**Oh no, we don't have a** spring here in Alaska,' explained the pump attendant as he filled my tank while I numbly gripped a cup of gas station coffee in both hands, stamping my feet and shivering furiously. 'It's either summer, or it's winter.'

'So, what is it now?' I asked, already knowing the answer.

'Oh yes, May is still wintertime,' he confirmed, and then seeing my crestfallen face added, 'but it's the end of winter.'

'But it was quite warm in Anchorage,' I said, hoping to extract some canny local weather forecasting involving freak heat waves along the length of the AlCan.

'Oh yes, of course,' said the old man sagely, 'Anchorage is different altogether; it's got its own climate, y'understand. You say you're headin' for Canada? The Yukon?' He chuckled knowingly. 'you just wait till you get up in those mountains, li'l lady, that's the real thing. Forget Anchorage. Y'know what they say—the only good thing about Anchorage is that you can see Alaska from there.'

'And watch out for the bears,' he hollered after me as my wheels crunched across the gravel forecourt, back out onto the deserted, frostbitten highway.

He was right about the mountains. I wound my way through a land so stupefying that I would occasionally find myself drifting into the middle of the road as I gaped at the enormity of it all, my head swivelling like the *Exorcist* girl. So much wilderness, so much space, just left to its own devices. The vastness was crushing. I felt like a tiny insect, beetling along in a land of giants. But something in me wouldn't let me stop and linger on these views; even passing my first glacier, I couldn't bring myself to pull over. After all the holdups and hiccups, now all I wanted to do was to ride and ride, just eat up the miles. At last, the trip had started and whatever had occurred previously and whatever might happen in the future didn't matter, because at this precise moment I was in a rare state of simple and unqualified happiness, to be found only in the act of being on the move, under your own steam. It would, however, have been unreasonable to expect this kind of serenity to last for more than a few miles, especially when the rain kicked in, a stinging icy Alaskan winter rain, comparable to riding slap-bang into a wall of needles. I was high up in the peaks of the Alaska Range now, almost at the treeline, fumbling for my waterproofs under a steely grey sky that grew ever thicker and heavier as each precious minute passed. Tonight's planned destination, Glennallen, was still several hours' ride away and the weather that lay ahead looked doomy and dark, the sky a dismal blanket of freezing fog to the east, my direction of travel. I checked the map for civilisation between here and there. Nothing. Well, what did I expect? I reminded myself that the purpose of this venture was to get away from it all, so I could hardly spend one minute admiring the lonesome wild beauty and then complain about the lack of Holiday Inns in the area. Anyway, I had my very own Holiday Inn right here on my bike: my trusty one-man tent. I decided to cut my losses, have an early night and get going first thing tomorrow morning when this inclement weather would no doubt have passed to reveal the first day of a glorious sparkling Alaskan summer.

The best kind of spontaneous wild camping is when you find a little hideaway in which to pitch your tent, off the beaten track, away from the road, where no local maniac or gun-toting landowner will seek you out. Fortunately, this was quite easy in Alaskan wilderness. A bumpy ride down a rocky path took me deep into the woods where incredibly, I stumbled upon what appeared to be a disused campground perched on the edge of a magnificent ravine that seemed remote enough for my reclusive needs. But hopefully not reclusive enough to house a family of bears, I thought, remembering the pump attendant's parting words of advice.

If there were such a thing as the Anti-Camping Lobby, setting up a tent in the pouring rain would be their ultimate campaign material, the clinching argument used to win over doubting campers. Surely there is no more dispiriting activity known to man. With the fading light and ever decreasing temperature, I have to admit to a few cries of 'What the hell am I doing?' as I stumbled around the slushy undergrowth, banging in pegs and tripping over guy ropes. By the time I was cocooned in my sleeping bag, fully clothed and sporting the winter camper's millinery of woolly hat and head torch, pretty much all my possessions had experienced some degree of saturation, ranging from slightly moist through to fully waterlogged. But nevertheless, racked with first night paranoia, I had painstakingly unloaded the bike with the intention of storing my entire luggage next to me inside the tent. Thus I found myself snuggling down alongside my soggy bags, boots, tools, crash helmet, a pile of damp leathers and a gallon of gas.

I lay there in the blackness, adjusting my city-bred ears to the concept of complete and total silence. I suddenly felt enormously vulnerable. Nobody knows where I am, it dawned on me. Nobody in the world. I hadn't felt so utterly alone since the time I got stuck on the outskirts of Melton Mowbray for seven hours while hitch-hiking from Bristol to Great Yarmouth.

It was about 3 A.M. when I first heard it. It woke me up, and I lay there absolutely frozen stiff with fear. I thought my heart would stop. Then I heard it again: THWOD.

Something between a thwack and a thud. Whatever it was, it was just a few inches from where I lay, right outside the tent.

And then again. THWOD.

This time behind the tent. A few seconds later, again. THWOD.

Oh Jesus, it was in front of my tent now. My heart raced, thumping audibly beneath my multiple layers of clothes. The sounds kept coming, with an agonisingly slow regularity. Like heavy, plodding footfalls, pacing a circle around me. THWOD . . . THWOD . . . THWOD. What could it be? Was it a bear that had sniffed out my Nivea cream? Or had some wildman of the woods spotted my motorcycle and come to steal it? I couldn't bring myself to move a muscle, I was so completely terrified, here all alone in the darkness, in this remote, isolated place at the top of the world. This was crazy, spending the night here, what had I been thinking? What was I going to do? THWOD . . . THWOD . . . it kept going, pacing round the tent. Sometimes there was a pause of a few minutes and I thought and prayed that whatever it was had gone away. But no. It would start over again. THWOD . . . THWOD . . . THWOD . . . always circling the tent in agonising slow motion. I hardly dared to breathe. My mouth was dry, my stomach knotted with terror, every muscle in my body tensed, from my clenched teeth down to my curled toes. I must have lain like this for half an hour or more, listening to these noises, my imagination running wild with gory images of my imminent demise and Gary the hotelier's catchphrase on repeat, like a stuck record: 'I bet you never thought your trip of a lifetime would start off like this. I bet you never thought your trip of a lifetime would start off like this. I bet you never thought your . . .' AAAAARRRGH! Enough! I couldn't just lie here like this all night, immobilised by fear. There was nothing else for it. I was going to have to investigate.

Making only the tiniest, mouselike movements, desperate to be as quiet as possible, I shimmied out of my sleeping bag and located the tent door zip. Another THWOD came from outside, just a few feet away. Oh God, help me! I held my breath, terrified of the dark, spooky outside world that lay beyond the safe confines of my cosy little refuge with its comforting aroma of wet leather and gas fumes. Slowly, steadily, I opened the zip by an inch. Icy air shot in like a jet. One more inch. More freezing gusts. And another inch.

And another, until there was just enough of a gap to slip my head out and face my tormenter. I gasped in awe at the sight that greeted me in the moonlight: a thick layer of blindingly white, virgin snow had enveloped Alaska.

THWOD.

Oh no.

Stiffening instinctively, I hovered in the entrance of the tent, my heart in my mouth. Now silence again. The seconds passed like hours. As I crouched there, poised, all senses on red alert, a pile of snow began to slip down the tent roof. I watched it slide slowly, steadily down the awning in front of me, gathering more snow and more momentum as gravity exerted its force and it finally fell to the ground, landing with a heavy . . . yep . . . THWOD.

My laughter bounced and echoed off the mountains, into the still of the night.

The memory of this first night in Alaska kept me amused over the next few days. I saw it as a sign, a timely reminder that things are never as bad as they seem. I would regularly laugh about it to myself, as I rode through the awe-inspiring landscape coated in the innocent white snow that had struck so much fear into my heart. Vancouver was my immediate destination, where I was visiting some old family friends, 2,200 miles down the road—the same distance as London to Istanbul. But compared with the rest of my journey ahead it seemed like a ride to the shops. Having a short-term goal to aim for served as a great boost to morale, and each day I would put between two and three hundred miles on the clock, stopping only for gas, food and the odd photo opportunity.

I'd love to wax lyrical on the Yukon scenery, but as the snow moved in, visibility dropped to just a couple of feet. The days following my entry into Canada were just one greyish white haze as the blizzards raged across the Northern Territories. The only other vehicles on the road were the snowploughs keeping this important

Cold, snowy nights in the Yukon

route open, cutting channels in the foot-high drifts that I followed with much gratitude. There was no one else on the highway; even the long-distance truckers were taking refuge in the cosy roadside lodges, and you could see why. They had log cabin interiors, blazing fires and hearty menus, and the idea of being unexpectedly confined to such a homely bolthole while snowstorms whirled past the window was reminiscent of the glee I remembered from childhood, when a sudden snap of bad weather would result in an impromptu day off from school.

'You don't wanna go out there,' one of the truckers advised me through a mouthful of maple syrup–drenched pancakes while I settled the bill for my own carbohydrate feast and prepared to tackle another fifty-mile stint. This was about all I could take before my toes turned blue and I lost all feeling in my fingers.

'Which way you headin'?' he asked.

'East.'

'It's worse in that direction,' another one added.

'There's snowdrifts down towards Whitehorse.'

'There's a light plane stranded at Haines Junction.'

'An' the highway's real bad for the next hundred miles or so,' piped up another, 'mostly gravel, 'n' holes all over.'

'Why don't you stay and wait it out,' they suggested. 'It'll pass in a couple of days.'

But for some reason that I still can't fathom, the need to keep moving was stronger than the need to keep warm. The truckers howled with laughter as I donned my extreme weather clothing. I'd picked up a new piece of kit in a gas station, the Emergency Poncho, ninety-nine cents for a see-through yellow plastic cape that I'd been saving for a day like this. Surely, this was just the kind of emergency it was intended for. To complement my new look I had also taken to wearing a pair of rubber washing-up gloves over my leather ones. Like a low-rent caped crusader, I trundled off into the snow, a mass of billowing yellow plastic flapping noisily behind me. Ten miles down the road my superhero outfit hung in tatters around my shoulders; this was clearly more than a ninety-nine-cent emergency.

There was something exciting about motorcycling in these extreme conditions, and even though I yelped out loud with the pain of my frozen hands and the speedo rarely nudged forty miles an hour, due to the potentially hairy combination of the porridgey white fog, loose gravel and random potholes, the experience seemed bizarrely appealing. This is exactly what I'm meant to be doing, I thought, this is about as different from sitting in a centrally heated office in West London as I can get. I tried to imagine what it must have been like up here when they built the highway during World War Two, after Pearl Harbour, with the threat of a Japanese invasion looming large. Thousands of men, soldiers and civilians alike, hastily bulldozing the 1,520 miles through an inhospitable wilderness in just eight months, following a tortuous route of old Indian trails and rivers to link up crucial U.S. airbases. Would they ever have dreamt that the AlCan would become one of the world's most celebrated road trips, drawing thousands of vacationers up from the Lower 48, looking for old-time adventure in their plush RVs during the summer months, causing traffic jams and congestion in overcrowded campsites from Dawson Creek to Fairbanks? Although I was suffering the ills of being here a little early in the season, I was glad to have the road to myself.

I felt I'd covered nearly all the elements of a classic AlCan adventure—whirling snowstorms, ropey road surfaces, a few close calls with wandering wildlife including moose, porcupines and a couple of coyotes. But there was one thing missing. My AlCan experience wouldn't be complete until I'd seen at least one bear—the trump card of the wildlife-spotting game and the hottest topic of conversation in this part of the world; all the locals had a bear story, but I was beginning to wonder if the whole thing was just made up for the benefit of visiting foreigners.

But to and behold, as if the Canadian Tourist Board had overheard my complaint, there he was, just strolling along the side of the highway like he owned the road. An extremely cute looking black bear with a little brown nose and an awkward lumbering gait. I couldn't believe my eyes! A bear, a bear! A real-life bear! I slammed on the brakes, leapt off the bike and whipped out my camera, quickly fitting the zoom lens; after all, I didn't want to get too close. He might look cuddly, but I wasn't keen to find out exactly *how* cuddly. Crouching in the long grass, I staked him out, snapping away, twitching nervously each time he looked in my direction in case he'd sniffed me out and fancied me for dinner. Must get rid of that Nivea, I told myself sternly, it's a damned liability. But he wasn't interested in my beauty products or me; he just ambled along gently without a care in the world. Wow! I kept exclaiming out loud, once I was safely under way again, I've seen a bear, just wait till I tell everyone, wait till they see the pictures, they won't believe it!

The following day I saw another one, and a few miles down the road I saw a couple more, and by the time I'd counted ten in a fifty-mile stretch, the novelty had worn off a bit. Bears? Oh yeah, they're all over the place, cluttering up the highway, nothing but common vermin if you ask me.

Despite this sudden influx of ursine furry friends I was still keen to carry on camping, although the reality of having one set of clothes and no washing facilities was beginning to make itself known to me, and probably anyone else that had the misfortune to come into contact with me. But Gordy, curator of the museum at Fort Nelson, an old fur-trading post on the British Columbian stretch of the AlCan, was made of sterner stuff than to be put off by a member of the great unwashed entering his repository. He pounced on me as soon as he saw the bike.

'I ride a Yamaha 1100,' he announced, 'come with me, I'll take you on a personal guided tour of the museum.' These words would have had me running for the exit twenty years earlier, but the museums I was dragged round as a kid didn't have stuffed elks, bear skulls and a trapper's cabin complete with dried pelts and evil-looking leg-hold traps. Gordy's generosity wasn't limited to the mere waiving of an entrance fee. 'Come and stay at my place,' he insisted when I enquired about local campsites. 'Don't worry, I've got a wife,' he added hastily, no doubt sensing my hesitation about heading off into the night with a mysterious museum curator, 'and she's used to me bringing home strays,' he said, as further encouragement. It was one of those will I won't I moments. Staying the night with a man I'd met only minutes earlier (well, it wouldn't be the first time, I could hear my mum saying), and if it all goes horribly wrong, I'll only have myself to blame. Just trust your instincts, I told myself, use your wits, this is what it's all about. And he does have a wife, I reminded myself, which is generally a good sign.

Putting any thoughts of England's favourite mass-murdering married couple, Fred and Rose West, to the back of my mind, I hopped on my bike and followed Gordy's Yamaha through town before we peeled off down a dingy side road into a tumbledown trailer park, each mobile home fenced in by a wall of automobile junk and vehicles in varying states of repair. He pulled up outside the one with the most motorcycles in the front yard.

'Well, here we are,' he announced cheerfully as I surveyed the situation, trying to keep my face expressionless.

His trailer looked worryingly dark inside and the rosy-cheeked wife in the gingham apron was nowhere to be seen.

'Shall I just wait here while you check it's OK with your wife?' I suggested craftily, passing off my paranoia as good old English politeness and wondering what on earth I was getting myself into.

'No, no, no,' he hollered, looking at me as if I was slightly unhinged, 'she won't mind, just come on inside.'

I peered through the window for any telltale meat cleavers or body parts but instead my eyes rested on a row of china figurines and I breathed a sigh of relief. Phew! There was a woman at large somewhere. Men don't have figurines, that was one rule you could rely on the world over.

Five minutes later, I was being urged to make full use of the facilities by Lee, Gordy's sweet, long-suffering wife. I wallowed in the piping-hot bathwater and plundered the plentiful supply of beauty products. Oh joy! This beat camping in the snow. Bath time was followed by dinnertime—a juicy roast salmon with all the trimmings. The beer flowed continuously, not least due to Gordy's self-confessed alcoholism, which he announced with cheery pride, keen to point out how he'd encouraged his wife down this slippery slope with him. 'She never touched a drop before she met me,' he beamed with the triumphant tone of a preacher who has successfully converted an atheist. Half native-Indian and an ex–long distance trucker, Gordy had yarns aplenty of the Canadian North, which I consumed with a salacious appetite, each one reading like a Yukon tabloid headline. Men killed in logging disaster! Hand-to-hand combat with bear in hunting escapade! Coyote kills child in trash can! Motorcyclist crashes headfirst into wall after all-day drinking session (guess who?). With each beer downed, the tales turned taller, while Lee, in her kindly way, gently corrected her husband's outlandish hyperboles: 'No, darling, the coyote didn't *eat* the child.' 'No, dear, you'd only drunk *two* bottles of whiskey when you crashed the Harley.' By the time I'd got the hang of the in-house beer can disposal system (squash it in your hand then lob it across the room), the talk had inevitably turned to bears and I found myself gingerly handling the teeth and claws of Gordy's latest kill. One thing was certain, I was a very long way from London.

Back on the road the following day, feeling slightly fragile but pepped up by the milk of human kindness, I finally entered Beautiful British Columbia. A day spent twisting through the Rocky Mountains was indeed awesome, but was followed by a few hundred miles of disappointingly dull landscape where the road cut through an endless expanse of pine forests, making for long days of dark and gloomy riding with no views except thousands of identical tree trunks flashing past on both sides. I was beginning to wonder if I should believe everything I read on the licence plates, but once again the tourist board's ESP kicked in and I was rewarded with a stretch of truly momentous motorcycling, the kind of riding that makes you grin from ear to ear, sing at the top of your voice and, if no one's looking, maybe even punch the air, Rocky style! A chap in a roadside café had tipped me off about a twenty-mile dirt road across the mountains that would link me up with Highway 99 into Vancouver—the famous Sea to Sky Highway—and what a piece of advice this turned out to be. These were the steepest, windiest routes I had encountered in my motorcycling life, proper biking roads boasting the most staggering scenery of the trip so far. Suddenly I was in a fairy-tale book that had sprung into life as I whizzed across colossal, snowcapped mountains, over fast-flowing rivers crisscrossed by dinky wooden bridges, past frothing white waterfalls cascading down the vertical cliff face onto the road in front of me, plunging deep into lush green forests, avoiding the odd bear (of course) and eking my way round a zigzaggery of hair-raising hairpin bends. Then the sun came out blazing and I was re-

The lonesome beauty of Canada's Rocky Mountains

minded why it was worth all the freezing cold and the wet, the delays and the hassles—for days like these. When strangers wave and smile at you from the roadside because they can just tell how much fun you're having.

Soon trees and bears gave way to skyscrapers and traffic jams, and the orange glow of city lights beckoned me into Vancouver via a multilane freeway. I rolled into town with a beaming smile on my face and found myself surprisingly happy to be back in the frantic pace of urban life, dodging the rush hour traffic and shouting obscenities at negligent car drivers, just like back home. I was getting into the swing of this.

Three

It wasn't until I woke up the next day in the alien comfort of
a family friend's guest bedroom at one o'clock in the afternoon, utterly exhausted and craving a hearty dose of healthy fruit and veg,
that I realised I'd knocked out Anchorage to Vancouver in ten nonstop days, running on pure adrenaline; gas station coffee and maple
syrup pancakes. Is this what Merle Haggard meant by White Line
Fever? I had it bad. If I carried on at this rate, I'd be in Ushuaia in
a couple of months and back home before I knew what had happened. I decided it was time to slow down the pace. This wasn't too
hard to do, considering the royal spoiling I was receiving from my
hosts, in their spacious hilltop home complete with spectacular
views across the city, washing machine, dryer, bath, a warm secure
garage (for the bike) and a bulging drinks cabinet (for its rider). I
didn't leave the house on that first day, instead relishing the opportunity to watch the rain lashing in off the Pacific Ocean through a
patio window rather than the usual smeared lenses of my riding
goggles. However, as I languished in the bath that evening, examining various bits of the Yukon as they floated up to the surface, the
irony of my pioneering urges being trodden into submission by the
lure of clean clothes and a few bottles of quality Chianti was not
entirely lost on me.

There was something familiar, homely even, about being in

Canada, a certain courtliness that I could only attribute to the influence of us demure English folk over the years. The first indication of this national decorum was the distinct lack of bullet holes in the road signs. Second, the local radio presenters were less prone to hysterical overexcitement and the use of ridiculous catchphrases than were their Alaskan counterparts. During my incarceration in the Eagle River Motel, I had often tuned into the Alaskan oldies station, Cool 97.3, a name which I can only assume referred to the average daily temperature, rather than the station's ethos. Here I would gorge myself on a repetitious diet of Motown classics and "Louie Louie" by the Kingsmen, enthusiastically presided over by Ed 'Hot Rod' Riley, an excitable fellow who not only told consistently unfunny jokes, but regularly fluffed their lame punch lines to boot. His co-presenter, 'Cool Daddy,' a gentleman who proudly broadcast under the slogan 'A married man . . . but available for parties' was slightly less bumptious but far sleazier and I soon had him singled out as an Alaskan Bush Company regular. Tuning into Vancouver's oldies station only compounded the genteel Canadian image when I discovered a mild-mannered chap, fronting the show in an almost apologetic manner, who meekly described himself as 'an eight-track player in a world of CDs.' But it was the anti-littering campaigns that illustrated the cultural divide most vividly. British Columbians were gently requested to 'Please Keep BC Clean' accompanied by a picture of a pretty pink and blue flower. Over the border in Alaska, a goony cartoon moose with a tire hanging from his left antler yelled 'DON'T TRASH ALASKA!' Predictably, there were a couple of well-aimed holes through his head from an angry resident who not only believed in the right to bear arms, but also the right to throw cigarette packets out car windows, whether the local moose contingent liked it or not.

When I did finally venture out of the house, it was down to the garage, to engage in a spot of routine maintenance on the bike. A swift oil change and a reassuring pat on the saddle seemed to be all that was required at this point, so I stripped off the boxes and bags and decided to take to the streets of Vancouver and enjoy the temporary experience of riding a luggage-free bike. There's a certain laissez-faire feeling one gets when travelling in another country, a sort of carefree sensation that your status as a hapless foreigner might help in getting you out of minor mishaps. So the sight of a police checkpoint on a leafy suburban thoroughfare didn't particularly bother me; even when they flagged me down, waving light sabre speed guns at me, I had no particular cause for concern. After all, although my little bike had many uses, breaking speed limits wasn't one of them. No, I had nothing to worry about here.

A burly, middle-aged, unsmiling cop motioned for me to park my bike on the sidewalk. I obliged. He looked angry.

'*No!*' he barked. 'Over there!' pointing to a spot about six inches from where I had taken position. Oh right, of course! Over there. Yes, that makes all the difference!

Crikey, I thought. I've got a right one here. Keep smiling. Tell them what you're doing here. It'll be fine.

'Can I see your driving licence?' requested Angry Cop.

I fished out my UK card-style licence.

'WHAT IS THIS?' he fumed.

'It's a British driving licence,' I replied in my plummiest English tones, resisting the temptation to preface it with, 'What ho, old boy!'

Angry Cop peered at the licence for some time, turning it over and over as if it were some rare and ancient document he'd unearthed.

'How do I even know you are permitted to ride a motorcycle?' he demanded snidely.

I pointed patiently to the picture of a motorcycle on the licence. Another minute was spent looking at the pictures of the vehicles I'm authorised to drive back home.

'But it's got pictures of everything on here,' he said, sounding both angry and confused, a lethal combination in an authority figure.

Oh no, I inwardly groaned. I'm going to have to explain the intricacies of the British driving test to a Canadian Mountie. I slowly pointed out that I was allowed to drive a motorcycle, a motorcycle with a sidecar, a car and various sizes of vans. To further make the point, I noted the lack of any pictures of buses, trucks and gas tankers on my licence. He grunted and paced towards the back of the bike. I could see what was coming next.

'WHAT IS THIS?' he yelled in disgust upon spotting my home-made number plate.

'It's a British licence plate,' I said unimaginatively.

'But . . . but . . . but . . .' he spluttered, barely containing his rage. 'It's a piece of plastic with letters on it,' he finally countered.

'Uh, yes, it is,' I responded.

We hadn't really got a repartee going at this point.

I told him the whole story of what I was doing here, how I had flown the bike into Alaska, that I was riding to Argentina. His eyes started glazing over.

He snatched the keys out of the ignition and I watched his knuckles turn white as he gripped them and my driving licence in his apelike hands. He glared at me menacingly and uttered the dreaded words.

'I need to see proof of ownership of this vehicle and your insurance.'

Aah . . . slight problem.

'I'm afraid I don't have my documents on me but I can bring them into a police station tomorrow,' I offered, thinking naively that everywhere is like England and wondering if there was any company in Canada that would back-date an insurance certificate (for a small fee, of course).

'YOU MUST CARRY YOUR PAPERS AT ALL TIMES!' he yelled. Blimey! Did I take the wrong road out of Alaska? I wondered. Am I actually in Russia?

'Anyway, how do I even know this motorcycle is yours?' he demanded.

Wow! He really is stupid.

'Well . . . let's think,' I proposed, just about keeping the sarcasm out of my voice, 'I'm English and this is an English-registered bike, and we're both in Canada. Just working on probability alone, it seems pretty likely that this is my bike.'

He thought about this for a while and seemed to see my point.

'Have you got insurance?' This was the sticky one.

'Yes,' I lied.

'What kind of insurance?'

'Oh, y'know, um, the usual kind,' I mumbled. I'm not very good at lying so I gave up at this point.

'I DON'T BELIEVE YOU HAVE INSURANCE!' he shouted.

Well done, Angry Cop. The detective inspector job may be yours yet.

He marched off to the car and made a series of frantic phone calls. I watched him behind the windshield, punching numbers into his phone with his fat fingers and gesticulating wildly as he relayed his victorious tale of catching an evil villain on a motorcycle. A while later he returned, still fuming, and began to bark short sentences at me in the style of a telegram.

'YOU CANNOT RIDE THIS BIKE. stop. IT IS ILLEGAL TO BE ON THE HIGHWAY. stop. YOU CANNOT TOUCH THIS BIKE. stop. YOU CANNOT PUSH THIS BIKE. stop. YOUR BIKE WILL BE TOWED AWAY. stop. DO YOU UN-DERSTAND? stop.'

I understood only too well.

With a flourish, he whipped out a large form and started taking down my details. Name, address, date of birth—the usual stuff. Then it got personal. He peered into my eyes.

'Blue,' he muttered, scribbling furiously. 'How tall?'

I told him my height.

'And what's your *real* hair colour?'

Cheeky devil!

'I don't know,' I replied truthfully, 'I haven't seen it since I was twelve.'

He took a step back and eyed me up and down as if I were a horse he was considering buying.

'Hundred and ten?' he asked.

'What?'

'HUNDRED AND TEN???' he bellowed impatiently.

'I'm sorry, I don't understand,' I replied, confused.

'Oh jeez, it's *stones* with you people, isn't it,' he said wearily.

Oh my God! He wants to know how much I weigh!

'Nine and a half *stones*,' I said through gritted teeth.

He smirked. 'That'll be a hundred and *thirty* then.'

Bastard! Mental note: Must cut back on the pancakes for breakfast.

He proceeded to write me out a ticket for $575, but I think he knew he was on to a loser. He handed it to me with the words 'I am fining you for riding without insurance. But I guess you won't be around to pay it, will you?'

I decided to reserve my right to silence on this one.

I heard a vehicle pulling up behind me. The tow truck had arrived. A roguish young man in greasy overalls jumped out of the cab and surveyed the bike with an interested eye.

'Great! A dirt bike,' he proclaimed. 'Any gas in this thing? I haven't ridden one of these in a long time!'

I forced a grim smile and realising this was my final chance, launched into a last-minute, desperate attempt to rescue my bike from the clutches of the steel claws that swung above our heads with all the doom of a hangman's noose. But it was too late. A mechanical whirring and clanking from the truck drowned out my plea and before I knew it, my trusty motorcycle was dangling forlornly in midair. Destination: the local vehicle pound.

Angry Cop stuffed a wad of scary official paperwork into my hands and whizzed off without a word in a self-important display of flashing lights and screaming sirens. The tow truck trundled off in the opposite direction and as for me . . . well, I just stood there, all helmet and no wheels. My head was spinning; it had happened so fast, I'd hardly had time to think, and now here I was, less than two weeks into my Pan-American motorcycle trip, with no motorcycle. Is there a sorrier sight than the rider without a ride? I wondered miserably, as I trudged through the empty suburban streets in the darkening evening gloom, helmet in hand, wondering what on earth I was going to do next.

Four

OK, so I thought I'd get away with it. I had considered buying insurance for the bike, albeit fleetingly, and I'd decided against it. You win some, you lose some. And if this whole trip was a series of gambles, then surely the odds were now set for a winning streak. After all, I reminded myself, I could have stayed at home, rotting away in the Pigpen and insuring everything up to the eyeballs—health, life, pets and the brand-new washing machine—just in case. Justincaseness is the enemy of adventure, I told myself stirringly, and I was ready to fight it to the bitter end. I might have lost this battle but I was going to win the war.

This was the spirited pep talk I gave myself while studying a map of Vancouver and plotting my next strategic move from my temporary operations headquarters—an uncomfortably swanky coffee shop I had stumbled upon, all blond wood, chrome and smooth jazz. I was easily the scruffiest person in the place but it didn't matter, because once you produce a map in public it's guaranteed that within seconds there'll be a helpful local hovering around, ready to offer a convoluted verbal version of the printed information in front of your nose.

'Tell me where you wanna go, and I'll tell you how to get there,' said the overly groomed man peering over my shoulder, a little closer than was necessary. He smelt cocky and expensive and wore a lopsided knowing smirk. Admittedly, not my ideal agony uncle, but feeling somewhat discombobulated by the events that had led me here, I welcomed the intrusion. I had a burning need to share the details of my saga with someone, anyone! I hoped he might offer up some local knowledge about bribing the tow truck company or loopholes in the insurance law, but he wasn't interested in the minutiae of my predicament.

'So, what are you doing over here on a motorcycle anyway, all on your own-e-o?' he enquired with a hint of suspicion in his voice, as if I wasn't quite playing by the rules.

I launched into a rambling explanation of my plans.

'Whoa! Hold on!' he said. 'Let me get this straight. This motorcycle of yours that the Mounties have made off with, you were gonna ride it down to Argentina?' He laughed incredulously, sliding into the seat next to me.

'Er, yes,' I replied, shifting uncomfortably towards the wall and breathing through my mouth to avoid smelling his noxious aftershave.

'Jeez!' he exclaimed, rolling his eyes and shutting the book he'd hitherto been absorbed in, awarding me his full attention. 'I don't know why women wanna do that kind of thing. I guess it's just so they can say they've done it.' He sneered disparagingly.

Slightly taken aback, I attempted to clarify my motives.

'Well, to be honest, I just fancied a bit of an adventure, nothing more complicated than that, really.'

He raised his eyebrows sceptically.

'And,' I continued, before he could get a word in, 'I'm upholding a good British tradition of exploration.'

'Jeez, you Brits!' he huffed. 'Still obsessed with colonialism and conquering the natives.'

My eyes fell on his book, *Find It in Five Minutes—Surviving the Information Overload of the 21st Century,* lying on the table between his cappuccino and his mobile phone. The scene resembled a lifestyle ad for a lifestyle I was keen to avoid. This was one native I would happily leave unconquered. I quickly gulped my coffee and made ready to leave.

'Hey hey hey . . . where are you goin'?' he said hastily, standing up, the smirk contorting his face into a caricature of smarm. 'Not so faaaaast . . . here's my number, gimme a call, we could get together while you're in town . . . where you staying?'

Rather than overload him with any more information this early in the twenty-first century, I decided to keep this nugget of intelligence to myself and made for the door.

A convoluted cross-town public transport farce, which by some miracle culminated in me arriving at my hosts' front door several hours later, only strengthened my resolve to rescue my motorcycle from the clutches of the Canadian authorities as soon as possible. The following morning I awoke with a jaw clenched from a night of anguished teeth grinding, and jumped out of bed, ready to do battle with bureaucracy. After grumbling down the phone to a slew of faceless insurance companies, I resigned myself to coughing up for a three-month policy that would cover my bike for Canada and the USA.

'Is that to include Alaska as well?' asked the voice at the end of the line.

'No, thank you, I've been there and got away with it,' I replied, keeping my bitterness light and jovial. I stapled the $575 fine into my diary as a memento, with a solemn vow that it would reside forever in the Overdue file. Armed with the most expensive fax I've ever had the displeasure to receive, the time had come to launch phase two of my crusade—the assault on the vehicle pound.

So far, I wasn't too impressed with Vancouver Man, and my venture in the drizzling rain to this desolate, razor wire–fenced enclosure on the outskirts of the city looked unlikely to alter this opinion. Admittedly, vehicle pounds, like scrap yards or landfills, aren't renowned as a hotbed of high-quality Y chromosomes, unless you like your bit of rough *really* rough, but I feared this experience would finally sound the death knell for the genteel Canadian image

I had previously nurtured. I strode purposefully across the yard, sloshing through grey oily puddles, towards a small wooden hut that I guessed to be the throbbing nerve centre of the operation. A group of men with blackened hands, wearing matching overalls contaminated with a cocktail of carcinogenic waste products, whistled and whooped from the other side of a chain-link fence. It was like a prison visit; I should have come with a file buried in a cake.

Inside the hut I rang a bell with an incongruously cheerful ding-dong tone and sat down for a long wait. A sign reminded me that the staff wouldn't take any lip from us lowly members of the public. But the walls, it seemed, were exempt from this rule. I studied the outpourings of the men and women who had sat here before me. BASTARDS, said one simply. SUCK ON THIS MOTHERFUCKERS, was another frustrated motorist's suggestion, accompanied by a useful illustration. YOU WILL DIE FOR YOUR SINS AND BURN IN HELL, promised one of God's children, proving that even the good Lord can't save you from the dreaded tow truck. A tiny window of reinforced glass separated the hunted staff from the baying masses as well as providing the only source of light in the cramped gloomy waiting area. This wasn't a problem until the vastly obese attendant appeared at the window, creating the effect of a mini solar eclipse, plunging the cell-like room into total darkness.

'Can I help you, ma'am?' enquired the rotund silhouette in a bored monotone.

Rummaging molelike for my paperwork, I relayed the story of my run-in with the Mounties.

'Oh yeah,' grunted the shadowy figure, 'you here on some kinda road trip? Fear 'n' loathing in Vancouver, eh? Heh heh, well, you'd better get used to it . . . hurgh hurgh hurgh.' He gurgled a laugh that could only emanate from someone whose BMI rating has rocketed off the scale, and then attempted to sting me for a range of spurious storage charges.

We argued bitterly for a while, he in the weary tones of a man that does it for a living, me with the quiet, controlled rage of a psychotic killer. I won. Light flooded the room as he shuffled off to look for my keys.

'Pete! Jimmy! Find this lady's motorcycle!' bellowed the Prince of Darkness from the doorway to a couple of inmates in the yard, throwing the keys in their direction before retreating into his hovel. Judging by his cadaverous pallor, it was the only fresh air he got all day.

I ventured warily beyond the chain-link fence. I wasn't looking forward to this part of the show—getting thrown to the grease monkeys. If only this was a musical, I thought wistfully. They'd perform a highly choreographed dance in their matching outfits before carrying me aloft to my waiting motorcycle, on which I would exit stage left, with a throaty roar and a billow of smoke, never to be seen again.

'Over here,' shouted a familiar voice. The tow truck driver who had so expertly whisked my bike away the day before beckoned me over to where it now stood, nestling between a crumpled truck chassis and a pile of buckled wheels. My heart skipped at the sight of the bike, as if I were being reunited with a long-lost friend. I wanted to give it a little hug, but fearing the derision of the less than sentimental workers, I settled for a friendly pat on the rogue licence plate.

'I bet you're glad to see the old beast again.' The tow truck driver smiled.

I smiled back, surprised. Maybe I'd been a tad presumptuous, earmarking him as a heartless Neanderthal oaf. If he could maintain even a hint of pleasantry, working in a place like this, where squalor and fury reigned supreme, I was impressed.

'Crazy, isn't it?' he said with a resigned shrug, seeing me survey the mountains of twisted rusting metal that surrounded us. 'And it wasn't all that long ago only the richest folk could own a car. Now look at it, they're just trash, y'can't get rid of the damn things. I'm sick of the sight of 'em.'

I nodded in empathy as I swung a leg over the bike, overjoyed to feel its familiar shape beneath me again, like the reassuring comfort of settling into an old favourite chair. We had over fifteen thousand miles ahead of us. From now on we'd better stick together.

'Canadian cops are bastards,' said the tow-trucker, less pensively than before, but not without feeling. 'You'd better get your ass over the border pretty quick. Mind you, they're no better in the States. I went down Seattle, month or so ago, got pulled over three times on I-5. Three fuckin' times! I was driving this beat-up ol' truck, min' you, and there was six of us in it, smoking shit and really haulin' ass!' He laughed at the memory, flicking his cigarette butt into the shell of a burnt-out car.

'I've got the law enforcement agencies of Mexico, Central and South America to look forward to,' I told him glumly.

He gave a sympathetic grin. 'Cops are bastards everywhere. But you'll be OK. You're lucky, I wish I was going with you, I've always wanted to make a big trip like that.'

I started the engine and clunked into first gear, slipping the clutch, itching to get going.

'Good luck!' he called out as I weaved around a couple of hub-caps, the glittering crystals of a broken windscreen grinding beneath my wheels. The place was a depressing dump, but as I accelerated out of the gate, splashing through the rainbow pools of oily water, I didn't care anymore. It didn't matter because I was back on the road and I could go wherever I wanted. It was an exhilarating sensation.

I hung around Vancouver for a few more days, but my heart was elsewhere, somewhere farther on down the road. Somewhere in sun-soaked California, riding through towns with song title names, sleeping out under a star-spangled sky, or soaring across the Golden Gate Bridge into the hubbub of San Francisco. It was time to move on. I bid a farewell, both fond and sad, to my friends and headed for the U.S. border. The crossing was quick but stern, with just a quizzical glance from the border police at my alien licence plate. A mile or so later, I pulled into a run-down gas station on Interstate 5 to call some friends of mine in Los Angeles with the good news—they'd let me into the Land of Opportunity and I was on my way south! But after I threw two dollars' worth of nickels and dimes into the sticky pay phone and got precisely nowhere, an enormous woman sporting poodle-permed hair in the next booth overheard my English venting of frustration.

'You having some troubles, honey?' she enquired with a kindly, maternal chirp of a voice.

Great! She was just what I needed at this moment—a real-life American to guide me through AT&T's undoubtedly efficient and customer-focused telecommunications system.

'Hey, baby, hang tight, I'll come and help you in a minute,' she called through the scratched, bleary glass that divided us. 'I just gotta call my daughter to tell her to go to work. She's in the military y'know, but she can't ever get outta her bed.'

Crikey! I thought. Don't tell the enemy. But the daughter snoozed soundly as Mom bellowed a verbal reveille to an unresponsive ansaphone.

'Gee, well, I tried . . .' muttered my self-appointed aid as she squeezed her terrifying bulk into my booth, forcing me into the Urination Corner. She punched the number in several times, with no success.

'Goddamn piece-of-shit phones,' she exclaimed, 'I don't know what's wrong with this goddamn country.'

As I murmured some sort of noncommittal, sympathetic response she made a magpielike snatch into my purse, emerging with a handful of shiny quarters that she rammed violently into the slot. Her body language suggested more erratic behaviour was to follow, so making a break for it, I inhaled as deeply as possible, easing past her nylon-clad, unsupported bosom with some difficulty and watched with a mixture of shock and awe as she became increasingly furious on my behalf.

'Motherfucking piece of shit!' she yelled, landing a fleshy right hook on the side of the phone. I was half grateful and half mortally embarrassed. She'd seemed so, well . . . wholesome.

'Goddamn it! I'm gonna call the operator,' she announced. 'They can't get away with this shit!'

I made a few feeble protestations but I knew it was no good. She was waging a one-woman war on faceless corporate America and who was I to stop her? Avoiding diplomacy at all costs, she launched into a furious tirade to the utterly disinterested operator.

'We've just wasted three fuckin' bucks in your piece-of-shit phone! What ya gonna do about it? What is fucking wrong with you goddamn people?!' she ranted. There appeared to be complete silence at the other end but this only encouraged her further.

'I said . . . what ya gonna fuckin' do about it? Ya hear me?' she shrieked, her fury finally culminating in an outburst of sheer modern-life frustration: 'FUCK YOU!!! YOU GODDAMN MOTHERFUCKERS HAVE TO START TAKING RESPON-SIBILITY FOR THIS SHIT!'

Bang! The sticky handset returned to its cradle, quivering.

Looking altogether more cheerful now, she waddled out of the booth with an almost Zen-like serenity and heaved herself into her car. 'I'm sorry I couldn't help, honey,' she apologised, leaning out the window with a beaming smile. The national catchphrase hung in the air as she bid me farewell with an arm-wobbling wave: 'Have a nice day!'

I stood there for a moment, a little poorer in the material sense, but spiritually enriched by my brush with this American antihero. I pondered my decision to incorporate the USA in this journey of mine. After all, one of the burning desires behind this trip was to escape these infuriating skirmishes with twenty-first-century bu-reaucracy and incompetence that grind us down every day. I was seeking some authenticity, some down 'n' dirty reality. I wanted to ride into the wilderness, sleep under the stars; just me and my mo-torcycle . . . get back in touch with the elements. I'd spent too many years staring at a computer screen in London media-land;

Stars and stripes everywhere. A warm welcome in the U.S.A.

now I wanted out. Goddamn it, I'd even pared down my makeup kit to survival status: mascara, nail varnish, eyebrow pencil and a couple of essential lipsticks—I was taking this whole thing very seriously. Like my telephone assistant, I'd had my fill of modern life's irritations, but maybe the States wasn't the best place to go to escape them.

This is still the beginning, the easy bit, I reminded myself; and with luridly concocted images of the nitty-gritty that surely awaited me down the Pan-American Highway, I jumped on my motorcycle and headed on south once again.

In Washington State I had the good fortune to be taken in by fellow BSA enthusiast Barb, and her fiancé, Rory, who put me up for the night in a display of good old-fashioned American hospitality.

'If I had a garden, this is what I'd want it to be like,' I said to Barb, as we trekked past her countless motorcycles in various states of repair all over the rambling yard. In the garage I was introduced to Britney, a BSA 441 Victor, Barb's pride and joy, and my ultimate dream bike, which had me drooling enviously. Nonmotorcycling Rory didn't share my and Barb's enthusiasm for classic British Iron, or in fact, anything to do with motorcycles, and in a display of modern-day role reversal, he busied himself in the kitchen preparing an enormous feast while Barb and I knocked back a bottle of port and talked bikes bikes bikes.

I was on the road the next morning, swearing I'd never eat or drink again after Rory's total lack of portion control the night before. I was spoilt for beautiful rides through Washington State and Oregon, and I passed by Mount Saint Helens through high mountain with snow still on the ground. But Oregon's rainy reputation was unfounded and I arrived in Portland to find the city cooking at ninety degrees. Not that I was complaining, with the blizzards of Alaska still fresh in my mind; it was everything I had hoped for.

The USA was proving to be endless fun. I had plenty of folk to visit and there were friendly people everywhere. But I also had White Line Fever bad—that old gnawing obsession with what lies ahead, and an inability to simply be in the time and place. The map is always tempting and beckoning, calling you, 'Come hither . . . look what joys await you down the road.' But it's a disease of the restless optimist and a sure-fire defence against disenchantment. No need to feel disappointed by a stretch of dreary scenery, an inedible meal or the rude pump attendant, because you're always just passing through, on your way to a place where the water tastes like wine and the sunsets are so beautiful they'll bring tears to your eyes. So off you go, counting down the miles to the next Promised Land, until you get there and out comes the map, and the dreaming and counting start all over again. I felt almost guilty about this to begin with, under pressure from an imagined omnipresent tourist board that scorned my shunning of museums and art galleries and scolded me for not studying the local history or some other worthy pursuit. It took me a while but I eventually came to terms with my restlessness, simply because, right or wrong, it was an itch I enjoyed scratching. A road trip isn't about being somewhere, I reminded myself, it's about going somewhere, and ultimately, that was all I wanted to do.

And what better part of the world to live out my hobo dream than the freewheelin' West Coast of America? The famous Pacific Coast Highway, a winding ribbon of blacktop, simmering under a guaranteed sixteen hours of ozone-free California sunshine each day, proved the ideal route to indulge my *Easy Rider* fantasies (although sadly not the ones involving Peter Fonda).

And I wasn't the only one. In stark contrast to my experience in Alaska, the road was teeming with American motorcyclists answering the call to arms. Or as Walt, a bearded, longhaired Goldwing rider taking a break in a roadside diner, put it, 'It's summer, it's California, what ya gonna do? Ya gonna ride the PCH, right?'

'I'm inclined to agree,' I said.

'You guys!' he roared with laughter. 'You sure talk funny! Gee, that is so cute! Is that a real accent, you ain't shittin' me, are ya?'

I assured him with crisp enunciation that yes indeed, this was a real accent and that no, I couldn't be accused, to use his vernacular, of shitting him. The conversation flowed with the ease of two strangers on common ground, as we put the diner's Bottomless Coffeepot to the test, our talk eventually turning to the ancient Californian redwoods that lined our route along the coast.

'Do you have forests in England?' he asked me with genuine curiosity.

It was too good to miss.

'Oh no, England doesn't have forests,' I explained. 'There used to be one called Sherwood Forest but they cut it down to build a car park.'

'Shit, man, that's too bad.' He shook his head. 'I ain't what you'd call a, y'know, tree-huggin' kinda guy,' he said, 'but why the hell they wanna cut down your only forest? We wouldn't stand for that kinda shit in America.'

I shrugged helplessly.

'You know Woody Guthrie, right?' he demanded, all fired up by the injustice of the Great British Forestry Scandal.

Oh no, please! I knew what was coming next; my toes were pre-curled in embarrassed anticipation. Please don't sing, please don't sing, I prayed silently.

But he was off.

'This land is yoooour land, this land is myyyy land,' he warbled, looking me straight in the eye, 'from Califoooorn-ya to the New York Iiiiii-land . . .'

I squirmed and smiled bravely until he petered out in the second verse, lamenting the fact he'd forgotten the rest of the lyrics.

'Too much weed, man.' He laughed, tapping the side of his head. 'I used to know that one all the way through.'

With a convoluted biker's handshake and a farewell holler of 'Keep the rubber side down!' he rumbled away north and I set off ever southwards, following the legendary twists and turns along the edge of the land. With the sun sinking away to my right, smoulder-ing pink and orange over the Pacific, I understood exactly what Woody and Walt were on about.

Despite my initial misgivings about the USA following my brush with the poodle-permed porker in the phone booth, I was having a ball. Life on the road suited me. I could feel the grind and the tedium of my office-bound existence slipping away, relegated to just a bad memory of something I used to do, once upon a time. My shoulders were loosening, my mind was opening, the sneers and jeers of cynical London life didn't seem to fit anymore. Life was all peace, love and understanding. Oh horror of horrors, was I turning into a hippie? Damn this beastly West Coast vibe!

Unnerved by this perturbing concept, I shared my fear with Christine, a friend of a friend I had been given instructions to look up in the seaside town of San Luis Obispo. She was a cool, peroxide-blond rockabilly chick, a veteran of Californian plastic surgery and hard living, who cruised the streets in her vintage Chevy pickup bearing the licence plate LADY LUCK. She knew just the man who could help me. We necked a few Jack Daniel's in a burrito joint, and before I could change my mind, ducked across the road into a tattoo parlour where I was introduced to an elaborately decorated Mexican man with a goatee beard and the unlikely name of Chewy. What the hell, I reasoned, if you can't get your first tattoo done while half cut on a motorcycle road trip, what can you do?

I sketched out an old fisherman's anchor surrounded by red roses and instructed him to etch this image onto my left hip. This eye-watering explosion of hard liquor and searing pain effectively exorcised my inner hippie child, but made the sporting of my leather trousers slightly uncomfortable for the next couple of weeks.

Most crucially, though, this American stretch was serving its purpose. My route from north to south was no accident; I had figured that starting out in the Land of Plenty would gently ease me into my adventure. I could get into the rhythm of life on the road and work out any teething problems with the bike, without the added difficulties of trying to communicate in Spanish amidst the potential mayhem of a Latin American country.

My theory was put to the test one morning in Northern California when, riding along in my usual fashion, singing Beach Boys songs and wondering where to stop for my pancake and maple syrup fix, I happened to glance downwards to spy my normally scuffed black leather boots in a state of unusual shininess. I pulled over in alarm to discover my feet and the rear wheel slathered in engine oil. Uttering a few choice words of Anglo-Saxon origin, I dismounted and sank to my knees to inspect the damage.

Five

I had an inkling what might have gone wrong. A few days previously, while staying with my motorcycling friends in Oregon, we had fitted a kick-start to the bike, planning ahead for the inevitable flat battery that would render my electric start useless. Upon replacing the engine cover, the gasket had disintegrated and the only option had been to employ a tube of rubbery gunge trading under the optimistic title Instant Gasket—which clearly wasn't living up to its name. Feeling somewhat cheated, I made a mental note to introduce the manufacturers of this product to the Trade Descriptions Office, should I ever find myself with a truly empty life.

I knew I had to face the facts and drain off the remaining oil to work out how much I'd lost. But I needed something to drain it into, and some way of measuring the quantity. What I needed was a measuring jug, but where on earth was I going to get one of those? The nearest town was an hour's ride away and I didn't want to risk it with a leak of these proportions. I remembered passing a gas station a mile or so back; it was my only option. I would push the bike there and hopefully they'd have something that would serve the purpose.

'

. . .

'*Good morning,' ma'am,*' said the elderly man on the forecourt. He was immaculately turned out in the gas company's
branded overalls and diligently washing the windscreen of a pickup
truck so huge he had to stand on tiptoe to reach. I panted at him for
a while, out of breath from a mile of grunting and shunting my
fully loaded bike under the sweltering rays of the California sun,
but finally managed to explain my plight, ending with a breathless
plea for a suitable receptacle.

'So (gasp), I was wondering (gasp) if you had any sort of con-
tainer, like a measuring jug (gasp) or something like that (gasp) . . .
or even an old oil bottle . . .'

'A measuring jug, ma'am?' The old man smiled, wringing out
his cloth. 'Let's have a look-see.'

I followed him into the shop.

'Ya wanna plastic one or a metal one?'

'Er . . . a plastic one, I guess,' I said, dumbstruck at the sight before me.

'Ya want clear plastic or white plastic? And what size is it you'll
be needin'? We gotta quart, a pint, half a gallon, lemme see, what's
this? Oh yes, this one's got a lid, ya need one with a lid? Now, if you
see here, this one's got the measurements on the inside *and* the outside. An' this one's gotta special rubber handle so it don't slip outta
your hands.'

'I'll take it!' I cried rashly, thrusting a handful of greenbacks
onto the counter. God bless America! Give me choice! Give me
consumerism! I spent the next twenty minutes examining all the
other jugs, in case there was a slightly better one that I should have
bought instead.

Under the welcome shade of a redwood, I discovered the horrible truth. Fifty millilitres of black gold sat in the bottom of my
clear plastic, nonslip-handle jug. The Serow's oil capacity being one
litre meant this wasn't a happy calculation. But I was grateful I'd
spotted it when I had; hopefully not too much damage had been

done, and besides, I was feeling rather pleased with myself. After the kick-start fitting, I had made it my business to buy a Complete Gasket Set from a Yamaha dealer in Portland, with the foresight that there might be more engine work in the months ahead.

'This is what it's all about!' I told myself, rolling up my sleeves in what I considered to be hearty Rosie the Riveter fashion. 'Oil leaks, roadside repairs, all part of life on the road. No problem!' I dug out the gasket set from the depth of my luggage and laid out the contents on my leather jacket. There were some little rubber rings and some bigger rubber rings and paper and metal gaskets in varying shapes and sizes, but none of them seemed to be the one I wanted. I laboriously matched them all up to their correct positions, leaving one glaring omission. My heart sank as I forced myself to accept the harsh truth—I was the proud owner of an Incomplete Gasket Set. The Trade Descriptions Office was gonna be real busy at this rate.

A shadow fell over my display; the old man of the garage had come to join in the fun.

'You all right, ma'am?' he asked. 'Looks like you got yourself one slippery ol' problem here.'

'Oh, it's not so bad,' I said, faking confidence. 'I'll refill the oil and just limp along till I find a motorcycle shop where I can order what I need. I'll be on my way in no time.'

It was my only option but the truth was I didn't have a clue where the nearest motorcycle store was or how long I would have to wait around for the part to arrive.

'So,' I continued, rising to my feet, 'I guess I'd better buy some oil before I go anywhere.'

'And what kinda oil would you like, ma'am? Ten-forty? Twenny-fifty? Mineral? Synthetic? We got Shell oil, we got STP, we got one with additives, cleans your engine while ya drive. . . .'

Oh crikey! My head was spinning with the Californian combination of sunstroke and consumer choice. I sat down again.

'The cheapest,' I groaned miserably, 'it'll be all over the highway in half an hour.'

I bought as much as I could carry and just as I was about to pour it in, I experienced a rare flash of illumination: *ZING! Maybe the bolts on the engine cover are loose.* Admittedly, in the world of engineering's inspirational lightbulb moments, this was little more than the flicker of a twelve-volt turn signal, but nonetheless, I felt rather pleased when a wiggle with the screwdriver confirmed my suspicions were indeed correct. 'Aha! Well, that explains a lot,' I announced positively. Maybe I'd cracked it! Buoyed up by what I considered to be my mechanical ingenuity, I set about enthusiastically tightening the bolts until sure enough . . . KERRRUNCH, the inevitable happened.

I sighed the deep despairing sigh of one whose good fortune has been cruelly reversed by her own ham-fisted bungling.

'Oh yes, I've cracked it, all right,' I muttered as I examined the ragged bolt head that I held in my palm and the other half, jammed deep in the hole. The whole affair was a shambles from start to finish, and now I wouldn't be able to fix it here, I would have to get hold of a stud extractor to remove the broken bolt.

By the time I arrived on the outskirts of the next town, the last drops of fresh oil had dribbled their way into the outside world, soaking back into the ground from whence they came. I struggled to find a silver lining in this dark cloud of a debacle, but the only one I could come up with was that I wouldn't have to polish my boots for a while. It was then that I spied the familiar red block letters jutting out from a building on the opposite side of the road, partly obscured by an overhanging tree. At first I could only see the H and the A, but I knew them straight away. As I swung a hard left across the street, the whole sign came into glorious view: Y-A-M-A-H-A.

Tony the mechanic greeted me like an old friend and upon hearing my tales of oily woe, steered me towards the store's computer system.

'It's an XT225, yeah? What year?'

'Ninety-four.'

Reassuring tapping noises came from the keyboard.

'And you need the right crankcase cover gasket?'

'Um . . . yes.'

More tapping.

'Yeah, got one of those in stock,' he announced casually. 'I can probably do it later this afternoon.'

I gaped at him in wonderment.

'You've got it in stock . . . and you can fit it today?' I yelped excitedly.

'Yeah, shouldn't be a problem,' he said.

I wanted to hug him but fearing it might give the wrong impression about my preferred payment method, I settled instead for jumping up and down on the spot.

As it turned out, Tony was a deeply committed Anglophile, and once I'd revealed my previous incarnation as a steadying hand at the tiller of the British Broadcasting Corporation (or at least, that's how he chose to perceive it, and who was I to spoil the fun?), he conducted our entire transaction in a highly exaggerated English accent, throwing in classic lines from *Fawlty Towers* and Monty Python and occasionally slipping into a convincing cockney brogue that he claimed to have learnt from his self-confessed addiction to *EastEnders*.

'Cor blimey, luv, put the kettle on! Did that sound right? I love British TV.' He beamed. 'I get the BBC on cable and I've got all the *Red Dwarf* videos,' he added proudly, breaking into a stirring rendition of the theme tune.

'So, have you met John Cleese?' he demanded as he silly-walked around the workshop.

'Er, no,' I said apologetically.

'How about Dirty Den?'

'Um . . .'fraid not,' I replied regretfully, racking my brain for a firsthand celebrity sighting. 'I did see Jeremy Clarkson in the

White City canteen once,' I offered hopefully, but Tony seemed underwhelmed by my tales of jostling at the salad bar with the *Top Gear* host.

'So what did you do at 'Auntie Beeb'? Were you a 'big cheese' who gave up the rat race to see the world?' he enquired, laughing gleefully at his use of these English expressions.

I explained that in the scheme of things, I would probably be better described as the scrapings from the director general's discarded Philadelphia wrapper, shattering his illusions once and for all. But he didn't seem to mind; as long as I laughed in the right places during his word-for-word rendition of the Parrot sketch he was happy.

I declined Tony's invitation to dinner; grateful as I was, I feared it would be too much like being back in the Pigpen. Instead, I made up for lost time in the waning daylight, riding until dusk in a state of oil-tight bliss before making camp on the beach, keeping a respectful distance from a gang of sunbathing sea lions, whose resonant hoots acted as a handy alarm call the following morning.

It was with a mixture of regret and anxiety that I realised my jaunt down the States was coming to an end. Los Angeles was just a couple of days' ride away, where I was planning on visiting my friends Joe and Lara, and doing some essential work on the bike, but it would be my last stop in California, and as far as I was concerned, my final halt for Western Civilisation as I knew it. From L.A., it was a straight shoot through into Mexico, crossing the border at Tijuana, a name on a map alluring as it was terrifying. Tijuana—a notorious frontier town, a hotbed of fighting, whoring and gambling, where desperate Mexicans running north for a better life cross uneasy paths with underage Americans southbound on their equally desperate but very different missions. I was taking an ostrich approach to the post-L.A. stage of my trip. I rarely gave it any thought, partly because I couldn't really imagine it, but mainly because the idea of leaving the cosy bubble of my American road trip fantasy was just too much to contemplate.

But if there was to be something that would kick me out of my Bottomless Coffeepot world of convenience and get my adventurous juices flowing again, it would be the synthetic, superficial whirlwind of plastic surgery and celebrity diets that is SoCal. Or so everyone in Northern California told me. Prior to my arrival in the Golden State, I hadn't been aware of the cultural and latitudinal divide that bisects California into NoCal and SoCal, or as some folk would have you believe, into good and bad taste, but it was a subject that the locals warmed to with a civil-warlike zeal: 'They're just a bunch of self-obsessed airheads down there' versus 'They're up their own hippie asses in SF.' 'It's all plastic boobs and fake tans in L.A.' versus 'They're a bunch of granola-eatin' faggots.'

No matter what side you were on, you couldn't deny it, there was definitely something afoot. I first noticed the change around Santa Barbara: the driving was getting faster, the blondes were getting blonder, and the breasts were getting bigger (although less convincing). I was in SoCal and I was having trouble keeping up.

'I don't mean you no offence, lady, but I don't think you should ride that lil' motorsickle on the L.A. freeways,' shouted an orange-skinned man from the tinted window of his shiny black 4WD. A series of face-lifts had left with him a tautness of skin and a visage so expressionless, he was destined to live out the rest of his days as a Thunderbird puppet look-alike.

This unfortunate candidate for My Plastic Surgery Hell was queuing behind me while I filled up the bike at a busy gas station near Ventura. He was bombarding me with all sorts of useful advice, but the problem was I could barely hear him thanks to the promotional efforts of the gas company that involved a giant clown on stilts dancing around the cars to a continuous loop of "Pump Up the Jam" blasting out at cone-busting volume over the forecourt PA system. It was ninety-six degrees and without the breeze of riding I was overheating fast. Sweat dribbled down my face in the sickly heat of the fume-laden air as I watched the clown flailing his extended limbs and lunging at small children, forcing them to dance with him in the name of commerce. I strained to catch the advice of my puppet-faced SoCal adviser.

'Sorry, what were you saying?' I shouted at him.

PUMP UP THE JAM, PUMP IT UP . . .

'It's dangerous, man! I seen you coming down the highway, you gonna be the slowest vehicle on the freeway.'

. . . PUMP UP THE JAM!

'I don't know where you've come from,' he continued, bellowing to be heard, 'but folks drive fast in this part of the world. You are on the wrong machine, lady.'

I was about to respond but the words choked in my mouth at the sight of the dreaded clown approaching, dancing in my direction. He was coming straight for me. I had to get away but my Thunderbird-faced friend wasn't finished yet, he was still bawling at me over the music.

'. . . an eighteen-wheeler goes past ya, you'll be blown away. Splat!' he yelled, whacking his right fist into his left palm in time with the music. PUMP IT! PUMP IT! PUMP IT!

'. . . like an itty-bitty fly on a windshield!'

PUMP UP THE JAM! PUMP IT UP!

I had to admit, it didn't sound like much fun, but as a lifestyle choice it was preferable to being here right now. The clown was getting nearer, but an accidental swipe at a Land Cruiser's wing mirror with his extended arm had caused a minor fracas with the Botox-faced blonde behind the wheel, and bought me a few crucial seconds. A child was screaming relentlessly somewhere in the back of Thunderbird Man's enormous blacked-out chariot.

'Like I said,' he was still shouting above the cacophony, 'I don't mean you no offence, but over here we'd use that lil' thing as a farm bike, y'know.' He raised his voice further as his offspring reached a piercing crescendo. 'LIKE FARMERS USE FOR GETTIN' ROUND THEIR LAND.'

'Yes, thank you for that explanation.' I smiled weakly.

The clown had extracted himself from the wrath of the Land Cruiser owner and was back on course, heading straight towards me. I hastily screwed the cap back on the tank and started the bike, hoping to swerve round him, but it was too late. He was blocking my escape route, bouncing around between the two cars in front of me, singing along and handing out sweets, while the inhabitants of the vehicles leant out of their windows, laughing and smiling.

I looked around me in amazement; no one seemed alarmed that a routine trip to the gas station involved being aurally assaulted by a deafening Technotronic loop and physically harassed by a gigantic gyrating clown. Not only did they not mind, they actually appeared to be enjoying it. I imagined the violent protests should this promotional endeavour ever be replicated across Merrie England. Maybe I was just an uptight Brit, but I had to get out of here.

With a blast on my horn I gunned it past the clown with millimetres to spare, sending his false limbs whirling like a wind farm.

'Ya tryin' to fuckin' kill me?' screamed his garish scarlet smile.

It didn't seem like such a bad idea, but for now I would settle for getting out of this nightmare as quickly as possible.

I tore out of the exit into the steaming congestion of Highway 101 south, gasping a lungful of hot heavy air before a concrete tunnel delivered me into the ceaseless high-speed swarm of the L.A. freeway system. How can one city have so many motorways? I wondered, trying to remember my route as cars and trucks shot past me at double my speed, overtaking me with inches to spare. Windows up, AC on. All powerful in tinted-glass anonymity. Peeling across the lanes to join another freeway from the east, more cars pouring in from the west. Grey junctions and green signs. Next exit Interstate 10. Next exit Interstate 405. Compton. Santa Monica. San Bernardino. Super-size American portions of spaghetti-junction intersections. Flyovers flying over more flyovers into smog-drenched, elevated oblivion. You could drive around L.A. for weeks and not see anything. Did people live and work and eat and talk in this city, or did they just keep driving? The roving, rambling, easy livin' of the Pacific Coast highway was just a memory, and it seemed to belong to another country. As I repeated my directions aloud, hammering them into my memory over the relentless white noise of this real-life slot car track, it occurred to me that Tijuana might actually come as something of a relief after SoCal.

But my relief came sooner than Mexico, in the shape of L.A.'s warmest welcome from dear friends Joe and Lara. If riding a farm bike into L.A. on its big ol' freeway system was like getting the middle finger from a city, this was like coming home for Christmas. Joe, the epitome of laid-back cool and quiet competence, was quick to offer his expertise and fully equipped, if haphazardly organised, workshop. He earned his Yankee dollar managing properties in downtown L.A. in a seemingly effortless manner, leaving him plenty of time for tinkering with beat-up vehicles and the renovation of their rambling old house, a rare turn-of-the-century building in the cut-and-thrust City of Angels. Lara, a fun-loving escapee from Illinois with a Midwestern heart of gold, had conjured up a tray of homemade chocolate brownies and a dazzling itinerary of Tinseltown fun. She implored me to stay with them as long as I liked.

'We'll go down Sunset Strip, do a tour of Hollywood, see the Capitol Records building, then we'll cruise along Mulholland Drive. And we've got to visit the Gene Autry Museum and we'll go down to the L.A. River, where they filmed the drag race scene in *Grease*.'

I was most excited at this prospect.

'We can go surfing,' she continued, 'and count the plastic tits on Venice Beach.'

'What happens if you don't get an even number?'

'Unlucky!'

'And we'll walk around downtown and see all the crackheads and hookers.' Hooker spotting was one of Lara's favourite pastimes.

'But tonight, we're going to have a truly L.A. experience,' she announced, 'we're going to Jumbo's.'

Joe groaned and hastily invented an excuse.

'Looks like it's gonna be a girls' night out then.' Lara winked. 'You are gonna love it!'

I didn't know how long I would stay in L.A., but I could already see it was going to be hard to leave. I spent the rest of the day just slowing down and settling in, enjoying the prospect of having a temporary base from which to prepare my break for the border. As I caught up on my e-mails, I called Lara over.

'Look, read this!' I exclaimed, pointing at a message entitled 'Girls On Bikes' from someone called Rachel Delavaud.

Hello Lois,

Saw your website. I've travelled overland from the UK (I'm French but lived in London for years) on the back of my boyfriend's bike for the past two years. By Australia I couldn't wait to get my own bike. I learned to ride and bought a KLR 250 (I'm small too). We shipped our bikes to LA and they've just arrived. I'm not sure about my route next but I'll be riding on my own most of the time so I'm glad you're out there too. Let me know how you get on in those leathers. I have ripped jeans, battered motocross boots and a cheap jacket . . . doesn't look nowhere near as good.

Rachel

'Wow,' said Lara.

'Wow,' I agreed, 'she sounds cool.'

'Says she's going to be riding on her own. I wonder what happened to the boyfriend?'

'Mmmm . . . I wonder.'

We speculated wildly, concocting various lurid theories.

'E-mail her back,' instructed Lara, 'tell her to come and stay with us.'

'Really? Are you sure?'

'Yes!' she insisted, always the hostess. Joe hadn't been consulted but it was assumed he wouldn't mind a French girl on a motorcycle showing up at his house.

Thanks to a combination of lightning-speed electronic mail and sheer chance, Rachel and her KLR250 arrived later that evening. Petite with a mass of brown curly hair and big brown eyes, she looked about fifteen, although she assured us she was twice that age. Her motorcycle, which despite falling into the farm bike category, being powered by only 25cc more than mine, looked enormous beside her and we were all suitably impressed when we discovered it was kick-start only, although Rachel admitted to occasional cravings for electric assistance in that area.

'I'll ask her if she wants to come out with us tonight, shall I?' I asked Lara, while Rachel wheeled her bike into the backyard.

'Well . . .'

'What?'

'Well, maybe we shouldn't go to Jumbo's then.'

'Why? What is Jumbo's exactly?'

'Well . . . y'see, it's a strip club.'

I fell about laughing.

'Oh no! We've just invited this girl to stay with us and now we're taking her to a strip club; she'll think we're roping her into some sort of illegal sex trafficking ring or something. We don't even know her, she might be really offended.'

'It's not a normal strip club, though,' explained Lara. 'It's not, y'know, lap dancing and big hair. All the girls that dance there are like, slightly fucked up, well, I mean, they're normal. Y'know, some are a bit fat, or not that good-looking, or they've got bad teeth or something. And they choose their own music, so it's quite different from like, a cheesy Spearmint Rhino joint. And apparently, Courtney Love used to strip there, before she was famous,' she added, as if that gave it some respectability.

We were laughing at the potential awkwardness of the situation when Rachel appeared.

There was a moment of uncomfortable silence.

'Oh. Hi. Everything sorted? Good. Look, we were planning on going to a strip club tonight where all the dancers are slightly disfigured in some way. Would you like to come?' I blurted out.

Lara looked at me, aghast.

'Yeah, sure, why not?' said Rachel with a cool Gallic shrug.

Jumbo's sat squat and unprepossessing amongst a row of low cinder-block buildings on a quiet neighbourhood street flanked by fast food joints and insurance companies. Inside, it was a different story. The place was hot, sticky and heaving with patrons of both sexes and all ages and persuasions. 'She's my favourite,' declared Lara, once we'd pushed our way back from the bar with a round of beers, as she carefully placed a handful of dollar bills on the stage in front of a curvy Mexican girl with Playboy bunnies tattooed on her ankles and dressed in nothing but a miniscule red tartan kilt. She was hanging upside down, her legs wrapped round a pole in the middle of the stage, writhing vigorously to the Southern rock grind of 'Sweet Home Alabama.' When she smiled you got a lifetime of dental ambivalence but I guessed that any spare cash had been spent on a more important set of attributes. And sure enough, her breasts would have given Isaac Newton pause. In fact, they didn't move during her entire performance, appearing to be formed from two solid hemispheres of moulded polypropylene coated with a thin layer of pale brown skin. Her arms were covered with randomly distributed bluish-black inky scrawls, as if some brutal backstreet tattooist had honed his craft on her, back in the bad old days, before she broke free and ran away to L.A. with dreams of becoming a movie star, stopping only in Georgia to garner an appreciation for the recorded works of Lynyrd Skynyrd. Or maybe I was getting carried away with my imaginary biography of this mysterious muchacha. Whatever her story, she was a great dancer and, despite her obvious flaws, undeniably and strangely attractive. This was more than could be said of the next one up, a lumbering woman in her late thirties with bovine features and an ill-fitting floral bikini who opened her act by violently flogging the stage with a leather bullwhip, adopting the ungainly stance of a rookie transvestite. Her lined face and thin lips suggested a lifetime of cruelty, dealt and received, but I felt for her when the music inexplicably stopped halfway through her routine and the poor woman was forced to clump offstage and wade topless through the audience to administer a beefy Fonz-style thump to the jukebox to get the proceedings underway again. We found ourselves rubbing up against her leathery shoulders later that evening, in line for the loo where she was discussing the pros and cons of having your makeup permanently tattooed on your face with a fellow dancer.

'Well, they fucked up my lips,' her friend was complaining, pouting into the mirror while absentmindedly tugging at a sparkly silver G-string wedged between her sculpted buttocks. She turned round to show a garish drawn-on mouth of Mick Jagger proportions.

'Yeah,' rasped the scary stripper in a voice not unlike Keith Richards's, 'you should sue their ass. What colour ya call that anyway?'

'I dunno,' said Mick, lips a-flubbering. 'Sex-toy pink?'

The lengthy queue for the toilets provided an opportunity to quiz Rachel on the circumstances that had brought her here to L.A., determined, as Lara and I were, to discover what had happened to her absent boyfriend.

'Things just weren't working out,' she told us glumly, 'travelling together for all that time; we were getting on each other's nerves.'

'So you've split up?' I ventured.

'Well, I don't know. He said he wanted to ride on his own for a while. He gets annoyed because I can't keep up with him sometimes.'

'So where's he gone?'

'He wants to tour around the States, so we might meet up again at some point, I just don't know . . .' she trailed off, looking miserable.

'I suppose it's quite natural to start annoying each other if you're together all the time,' I said. 'You probably just need a break for a little while.'

'Did you want Austin to come with you on your trip?' Lara asked me.

'Well, obviously I miss him, and in a way it would have been nice, but I really wanted to do it on my own, because that's what I'd set out to do before I met him. But I'd love us to do a big trip together in the future; he'd be my perfect travelling companion.'

Rachel looked sceptical.

'You can never tell,' she said knowingly, 'relationships get very strained on the road. I would never have thought that this would have happened with me and Simon.'

'Well, don't you worry about him!' said Lara, trying to lift the mood. 'You can stay with us for as long as you want, it'll be great fun!'

'Thanks,' said Rachel with a wan smile.

Back at the house the next day our partying was put on temporary hold as Rachel and I got on with some down 'n' dirty bike work. But the baking July heat meant that attempting anything remotely strenuous outdoors was a recipe for instant sunstroke, especially for an unacclimatised pasty Londoner. Fortunately Joe and Lara were the type of hosts that every motorcycle traveller dreams of visiting, and positively encouraged the changing of motorcycle tires in their living room. The Serow's clutch had also been showing signs of weariness, and on inspection I discovered it needed the friction plates replaced, a procedure I had never attempted before, but after some studying of the manual and quite a lot of head scratching, I felt was in my capabilities. My final upgrade was the biggest, loudest horn I could find, convinced that I'd be blasting it around blind corners on treacherous mountain roads while drunken Mexican truck drivers bore down on me shouting, *'Caramba!'*

Although, the truth was that I had no idea what they'd be shouting. My Spanish hadn't really progressed since I skipped out on the sex-crazed Argentine and his Wednesday-night Reclaim the Malvinas sessions. Lara had taught me a couple of words, pointing out signs as we drove around L.A. and purposely taking Rachel and me to Mexican eateries where no English was spoken. Chomping on a rubbery *quesadilla* in such a place, Lara nudged me, pointing to a yellow triangle warning of a slippery floor, bearing the instruction CUIDADO!

'KWEE-DAH-DO,' I said, dutifully taking my cue.

Lara screamed with laughter.

'You gotta work on the accent,' she said between fits of giggles, 'man, you sound so funny, saying those Mexican words in that lovely English lady's voice, like Jane fuckin' Austen!'

My second attempt in a more husky, Claudia Cardinale–style tone prompted further merriment.

'Don't worry,' Rachel interjected, 'I've been thinking, I'd like to go to Mexico too and I speak Spanish, so I can teach you some as we go along.'

'Brilliant!' I squealed excitedly, delighted by this announcement. 'You speak Spanish? Amazing!' I couldn't believe my luck.

'Well, I did a degree in it, but I'm a bit rusty,' she said nonchalantly.

'Rachel, you dark horse!' exclaimed Lara.

Rachel smiled self-consciously and I grinned back at her. I had a feeling that maybe, things might work out just fine south of the border.

Six

But Rachel's good news was tempered by her announcement that she would have to return to England in a few weeks to earn some cash in order to continue her travels at a later date. Although I was thrilled to have her as a riding companion for just this short stretch, the news made me aware that my apprehension about what lay ahead was still bubbling below the surface of my overactive mind.

I had no idea what to expect from Latin America, and like most people whose travels have been confined to First World countries, I was assuming the worst. My predicament wasn't helped by the horror stories I'd been fed over the last few months throughout my journey in the USA. Even the most enlightened North American, it seemed, possessed an inherent fear of the southern Spanish-speaking territories. My mind kept returning to a scene in a San Francisco bar, where I'd made the mistake of discussing my plans with a group of local motorcyclists, on the assumption they'd share my enthusiasm.

'You're going to do *what*?' they had spluttered incredulously.

'Are you insane, girl? You're going to ride through Mexico, Honduras, all those crazy places *on your own*?'

'You'll get raped,' stated one of my doom-mongering companions in an alarmingly matter-of-fact manner.

'They're, well, y'know . . . *different* down there,' volunteered another, slightly more tactful member of the party.

I barely had a chance to explain that 'different' was exactly what I was after, before a frenzied babble of hysteria had taken over the table, their neglected beers turning still and warm as they traded sensational tales of death, drugs and violence south of the border.

As a result of this drip feed of propaganda, I embarked on a highly unnecessary shopping spree, my fertile imagination encouraging me towards the type of fear-based bulk purchasing that any motorcycle traveller should know to steer clear of. Supposing they don't sell contact lens solution in Nicaragua? What about tampons? Do they even know what they are? Maybe they use old rags . . . and what if I can't get factor 30 sun lotion? And so it went on, until I struggled out of Wal-Mart, laden with all the trappings a paranoid Latin America–bound Westerner could desire.

'Oh dear, where are you going to put all that?' asked Rachel, as I attempted to force my emergency supplies into my already bulging luggage.

'I'll fit it in somewhere,' I replied optimistically, 'maybe some of these books will have to go.' I lived in fear of running out of reading matter and as a result was guilty of operating a mini mobile library. After three weeks of fun-filled procrastination in Los Angeles we were getting round to the idea of moving on, and a quick check of the calendar revealed that time was now of the essence.

'Look!' I said, alarmed, showing her the U.S. visa stamp in my passport. 'My ninety days run out tomorrow, it dates from when I arrived in Alaska, not when I reentered the States from Canada. We'd better get packing.'

It was to be our last night in Los Angeles and a sad occasion for all, except maybe Joe, who we suspected had entertained our international banshee conference for long enough, patient fellow that he was.

I was on the move again and I felt the usual mixture of sorrow and excitement that follows a prolonged stay in one place. On this occasion I was also riddled with nerves, but as I squirmed restlessly in bed that night, eyes glued open, the hum of the freeways buzzing in the distance, it occurred to me that my anxiousness was just a natural, if unwanted, by-product of adventure—the tarnished flip side of the shiny golden coin of excitement. And all I had to do was to flip it over . . . and start getting excited. It really was that easy.

The multilane freeway south towards Tijuana was packed solid, the blacktop steaming and sticky in the midday sun. BORDER WITH MEXICO 5 MILES. BORDER WITH MEXICO 3 MILES. The signs began appearing regularly, the thrill rising with each one. *Wow! This is it,* I exclaimed inwardly, *I'm really doing it.* Only now was the reality hitting me. All the original urges that had inspired my journey in the insipid confines of the Pigpen came rushing back: I wanted the uncertainty, the unease, the strangeness of it all. I was relieved to find that I still possessed a gnawing desire to be somewhere that bore no similarity to anywhere I'd been before, to explore places where the climate, the landscape, the language, were all alien to me. Where the people around me were clearly from a different stock, where I could visit a fruit stall and be faced with strange and exotic wares, or peruse an entire menu and still have no idea what was on offer. I wanted adventure. That was what I had come for.

Maybe I was transferring my own excitement onto my fellow road users, but there seemed to be an air of anticipation and expectancy in the sweltering line of cars and trucks that slowly edged towards the frontier. As if on the other side of that chain-link fence, the road would open up and the real fun would begin. But the dark side of this famous international border, where hundreds of migrating Mexicans die each year from heat exhaustion, thirst or in road accidents, was made apparent by signs along the freeway in a style usually associated with warnings of wild animals on the road. The word CAUTION in black letters on a yellow background accompanies the silhouette of a fleeing family that manages perfectly to capture the very essence of being on the run. The father leads the way, head down and determined, the mother is struggling to keep up, movement restricted by a knee-length skirt, her right hand grabbing the wrist of their young child, whose feet barely touch the ground as she is dragged along, pigtails flying, into the land of opportunity. To capture a nation's desperation in a simple road sign is quite a skill, but the irony that I was escaping into the land that they were so eager to leave wasn't entirely lost on me.

We arrived at the cluster of buildings that marked the end of the USA, and it was time to deal with my own border-crossing formalities. Thank heavens for Rachel and her degree-level command of Spanish. We parked up the bikes and set off on our paperwork trail. I had no idea what was going on, so I followed her around, doing what I was told and saying *"Gracias"* to men in uniform. We traipsed between dowdy government buildings, along featureless corridors, in and out of grey airless offices. We waited for slow grumpy bureaucrats to fill out forms in triplicate, we watched important little men banging big rubber stamps and eventually we signed all sorts of funny bits of paper.

Mexico was officially ours for the taking. Or so I thought. But the lady behind the desk had one final question for me. 'How many dogs in the car?' she demanded in heavily accented English.

'Um . . . er . . .' I replied, in mucho confusion.

I was a little lost for words, even in my mother tongue, but eventually succeeded in conveying the necessary information regarding my chosen mode of transport by standing feet apart in the middle of the customs office, arms outstretched as if gripping my handlebars and making loud motorcycle revving noises. 'VROOOOM! VROOOOM!' I was hoping one of the more hip pen pushers would take the cue and utter the immortal words: 'Is that Jimmy's ring you're wearing?' at which point the entire office would break into a storming rendition of 'Leader of the Pack.' Sadly they allowed the opportunity to elude them.

'How do we get back to the bikes?' I asked Rachel once we'd

been fully processed by the system and spat out into the sweaty chaos of the outside world. Our mazelike meanderings had left me slightly disorientated.

'I think it's up this street, turn left and then back through that big revolving metal gate.'

It wasn't until we'd worked up quite a thirst trying to force a ton of maximum-security steel to revolve in the opposite direction that we realised our foolish mistake. The gate was one-way only—south. Our paperwork trail had somehow led us to enter Mexico inadvertently, and now here we were in the thick of Tijuana, surrounded by strip clubs and sombrero stalls, while our trusty motorcycles sat safely ensconced in the USA, on the other side of the busiest and most stringent border crossing in the world.

'Oh crikey! What are we going to do?' We looked at each other aghast and burst out laughing.

'Let's scale the fence and head back the way we came,' I suggested.

'We can't do that! We'll get arrested, or even shot!' Rachel protested.

I had to concede she was probably right; the border was teeming with stern-faced, gun-toting guards just itching to make mincemeat out of a couple of hapless have-a-go wetbacks. And even if we were to make it over the barbed wire and metal spikes, there was a strong possibility of emulating the plight of the fugitive road sign family: dodging eighteen-wheelers on Interstate 5, our progress hampered by unsuitable clothing.

'There's nothing else for it,' said Rachel, 'we'll have to join that massive queue on the other side of the road and officially reenter the USA.'

It was a tedious business, all right, but the lengthy procedure gave us ample opportunity to study our fellow foot passengers. A curious combination of California housewives stocking up on cheap Mexican cleaning products, college boys recovering from the previous night's underage drinking spree and roly-poly Midwesterners clutching toy donkeys, excited by the fact that they'd visited Mexico for the day . . . and survived!

Rachel's French passport prompted a scathing comment on her nation's refusal to back the war in Iraq. Thank heavens for Britain's 'special relationship' with America, I thought as I handed over my documents, grateful to Tony Blair for his sycophantic chumminess with George Bush. My U.S. visa expired that day and technically, a fuss could have been made. But no! Upon detecting my citizenship, the immigration official leant towards me with a conspiratorial air.

'Together we're gonna get the folk that have caused all this darn trouble,' he assured me.

We briefly discussed the Beatles (good), English weather (bad) and Princess Diana (dead). I threw in a 'Cor blimey, guvnor' for good measure and once again I was in the land of the free, under specific instructions to have a nice day.

And five minutes later we were back in Mexico, this time on two wheels, having finally worked out the correct entry gate. As we left behind the tacky mayhem and frontier desperation of 'TJ' (as its regular visitors like to call it), a two-lane highway rolled out ahead, beckoning us south down the Baja peninsula. This was Highway 1, the only sealed road on this narrow strip of land, the rest of Baja being served by a maze of enticing dirt tracks and trails, hence its Mecca-like status as an off-road-adventure playground. Here in its northern stretch the road followed the twisty west coast with spectacular cliff-top views of the Pacific Ocean, the density of its dark blue waters relieved only by strips of stark white surf rolling rhythmically into shore. There were copious reminders to keep our eyes on the road, though, in the form of the decorated crosses and homemade shrines lining the roadside in tribute to those who had met a sticky end on these dramatic curves. And indeed, when we peered cautiously over the edge of the cliff we spied a collection of crumpled vehicles showcasing several eras of car design, each in relative stages of decay: an early VW Beetle, a couple of boxy eighties pickups and a very Starsky and Hutch bright red muscle car. The drop was so great that from this vantage point the pile of wreckage took on the appearance of a miniature scrap heap of long-forgotten Matchbox toys.

Musing on the fate of the unfortunate drivers of these cars, I narrowly escaped joining them, thanks to an opportunist wasp seeking out good times in my underwear. An angry buzzing sound emanating from my Elle McPherson bra (does that count as product placement? If so, I could do with a new one) sent me into wild spasms as I attempted to steer a steady course while groping and bashing at my left breast in frantic desperation. 'AAAAAAARGH,' I screamed to Rachel, who had come alongside, curious as to the cause of my sudden erratic riding. 'THERE'S A WASP IN MY BRA!' I yelled in explanation over the noise of the engine as I jerked and zigzagged down the road, swerving around a sharp bend straight into the path of an oncoming truck. BEEEEEEEEP! came the horn. Oh Jesus! My first *Caramba!* moment. I beeped back. The driver's eyes met mine for a split second as I dodged the truck's wheels in the nick of time, still rummaging urgently for the captive critter. I briefly glimpsed the jumbled look of fear and disbelief that passed over his face as he realised how narrowly he had avoided squashing a young lady, apparently in the midst of some motorcycling mammary excitement. With some difficulty I managed a one-handed emergency stop and yanked my bra up around my neck, freeing my winged tormentor. Incredibly, I had escaped without a sting.

A landscape of shantytowns and unfinished construction projects flashed by on the opposite side of the road as we continued southwards, looking for a place to camp. The developed world was now firmly behind us—this was it for the next fourteen thousand miles. The steep scrubby hillside was dotted with makeshift structures that were clearly the long-term residences of the less fortunate locals. Constructed from a mass of corrugated iron sheets, scraps of wood and frayed tarpaulins, and overrun with ragged chickens and dogs, these family homes existed just a few miles from the synthetic shopping malls and SUV-choked suburbs of Southern California.

'We're rich gringos from now on,' I observed to Rachel.

' "Gring*as*," she corrected. ' "Gringo" is the masculine.'

I had a lot to learn.

The long hot day melted into a perfect summer's evening and the lure of the Pacific was just too much to resist. A rocky gully led us to the sea, where we swam under the pinkish glow of the setting sun, drying off in the warm breeze as we set about pitching our tents for the night. Our dinner of tamales was procured from a roadside stall.

'What exactly are these?' I enquired warily, as a greasy paper bag containing a dense waxy lump was stuffed into my hands.

My knowledge of tamales was gleaned only from old Robert Johnson songs and I had imagined them to be some spicy Southern fare, rather than a mundane mash of corn in a cornhusk. My fantasies of *exótica mexicana* were further dashed by the sight of the sweat-soaked proprietor scooping a rogue tamale off the ground and slamming it back onto the soot-caked griddle.

'Er . . . *muchas gracias, uno* is enough,' I assured him in response to his offer of *'Más?'*

Sitting outside my tent writing in my diary and watching the sun slipping away into the sea, I spotted a flicker of movement out in the water that dragged me away from my first entry of Mexican memoirs, which so far consisted of not much more than *MEX-ICO!!! OLE!!!* a sketch of a sombrero and far too many exclamation marks than were strictly necessary.

'Look, Rachel.' I called her over excitedly, pointing into the distance. 'Dolphins leaping over there.' It was a perfect finishing touch to the day and I slipped into my sleeping bag to the sound of waves crashing against the rocks and my head buzzing with a combination of excitement and satisfaction. My scribbled, torchlit diary entry reveals: . . . *today I had a moment of sheer joy, I was swimming hard out*

*to sea past the waves, with just the cliffs in view. I thought to myself
'WOW! I'm swimming in the sea in Mexico! I was grinning like mad.'*

The following day's entry suggests a slight change of mood:
*Woke up in complete agony with my entire face swollen up and unable to
open my right eye. . . .'*

Shortly after the wasp incident, we had pulled into a U.S.-style
caravan park packed with rows of American RVs and unhappy holidaying families. This pitiful dump was under occupation by an
army of fighting, screaming children and their miserable parents,
apparently leading by example. Somewhat bizarrely, there was also a
cage of wild-eyed, mangy circus animals at the entrance, serving no
obvious purpose, except possibly to illustrate what visitors should
expect from their holiday. Fortunately, our plan was solely to launch
an assault on the ice cream parlour and then withdraw. While delib-
erating between the curious flavours of Rose and Tuna (the latter
turned out to be Spanish for 'cactus fruit,' thankfully), another
pesky insect bit me. Now just a few hours later, my face was increasing in size at a tangible rate, the bone structure fully concealed
under a mass of hot puffy flesh, its colour and texture reminiscent
of a burn victim's skin graft. My right eye was sealed shut, rapidly
disappearing into the encroaching swollen tissue, and oozing some
unspecified sticky goo. 'I knew we shouldn't have ventured into
that place,' I bemoaned to a concerned Rachel. 'There was something weird about it.'

'Probably that caged lion and performing monkey at the front
gate,' she reminded me.

So much for my valiant entry into exotic lands. My pasty English skin had already been struggling under the intense sun and
now it appeared I was allergic to the local bugs to boot. 'Oh, to be
a tough-skinned swarthy type,' I sighed wistfully. 'Maybe I'm not
cut out for these climes, I should be tramping round Scotland or
something more suited to my Anglo-Saxon complexion.'

'All that spirit, knocked out of you by one little insect!' exclaimed Rachel.

But she was right. I felt crushed by the prospect of what I had taken on. I still had another fourteen thousand miles ahead of me through a list of countries of which I had very little knowledge, except that each one was a byword for violence, corruption, civil war, rabid dogs and tropical disease. El Salvador, for crying out loud! Who wants to go there? To compound my unease, Rachel, my trusty interpreter, was returning home in a few weeks and I could barely speak a word of Spanish, let alone understand what anyone said to me. Now my face had turned into a colossal red, swollen, burning blob, and I had temporarily lost the use of one eye. And all I'd done was bought a Tuna-flavoured ice cream! What on earth was I thinking—planning a road trip through these wretched places alone on an underpowered, overloaded motorcycle?

'Sorry to put our adventure on hold, Rachel,' I apologised, 'but we're going to have to find somewhere to hole up for a few days until I can see properly again.' We set off in search of a cosy nook. My bizarre looks caused quite a stir along the way and each time we stopped at a gas station or roadside café, I was peered at by leathery-skinned locals. *'Dios mío!'* they would cry before breaking into a babble that I took to mean 'What the hell happened to you?' Having already become adept at charades due to my lack of linguistic prowess, I would respond with a loud buzzing noise while moving my pointed index finger swiftly through the air before jabbing it into the side of my face accompanied by a special *zing* noise for climactic effect. This seemed to entertain the audience no end, although I'm not exactly sure which part of my circus freak act they found the most amusing. 'Roll up! Roll up! See the balloon-faced lady on a motorcycle!' I was convinced they were saying, as they giggled knowingly amongst themselves. It was bad enough being the *chica en la moto* everywhere I went, but now my newly acquired disfigurement only added to my novelty value. Forget anonymity for the next six months—I had to accept I would be stared at, pointed at, interrogated and, if I got really lucky, poked and mauled during the remainder of my journey.

Once I had come to terms with the fact that my appearance suggested either a key role in a travelling side show or a heavy involvement in a Tijuana bar fight, we limped our way to the coastal town of Ensenada for three days of enforced rest in a cheap but seemingly clean hotel located down a grotty side street. 'Blimey, this place is a bit grim,' I observed, taking in the vista of open drains and pothole-strewn pavements that promised a sewagey nighttime stumble under the flickering low-wattage street lamps. *'Hola, chica'* came the gruff voice over my shoulder as we began the motorcycle traveller's most hated task of unloading the bikes. A slew of attentive men had appeared from nowhere, galvanised into action by the appalling sight of women carrying bags. 'No, no, no!' they exclaimed almost angrily every time we attempted to lift anything heavier than a glove. We thanked them politely for the offer and carried on with the job in hand, but it was too much for our chivalrous porters to bear. 'OK! I surrender!' I cried, flinging down my luggage with a suitably princess-like flourish. As I sat back to watch a line of obedient men carting my possessions into the hotel, I realised that any feminist principles were best left at the California border. 'Sorry, *chica,* you can't bring any of that women's lib into Mexico,' I imagined the customs official saying as I unwittingly tried to enter via the gate marked NADA QUE DECLARAR.

'OK, I'm getting the hang of this,' I called out to Rachel as I took a tour of our cell-like room. 'The turning on of a tap can no longer be assumed to result in the flow, or even trickle, of water. Correct?'

'Correct.' She nodded sagely, her previous travel experience in flea-ridden hostels in India making her an old hand at this.

'And the bare wires are no immediate cause for concern?'

'They are *de rigueur,*' she confirmed.

'And the loo roll goes in the overflowing bin that hasn't been emptied for a week—*not* down the loo?'

'Yes,' agreed Rachel, elaborating further, 'it's quite surprising how quickly one gets used to squatting down in close proximity to a stranger's used toilet paper.'

Admittedly, we weren't staying in the most exclusive part of town, as was evident along our street, where the cheaply constructed breeze block buildings sported neon signs, their messages flashing furiously in lurid pinks and reds while music pumped forth at top volume from behind the unmarked doors. All the signs were in English. GIRLS! GIRLS! GIRLS! screamed one. TOPLESS GIRLS DANCE 4 U! countered its neighbour. But the scene I found most disturbing was the venue that promised HOT NUDE GIRLS! while simultaneously blasting out 'Catherine of Aragon' by Rick Wakeman. What sort of stripper could you expect to find in there, grinding her way through the back catalogue of a prog-rock has-been? Even Jumbo's wouldn't sink that low.

It didn't take long to work out that all was not as it seemed at our unassuming hostelry. The ladies at reception were friendly enough if a little world-weary in appearance, but the place was almost empty despite the holiday season being in full swing. We soon discovered it wasn't until the sun went down that the Hotel Rio came to life. Our first clue was the sporadic sightings of heavily made-up women squeezed into tight-fitting clothes who flitted silently across the courtyard. Later, a group of surly men began to congregate at the front door, chain-smoking and bantering while all the time glancing furtively up and down the street. But it was the complimentary condom in the bedside cabinet that finally clinched our detective work. Yes indeed, our 'budget hotel' was in fact the local brothel, and they were doing a roaring trade.

'Hey, we could make a few pesos while we're here,' suggested Rachel. 'They'll pay good money for a white woman.'

'How much for a one-eyed red one?' I groaned as I proceeded to douse my entire body in super-strength insect repellent and nailed my mosquito net to the wall, with me inside it. The splatters of blood from previously swatted mozzies that decorated our room were enough of a warning for me. I wanted revenge on the insect world and I was ready to kill, armed with a hefty Jackie Collins bonkbuster.

'That's all it's good for,' sniffed Rachel, whose holiday reading tastes were a little more refined.

'You're just denying the call of your white-trash inner woman,' I countered in defence. But in truth, I doubted she had such demons inside her. Being French, she was so typically sophisticated that even on her motorcycle travels, she carried a small bottle of perfumed oil solely for the purpose of slicking down her immaculately plucked eyebrows.

The time passed slowly and we amused ourselves easily enough, taking in the atmosphere of Ensenada, an uneasy mix of working port town and trashy tourist trap. The days were too hot to encourage much physical activity but come dusk, we would venture out down the rubble-strewn streets, the lingering diesel fumes hanging heavy in the muggy night air. With eyes straight ahead and a resigned look on our faces we would stride past the hissing men who skulked around our neighbouring entertainment venues, into the centre of town, searching for something vaguely resembling a Mexican delicacy.

But soon enough, and in keeping with the aims of the Hotel Rio, I found relief from my inconvenient swelling and we were back on the road once more, tackling the melee of honking horns, smoke-belching trucks and ambiguous road signs that would come to define our ride through Mexico. We were heading away from the coast, our destination a remote ranch in the middle of the peninsula, accessible only by a series of dirt roads and trails that form part of the course of the famously gruelling Baja 1000 off-road race. It was a real thrill to know we were following in the tire tracks of so many legendary bikes and cars that have raced these very routes since 1967. As we left Ensenada and the coast, the temperature soared and we soon found ourselves surrounded by nothing but stark desert scenery. As someone used to the toy-town, patchwork greenness of England, I was fascinated by this strange and alien landscape. The oven-hot stillness of the air seemed to slow the passing of time and I sat mesmerised in the saddle, the little engine puttering away, transporting me gently across this weird and wild land in a state of dreamy delight. This was it, this was what I had craved for so long. And now I understood it was the emptiness that I'd been itching for. All that open space to wander off into and get lost in; there was nowhere you could do that back home. I was thrilled to see the cartoon-like *saguaro* cactus with their sticking-out arms that until this point in my life had existed only in moulded green plastic form at bogus Mexican restaurants. And here they were for real, in the spiky green flesh, hundreds of them, scattered across an endless lunar landscape of towering, mind-bending rock formations in dusky pastel pinks, oranges and browns. It was official: I had fallen head over heels in love with the desert.

I'm not too prone to Deep Meaningful Moments and have always felt slightly cheated by this fact. I think I should get more of them and assume that other people get them all the time. So here I was trying to force one on myself during a roadside stop in Baja, when a familiar V-twin roar shattered my semi-trance-like state. I turned to see two big ol' Harleys pulling off the main highway across the desert towards us, a pair of lumbering black and chrome beasts, complete with leather handlebar tassels. Their riders, dressed in the standard *Wild One* outfit of black leather and red bandanna, dismounted and swaggered up to us, the elder of the two adjusting his crotch with his left hand while offering me his right in a flamboyant high five.

'Allriiiiight!' he howled into the emptiness, and before we could respond, further utterances of amazement cut through the desert silence. 'Fuck-in'-hell! Fuck-in'-hell, maaaaaan! Check this *out!*' His arms outstretched, head turning slowly, surveying the scene. 'Two chicks, man, on bikes! Coooooool! This here is my son, Bubba,' he said, beckoning over to a slightly awkward-looking teenager dressed in an identical outfit. 'Man, we have ridden here from Canada' (more testicular adjustment) 'and we're going all the way down the Baja. What are you doin'?' I outlined my intended route. There was a moment's silence before Harley Dad threw himself on the dusty ground in an exaggerated mock faint before bouncing back up again to pump my hand zealously. 'Shit, man, I have always wanted to do that journey! That is sooooooo cool! Y'know what . . .' he continued, suddenly all thoughtful, 'if you pull something like that off in life, you ain't never gonna worry about any other shit ever again, right?' 'Right!' I assured him. He nodded slowly, pondering something. 'Hey, I know . . .' he exclaimed, animated again, his eyes flickering with inspiration. I could almost see the lightbulb over his head. 'You should write a book! Yeah, man, you gotta write a book about your ride! You could call it . . . um . . . err . . .' I waited politely, watching his face contort in deep concentration. 'I've got it, I've got it!' he cried, slapping his leather-clad thigh in excitement. Taking a moment to compose himself, he announced the title of my blockbuster novel in the slow, dramatic growl of a movie trailer voiceover: 'Gurrrrrl . . . on . . . a . . . mot-or-cy-cle!' A moment's awkward silence was followed by another round of jubilant high fives. 'Allriiiiight!'

Harley Dad and Bubba insisted on buying us lunch and all the ice-cold beer we could drink. It was 120 degrees Fahrenheit and they were picking up the tab. So we drank a lot of ice-cold beer. Dad bombarded us with tales of their two-wheeled adventure, boasting of their six hundred-miles-a-day stints, which clearly wasn't what Bubba had planned for his odyssey. 'Daaaad, it's not the destination, it's the *journey,*' he groaned in the voice of an exasperated, bored teenager who's consumed one too many Beat novels. Once the midday sun had moved around a little, our new friends paid up, good as their word, and roared off into the distance, keen to maintain their daily average. The waiter returned to our table; he was very sorry, he said, but he had forgotten to include the beers on the bill and could we settle up, please?

Back on the road, a little merrier and poorer than anticipated, we turned off the main highway into the thick of the desert, heading for the isolated ranch where we would spend the night. Mike's Sky Ranch is a famous pit stop in the Baja races, making it a popular halt for visiting dirt bikers. The route started off in pretty good condition—just a flat sandy track with suspension-testing corrugations cutting a straight line across the scrubby plains. But after a few miles, as we approached the mountainous spine that runs along the centre of the Baja peninsula, it deteriorated into a twisty, rocky trail, made all the more onerous due to a recent bout of unseasonably heavy rain. Without our luggage it would have been a piece of straightforward fun riding, but the extra weight made the going pretty tough and I was soon cursing my survivalist supply of contact lens solution and sanitary products. Rachel was a little apprehensive about the venture as she was unused to riding on dirt. 'Go as fast as possible and hope for the best,' I advised vaguely. But what the hell did I know? The 'If in doubt, gas it' school of thought had got me in trouble plenty of times. But she took me at my word and rose to the occasion like a pro. The ride threw up plenty of unexpected hindrances, over and above the standard rocks and sand that were already keeping us on our toes. Haring round one sharp bend, we came face-to-face with a snarling red bull in the middle of the path. My stomach churned with the city dweller's innate fear of livestock, but Rachel didn't miss a beat, so I followed blindly, heart thumping, not daring to look back. By the time the ranch came into sight the sun had moved low across the sky, casting long shadows and a reddish glow over the desert. But just when we thought it was all over, the track was crossed by a deep river. Once again, there was nothing for it but to plough through the water, safe in the knowledge that this was our final obstacle. We had arrived at our destination. We were wet, weary and dirty but received a hero's

welcome (well, a couple of beers on the house) and an eager inquisition from a group of California dirt riders who couldn't believe
we had ridden there on our heavily laden bikes. They invited us to
join them for dinner and fed us stories of their own heroics, which
I listened to politely and Rachel blatantly ignored. 'When I first
started travelling,' she explained to me later, 'I wanted to talk to
everyone I met, but now I find most people I meet are boring.' I
was intrigued by this comment and wondered if the same thing
would happen to me in time. For now, everything and everyone
was a source of novelty and excitement, but maybe a few months
down the line I too would have become jaded by the relentless,
rootless nature of constant travel.

'It's great to be sleeping outside again,' I declared as we set
up camp under a rare tree. Our brothel experience had given me a
touch of cabin fever over the last few days so I was happy to lie
there under the big night sky, wondering what lay ahead and relishing the eager anticipation that uncertainty brings. Another day of
blazing desert heat greeted us the following morning, the sun already high above us as we packed our bikes. Still keen for more off-
road fun, we decided not only to retrace our steps but also to ride a
forty-mile mountain track to pick up the main highway south
again. 'Come on, Rachel!' I cried, all fired up. 'Let's hit the trail!'
I'd like to imagine we roared off in a cloud of dust, but we probably just rumbled off gently. A detour for fuel took us into Valle de
Trinidad, a run-down one-horse town, forgotten by the rest of the
world, and possibly even by Mexico itself. 'Check out the gas station,' I said to Rachel, pointing at a couple of rusty, dented oil
drums on the back of a flatbed truck, presided over by two
painfully awkward teenage boys. 'They're obviously not used to a
couple of muchachas turning up on motorcycles!' said Rachel with
a smile, as the boys studiously avoided eye contact while funnelling
gas into our tanks.

We'd been warned about this town by the California dirt bikers the previous night, who, despite being regular visitors to Mexico, were still terrified of the place. 'Be careful in Valle de Trinidad,' they had advised. 'On Friday nights all the locals fight each other just because there's nothing else to do' 'Well, it does look pretty rough,' Rachel concurred, casting her eyes around the dilapidated main drag with its grimy-windowed restaurants and tire repair shops. The eerie ghost town silence was abruptly broken by a crashing sound followed by a cascade of excitable Spanish, the translation of which was unlikely to be found in my pocket dictionary. We swung round in time to see a shirtless man flying out of a barroom door, apparently propelled by something stronger than his own free will. It was only 2 P.M. 'Let's get out of here before the action starts,' I suggested.

The confusing network of unmapped tracks and trails across the mountains forced me to dig out my as yet unused compass to identify the route that would take us over the high desert range of the Sierra de Juárez and back to the cooler conditions of the Pacific coast. Using a compass and the position of the sun to navigate added a certain adventurous air to the proceedings, just so long as one could forget that San Diego was only a couple of hundred miles up the road. The terrain was rocky and rough, our motorcycles too heavily loaded and the temperature nearing 120 degrees again, but we continued undeterred. As we became tired, our bikes seemed more like a couple of overloaded Harleys than a couple of nimble 250-pound trail bikes. The sun burned ever hotter, but we had reached the point where pressing on was easier than turning back, and although dehydration and exhaustion were taking their toll, there was nothing else to do but keep toiling away across this barren landscape in the hope of finding civilisation.

'Are you OK?' I called out, seeing Rachel had ground to a halt in a rocky section.

'I've stalled,' she said, rolling her eyes in despair.

After half an hour of tinkering, fiddling and fruitless kick-starting in the scorching heat, we were still stationary and she was at her wits' end.

'I don't know what's wrong with it. We'll never get out of here!' she exclaimed miserably. 'We'll have to sleep by the side of the road.'

'We're at the top of a slope here, I'll try bump-starting it if you want,' I offered.

I climbed onto her bike, selected second gear, and with the clutch pulled in, freewheeled down the track as it descended the mountain. I quickly picked up speed and as I released the clutch, sure enough the engine roared into life.

'Hurrah!' I shouted, giving Rachel the thumbs-up with my left hand. But my moment of celebration coincided with the front wheel hitting a patch of deep sand at the bottom of the slope. I skidded out of control and before I realised what was happening, I had slammed her bike straight into the mountainside, smashing up the front end, snapping the mudguard and sustaining a few minor injuries of my own.

I was vaguely aware of Rachel running towards me shouting, 'Are you OK?' as I reeled away from the rock face, wondering if this was what I had meant by adventure. But wasn't it meant to be fun too? Maybe this *is* fun and adventure, I thought. The truth was, I wasn't really sure anymore.

'Yeah, yeah, I'm fine,' I assured Rachel sheepishly, rubbing my forehead. 'But I think I'll wear a crash helmet next time I want to drive into a cliff.'

My foremost concern was the damage done to Rachel's bike. I made an official apology. 'I'm really sorry, Rachel, we've only been on the road for five days, three of which have been spent in a Mexican knocking shop, and now I've crashed your motorcycle into the side of a mountain.' 'Don't worry,' she assured me kindly, 'it's nothing too serious.' We spent the next hour dragging her bike out of the ditch, amazed at how little strength we could muster between us. Another gruelling hour passed as we tried to get the bike started again but by now the light was beginning to fade and we accepted the inevitable—we were here for the night, in this remote, isolated high desert with nothing in sight but miles and miles of barren mountain range. 'How much water have we got?' I asked, already dreading the answer. 'About half a bottle between us,' replied Rachel miserably. 'And what about food?' 'One stale taco left over from lunch yesterday.' 'Yum.' *'Bon appétit.'*

It was while we were discussing the comfort ratings of different parts of the ditch that we heard the faint rumble, far off across the valley. We listened intently, neither of us daring to put our hopes into words. Then the yellow speck of the headlights came into view, slowly picking their way along this lonesome mountain track. We were jubilant to discover these lights belonged to a pickup truck full of young Mexicans who were more than happy to transport our bikes and us to the nearest town. The driver of our self-styled rescue vehicle was in his late teens and possessed a good grasp of English. 'Why motorcycles, not cars?' he asked us after quizzing us on our travel plans. 'Because they're more fun!' replied Rachel with an exaggerated cheerfulness. He took his eyes off the road for a moment and looked us up and down; filthy, tired, bruised and battered and then slowly surveyed his air-conditioned truck, his mobile phone, his stereo system. He smiled, and with a sense of irony and comic delivery beyond his years he simply replied: 'But not at this moment, no?'

I had to admit he had a point.

The following morning we awoke in a roadside motel somewhere. My entire body ached as if I'd taken on everyone in Valle de Trinidad—and lost. A layer of dirt coated my face and neck, my hair hung in crispy tendrils of dried sweat and dust, and as I forced my eyes open, I was greeted with the sight of a giant cockroach crawling across the floor towards my pile of grimy clothes. As I drew my head back under the nylon sheets, my heart sank. Is this what it's going to be like? I wondered to myself. Is this it? Am I going to spend the next six months filthy and exhausted in bug-infested foreign lands, unable to communicate with anyone, surviving on a diet of barely edible food? Is this what I meant by adventure? The prospect utterly overwhelmed me.

Rachel stirred awake in the next bed and as if reading each other's mind, we groaned in miserable unison. Then our eyes met and we began to laugh. We jumped out of bed, threw on our dirty clothes, Rachel squashed the roach with her motorcycle boot and we stepped outside into the glare of the morning sun, ready to fix our battered bikes and do it all over again.

Seven

We couldn't linger too long on the sandy trails of Baja.
With Rachel bound for Mexico City and her flight home, we
pressed on across the desert plains towards the southern port of La
Paz, where a ferry would transport us to the mainland, depositing us
in the resort of Mazatlán, halfway down the west coast and slap
bang on the Tropic of Cancer. Our desert run was broken only by
the irresistible temptation of a paradise beach on the Sea of Cortés,
the narrow strip of ocean that separates Baja from mainland Mexico. Riding the bikes onto the pristine white sand, throwing off our
clothes and running straight into the warm turquoise water was
truly one of those cheesy TV-ad moments. A little palm-thatched
shack tucked away at the end of the beach, serving the ubiquitous
Baja fare of fish tacos and margaritas, was enough to convince us to
hang around for several days longer than we planned, and it was
only the desire for a variation in diet that prompted us to finally
move on.

The other, less attractive factor that hampered our southerly
progress was the military checkpoints that cropped up with
paranoia-inducing frequency along the length of Highway 1. Initially they appeared quite intimidating, until we got the measure of
the routine interrogation.

'Here we go again,' Rachel and I would mutter to each other as a pimply, uniformed youth sporting an ornate, oversize peaked cap flagged us down importantly and instructed us to empty the contents of our luggage onto the dusty roadside. We would oblige willingly, mainly due to the fact that he had an enormous machine gun slung over his shoulder. More identically dressed and armed teenagers, distinguishable from each other only by their varying degrees of acne, would appear from the checkpoint hut to assist in the inspection of our possessions, either blushing or sniggering at any item relating to feminine hygiene or underwear. Then the questioning would begin:

'Where are you from?'

'England.'

'Where are you going?'

'La Paz.'

'Where is your husband?'

'No husband.'

'You have children?'

'No children.'

This summary of our domestic situation would elicit a look that hovered somewhere between confusion and irritation, followed by the final question.

'*Drogas?* Drugs. You have drugs?'

'No. No drugs.'

With the inquisition at its end, the bemused boy soldiers would send us on our way, the unspoken question written all over their faces: 'Well . . . if they haven't got husbands or children or drugs, then what can they possibly be up to?'

I felt a bit sorry for them at first, but in the end I figured that if I were a spotty, hormonal fourteen-year-old boy I'd be delighted if someone gave me a huge gun to play with. It certainly beats doing a paper route.

La Paz was something of a shock after the hypnotic, timeless travel of our one-thousand-mile desert ride. After two weeks in the arid emptiness of Baja, with only its hushed, dusty little towns and the odd passing truck to shatter the peace, we had drifted into a slow, dreamy desert frame of mind. And now here we were in a real town, bustling with shops, restaurants, noisy traffic jams and local men, who barraged us with obscenities dressed up as compliments every time we stepped out into the bustling, baking streets. On the bikes we garnered a certain degree of respect, but as soon as we exchanged our motorcycle boots and helmets for flip-flops and sun hats we were just another couple of gringas, at the mercy of the lecherous Latinos. We found sanctuary in the female-friendly confines of a lingerie shop, where we got so carried away with the excessive frilliness of cheap Mexican undies that we lost all track of time.

'Rachel,' I yelped into the changing room, 'it's four o'clock, we've missed the ferry!'

'Oh well,' she replied, emerging with a few pink lacy numbers to add to her pile of purchases, 'we'll just have to stay another day and do some more shopping.'

Feeling somewhat gung-ho and hopped up on holiday fever, I decided to use this downtime to risk a trip to the hairdresser. Up a quiet cobbled side street, tucked between an antiquated tailors shop and a crumbling but industrious cobbler's, I found a tiny salon where a weary middle-aged woman with mournful brown eyes was sweeping snippets of straight black locks into a furry pile. The shop was a little tatty round the edges and decorated with those black-and-white portraits that are the scourge of the hairdressing industry and must come as a bulk buy entitled Hair Disasters of the 1980s. But this was Mexico, not Manhattan, and I had to take what I could get. Armed with my Spanish dictionary and with Rachel assisting, I reeled off a series of words including 'dye,' 'cut,' 'fringe' and 'layer.' I even drew a picture of my perfect hairstyle. The woman smiled and nodded reassuringly, ushering me into the salon's only chair, unhelpfully upholstered in heat-soaked black vinyl that threatened to rip the skin off the backs of my legs with every movement. As she trimmed away carefully, smiling and nodding to my reflection in the mirror, wordlessly seeking my approval, it didn't take me long to realise that I had made a grave and terrible mistake. But already I was in too deep. In desperation, I flicked through my dictionary, spouting random words, unable to form the sentences, my frustration manifesting itself as an autistic babble of Spanglish. Rachel tried to help, but hairdressing terminology hadn't played a key part in her degree syllabus. My stylist (and I use that term generously) kept snipping and smiling, and I kept jabbering and pointing, despairing as I watched the abomination unfold before me, powerless to halt its disastrous progress. When it became too painful, I shut my eyes and asked Rachel to wake me up when it was over. With a final blistering blast of the dryer, my hair butcheress stepped back to admire her masterpiece and I, wincing, forced myself to face the true horror. I scarcely recognised the person that stared back at me from the mirror. I looked like the 'Before' photo in a *Ladies Home Journal* makeover feature. Her handiwork had aged me twenty years and created the bastard love child of Ronald McDonald and Barbara Bush. I wanted to strangle the woman with my sweaty bare hands.

'*Te gusta?*' she enquired hopefully. You like it?

I gave the predictable response.

'Oh, *sí, sí*. Yes, yes! Lovely! *Perfecto! Muchas gracias,*' I enthused, handing over the Mexican peso equivalent of two pounds fifty and rushing out the door, with Rachel in close pursuit making kind but essentially unconvincing comments about Charlie's Angels.

Fortunately for me, the time had come to don our helmets and fire up the bikes for the ride to the ferry terminal. On the map, the crossing of the Sea of Cortés looked like a short hop, Dover-to-Calais style, so on arriving at the ticket office we were surprised to discover that we were about to embark on an eighteen-hour, overnight sea journey. We were doubly surprised when the man behind the counter, who despite his civilian status was dressed in the military-style uniform favoured by even the lowliest Mexican bureaucrat, gave us very strict instructions about which ferry to board.

'For you *chicas,* the boat here.' He pointed to a rust-streaked hulk of questionable seaworthiness moored at the far end of the quay. 'This one . . .' he said, indicating another less than shipshape vessel with a long line of trucks and lorries already queuing to board. '. . . No. Not for you.' He shook his head.

'Not for you. *Entiendes?*'

We nodded but he continued.

'The boat here—*no mujeres, solo hombres,*' he said emphatically, wagging a stumpy index finger in our faces.

'What does that mean?' I asked Rachel.

'*No mujeres* means no women.'

We looked at each other, intrigued.

'*Por qué?*' she asked. Why?

The man shook his head again with extra vigour.

'*Los hombres,*' he whispered in a voice laden with doom, then a little louder, trying out his English on us, 'the men! They are cray-zeee!'

'Eighteen hours in this hellhole,' we said, almost in disbelief, as the lumbering iron beast cast off with a booming honk. Surely, even the boat full of crazy hombres couldn't be this bad? The airless passenger compartment was already rich with diesel fumes, leaching out from the engine that thundered in the hold beneath us, the wild antics of its untamed pistons causing the vessel's interior to quiver and quake like a Pennsylvania preacher. But our attempts to prise open the grimy portholes revealed them closed until further notice, sealed shut by years of slapdash paint jobs. It wasn't even as if engine maintenance and ventilation had been sacrificed in the name of soft furnishings. The seats were wobbly and threadbare with random eruptions of stuffing spewing out onto the scraggly carpet, and over the redundant portholes hung the shredded remains of pink nylon curtains, tattered and useless, swaying forlornly as the boat lurched and pitched its way towards the tropics.

'Eighteen hours?' was all we could think to say to each other. It seemed like an eternity. As darkness began to creep in from outside, the other passengers, mainly Mexican families and a few chain-smoking truck drivers, bedded down on the floor under heavy woven blankets. We followed suit and discovered the filthy carpet to be teeming with gangs of cockroaches out for the night, ranging in size from S to XXL. Eventually, I found a seat with most of its innards intact and passed those bleak and endless hours before first light scrunched up, clock watching and praying for daybreak. It was a long and lonely night at the world's worst pajama party. The truckers belched and farted, the children cried, the cockroaches stampeded, and as dawn broke, so did the toilets. Stagnant sewage backed up and brimmed over, carpeting the floor with a fibrous, putty-coloured sludge. I looked out the window and consulted my watch. Eighteen hours had come and gone and still there was no land in sight.

At least I didn't have to worry about the bikes, knowing they were safely strapped down in the hold. But this was only thanks to Rachel, who had spent twenty minutes testing international relations with a bunch of surly deckhands, persuading them not to merely lean our motorcycles up against the wall, but to tie them down to the floor. We'd considered it a pretty standard request, but just convincing them to give us a piece of rope had been akin to high-level negotiations at a NAFTA summit. I wasn't sure if their reluctance to take care of business was laziness or unhelpfulness, but I suspected this laissez-faire attitude extended beyond a few ferry company employees and was more a mild case of a national malady. This mañana way of life was all laid-back and charming—until you wanted to get something done properly. It was going to take a little getting used to for this list-ticking Londoner, but luckily I had all the time in the world.

Twenty hours after leaving La Paz we docked in Mazatlán, and entered a whole new world. The air hit us like a brick; heavy and humid with a sultry tropical heat that left us breathless and sticky before we'd even moved a muscle. The arid emptiness of Baja might as well have belonged to another planet. Even through the smeary portholes we could see a landscape of lush greenery, high-rise hotels and a coast lined with palm trees and exotic vegetation. I was first off the ferry, revving my engine at the front of the queue, gasping for the great outdoors, the open road, the wind in my hair and any other motorcycling cliché that would work as an antidote to a bad case of Mexican Cabin Fever. The instant the metal ramp made its clanking contact with terra firma, I was gone.

'*Despacio! Despacio!*' the port officials shouted after me. Slow! Slow!

As soon as we hit town, it was obvious that our ride down Baja had merely been a warm-up for what lay ahead. If Baja was Mexico-Lite, here was the real thing: the full-fat, high-cal version in all its messy and manic glory, slapping you round the face and bellowing in your ear. Suddenly there was more of everything. More people, more cars, more trucks, more fumes, more noise, more potholes, more dogs and cows and donkeys and barefoot children. Trouble was, we were all competing for road space.

'Which way do we go?' Rachel shouted at me, as we dodged and weaved our way through the chaotic streets.

'I dunno, I think it's up here,' I called back as I swerved to avoid a whining moped straining under the weight of three passengers and a crate of chickens.

'What? . . . Where?'

Bike-to-bike communication was proving tricky over the constant blare of honking horns.

'We're following signs to a place called Tepic,' I yelled, glancing down at the map strapped in front of my handlebars.

But after a while the signs ran out. And when they reappeared they were pointing the wrong way. An hour later, we were no closer to leaving Mazatlán. Then we found out what it really meant to have crossed the Tropic of Cancer. There was no warning, no little drip, no opportunity to say, 'Oh, was that a drop of rain?' Just end-of-the-world darkness followed by torrents of water, as the doomy black clouds did what they do best. Rachel and I instantly leapt into action without a word, rummaging for our long-forgotten water-proofs, buried deep at the bottom of our luggage.

'Look at it!' I cried in horror at the sky, mentally and sartorially unprepared for a soaking. I hadn't so much as sniffed a drop of rain since Canada. 'Look at it! This is Mexico in August. Isn't it meant to be hot and sunny?'

I knew I should have studied that book on weather systems a bit harder.

Rachel, having travelled through India during monsoon season, wasn't as perturbed as I was by the sluices that had opened above us. Within minutes the streets had turned to rivers. Women hitched up their skirts, wading knee-high through the grimy grey water to get to the market, piggybacking each other back and forth across the overflowing roads. Shopkeepers barricaded their doors with sand-bags, and rows of previously idle taxis, now crammed with passengers, plied their trade around the flooded town, making the most of the sudden rise in business. We too ploughed through the deluge, eventually succeeding in our quest for the route to Tepic. With the water level up to the bike's foot pegs, any sensation of riding on a road was now lost; we just had to hope there wasn't a pothole hiding beneath the water, waiting to swallow our front wheel and catapult us over the handlebars into the gushing torrent.

'My waterproofs aren't really living up to their name,' I observed after a while, feeling the telltale dampness against my skin.

'And why do they always leak in the crotch?' bemoaned Rachel, as we peeled off our outer layers to reveal our new look—Incontinent Biker Chick.

Starving hungry after our sleepless night, and now soaking wet, we had stopped for a much needed morale boosting lunch at an isolated roadside café that was no more than a few sheets of corrugated iron propped up by tree branches, and home to a peep of chickens running ragged around the dirt floor, pecking at our feet for scraps. The menu promised a number of Mexican delicacies, but each request was met by a shake of the head from the teenage waitress.

A Mexican jalopy tackles the flooded streets of Mazatlán.

'So what food *do* you have?' asked Rachel patiently, after we'd eliminated most of the list.

The dish of the day appeared minutes later, served with a take-it-or-leave-it flourish. Predictably, it was a taco.

'What's in it?' asked Rachel as I peeled back the thin doughy layer to reveal a scattering of dried insects.

'I have no idea,' I replied grimly, 'but the last time I saw something like it, they were crawling round the floor of the ferry.'

The waitress insisted they were shrimps but it didn't really matter what they were; a mouthful of the crunchy crustaceans was enough to ascertain that I would be taking the 'leave it' option. Thankfully, the one item on the menu that never ran out, even in the most run-down of Mexican cafés, was cold beer. As the rain hammered onto the rusty roof, the chickens squawked and flapped around us and Rachel picked miserably at her shrivelled shrimps, the waitress added insult to injury by playing a tape of the Scorpions' horror hit, "Wind of Change." I drowned my sorrows in the plentiful supply of ice-cold Tecate and hoped that if nothing else, the choice of track had some prophetic meaning.

Every day, all day, we rode stolidly through the torrid storms, heading up and away from the coast, along twisty mountain roads and through damp and pungent pine forests. I was surprised to find myself in such familiar scenery, and if it wasn't for the occasional sight of women carrying giant baskets of bananas on their heads or kneeling at a river, washing clothes on a stone, we could have been in Wales. Wanting to avoid the expensive tolls and tedium of Mexico's *autopistas*, we found ourselves sharing the neglected secondary highways with homicidal truckers and suicidal livestock, but as we approached the ramshackle little villages that were dotted along these routes, our main hazard was the rabble of stray dogs that met us on the edge of town, chasing along next to the bikes, yapping fiercely and nipping at our ankles, then bidding us farewell on the other side of town in a similar manner.

'I'm glad I had my rabies shots,' I remarked, examining a couple of teeth marks in the ankles of my leather trousers.

Each night we would turn up, dripping and muddy like the Creature from the Black Lagoon, at the first cheap hotel we could find, taking full advantage of the fact that we were most definitely Out of Season. We soon developed a routine: Check in. Go straight to the room. Try not to scare the other guests. Pour contents of boots down sink. Wring out soaking clothes in shower. Hang said clothes from every hook, hanger and light fitting until room resembles shantytown. Eat. Drink. Sleep. Ride. Repeat to fade.

One morning, feeling slightly soggy and sorry for myself, having once again endured the misery of wriggling into the previous day's sodden clothes, I attempted to inject a shot of optimism into the conversation as we prepared for another long, wet ride.

'Well, at least the bikes are running well,' I commented cheerfully.

This was of course the cue for the oil seal behind my front sprocket to give up, duly dumping half a litre of Mexolube on to the floor of a gas station floor just ten minutes later. In the time it had taken for the attendant to deposit seven litres of *sin plomb* into the tank and for me to hand over the necessary *pesos,* I had caused a mini environmental disaster. Rachel and I surveyed the oil slick below my bike that was fast spreading out across the wet concrete in glorious Technicolor.

'Oh God, someone call the Rainbow Warrior,' I cried in dismay, thinking I'd be in big trouble with the gas station staff. But luckily, or unluckily, depending on how you look at it, green issues aren't at the top of the agenda in the lives of average Mexicans, who in fact, seemed more concerned with fixing the problem, as they peered and poked around my motorcycle, eventually engaging the other customers and a few passersby in their examination.

'What are we going to do?' asked Rachel. I mused over the options. Could I limp along and keep checking the oil level every hour? How bad would it be once I was moving along? Where could I get a replacement seal?

I didn't have time to reach a decision before help was at hand, in the guise of local motorcyclist George, who had pulled in to gas up his 600cc sports bike. 'Follow me!' he instructed, beckoning, as he wheeled the wrong way up a one-way street. Rachel and I shot a glance at each other, along the lines of 'Well, why not?' and set off in hot pursuit, albeit on two wheels, to find our rescuer parked outside the workshop of the local moto mechanic, who, to our delight, resembled a young Che Guevara. Bikes of all ages and in all states of disrepair spilled out from the little garage onto the street, and in the style of motorcycle workshops the world over, the place was inhabited by a band of merry men, happy to while away their days smoking and talking about compression ratios. George ushered us into this cosy scene with a loud theatrical introduction, throwing the masculine dynamics of the workshop into disarray, as the men hastily swapped their usual banter for a reverential meet-and-greet.

'Maybe it is the first time two *chicas* come here on motos,' whispered George in my ear, enjoying his role as worldly boy-racer about town.

There followed some pointing (from me), some translating (from Rachel) and attempts at English from the group of eager onlookers. But there was no need for any of this garbled explanation. Che knew just what to do and it certainly didn't involve ordering parts from Yamaha. Judging by most of the traffic we had encountered on our journey through Mexico, the national approach to vehicle maintenance was 'keep it going, amigo!' This mentality combined with a generous squirt of sealant meant I was up and running again in less than half an hour. Back home they might call it a bodge, but if it was good enough for Che, it was good enough for me. The labour costs were alarmingly cheap, although George's insistence on a slobbery good-bye kiss from the pair of us somewhat took the feel-good factor out of the transaction. But no matter—we were back in the game, Mexican style.

'What are you going to do with your bike when you go back to England?' I asked Rachel later that day, as we settled down for dinner in a greasy, smoke-filled restaurant in the small town of Manzanillo, perusing the menu in the vain hope that it might actually reflect the contents of the kitchen, rather than the gastronomic fantasies of the proprietor.

'I'm not sure, I want to find somewhere to store it so I can come back and carry on when I've earned some more money,' she replied.

'You know what, a Mexican rider called Juan contacted me through my Web site while I was in L.A. he might be able to help, he lives in a place called Valle de Bravo, not far from Mexico City,' I suggested.

The heartwarming camaraderie of the two-wheeled travelling

community meant that invitations of help and hospitality from like-minded motorcyclists were a common occurrence.

'I'll drop him a line if you want,' I offered.

'Thanks,' said Rachel, then adding suspiciously, 'does he seem Ok?' her bike-bore detector on full alert.

'Yeah, fine, sounds really helpful. Y'never know, could be your lucky day.'

Rachel raised a groomed eyebrow sceptically.

'Have you heard from Simon?' I ventured. She had barely mentioned him since our conversation in Jumbo's.

Her face clouded over.

'Yeah, I've had a few e-mails. He's still riding around America but he's going back to London soon for a little while, but I won't be looking him up when I'm there.'

'Really?' It was my turn to raise an eyebrow.

'No, definitely not.'

I got the feeling that we hadn't heard the last of Simon, but my prediction was interrupted by the arrival of the waiter, who informed us in a most charming and roundabout way that the menu was no more than a figment of the chef's imagination and could he interest us in a plate of rice and beans?

I would miss riding with Rachel. I enjoyed her easy company and having someone to share the good and bad times with. But I had set off on this journey alone, and in a funny sort of way, I was looking forward to tackling the challenges ahead unaided; I liked the idea of living on my wits amongst the unpredictability of Latin America, if only to see how I would contend with the communication barrier, the rough roads, the bike maintenance, the notoriously corrupt border crossings and any other surprises that life on the road might throw at me. It was the adventure I'd always wanted, but I also knew there'd be times when I would appreciate some companionship. Rachel was reading my mind.

'I think I'll be able to catch up with you if I'm only away for a month or so,' she said. 'We'll stay in touch and arrange to meet up again somewhere in South America.'

'That'll be good,' I said. 'This woman I know in London called Amalia says she's going to come out and join me in Peru as well.'

'Who's she then, what bike's she got?'

'I don't know her that well, we've just got some mutual biking friends, but she seems like good company, so when she suggested it, I thought, why not? She got herself a Serow too—we thought it would make sense to have the same bike—she's got all her luggage sorted out, so she's really into the whole plan. She's going to fly the bike out to Lima and then we'll ride together down to Ushuaia. She's going to carry on up to Brazil after I go home.'

'Excellent.' said Rachel. 'Y'see, it'll all work out fine!'

'Yeah, I think you're right,' I agreed, as we tucked into our all-too-familiar dinner of *frijoles y arroz*.

Juan was more than accommodating regarding Rachel's predicament, offering his house for temporary storage of her bike and insisting that we come and stay with him in his hometown of Valle de Bravo. We arranged a rendezvous in a café where we took seats by the window and scrutinised every passing hombre as our possible host, accompanied by cries of either 'Oh no, I hope that's not him,' or 'Phwoarrr, I hope this is.' Our people-watching was interrupted by the guttural throb of a 650 dirt bike shuddering to a halt outside the café. In walked an impossibly tall man covered head to toe in mud. Juan had arrived, fresh off the trail. Beneath the splattering of dirt there appeared to be a kind, open face sporting a welcoming smile in proportion to his giant stature.

The three of us convoyed through the steep, twisty streets of Valle de Bravo to his house on the edge of town, encountering a whole different side of Mexico along the way.

'Valle de Bravo is where the rich folk from the city come for their weekend breaks,' explained Juan.

And I could see why. It was a gorgeous, clearly opulent little mountain town rising from the shores of Lake Avandaro. Its red-roofed, white stucco houses were reminiscent of Switzerland, with flowers spilling from their wrought-iron balconies and doorways onto the pretty cobbled streets. Still reeling from our shrimp shenanigans, we were also excited to spy a range of Cordon Bleu restaurants with views across the lake, where later that evening, Juan began his whirlwind of faultless hospitality, treating us to a mouthwatering Italian meal before rounding up the night in a dimly lit hideaway club where an elite bunch of dapper young Mexicans draped themselves over the minimalist furniture, filling the darkened room with clouds of telltale aromatic smoke and what I assumed to be meaningful discourse. I struck up a conversation with a foreign correspondent from a Mexican TV channel who had spent some time in London with the BBC, and I enjoyed listening to his observations on the differences in social etiquette between our native countries.

'In London,' he remarked, 'you are invited to dinner at eight in the evening and you must arrive at that time. You come later, it is a terrible crime. And of course when a person leaves the room, the other people, they all talk about them. They come back in the room—everyone is smiling and polite. In Mexico we do not hide so much, we speak to their face. In England, the truth is hidden behind your good manners.'

I laughed out loud at his take on the farce of British polite society, imagining this affable man attempting to tiptoe his way through the minefield of London media politics.

'The Latin way is more emotional, you know,' he continued, 'we speak what is in our minds, we say how we feel. It is very different, I did not like it so much in London.'

Staying with Juan was a crash course in the Latin Way. No subject was taboo, and despite considering myself to be one of the franker natives of Blighty, even I found myself squirming occasionally, while the more insular, reserved Rachel went into total shutdown mode. Over the following days, we rode Juan's emotional tidal wave of broken hearts, multiple marriages, painful divorces, sex, drugs, politics, religion and any other subject that would elicit a look of horror and a sharp kick under the table at a polite North London dinner party. I must admit to perversely enjoying this forthright cultural exchange, and while Juan would prepare dinner, chopping exuberantly at a heap of exotic wild mushrooms and fresh herbs, I would listen to his tales of life, love and whatever else was in the mixing pot that night, usually spiced up with some spiritual meaning or message.

One evening as we were protesting his excessively generous hospitality in that terribly English way—'No, no, I insist,' etc.—he stopped what he was doing and turned to us, almost annoyed at our polite remonstrations.

'I must tell you a story,' he said, 'it is very important. You must listen carefully.

'When I split up with my wife, I was so sad, really, really sad. My heart was broken in two. I could not bear it so I went away, to the north of Mexico, to a place called Copper Canyon. It is very beautiful there and I just wanted to walk and walk. I met an old man who was a guide, he had lived there all his life and he knew the canyon, every twist and turn. I said to him, "Take me walking. I want to walk for days and days. But I want to do it like you, I want to know it like you know it." First he said no, that it was too hard, the way he travelled. He carried nothing but his knife and a pack full of water and dried maize, and walked from dawn until dusk, sleeping on the ground. I said to him, "That's how I want to do it, just walk in the canyon, in the silence, with nothing." Still he refused, but I begged him to guide me and in the end he agreed. So that is what we did, drinking only water, eating only dried maize that we carried with us, nothing more for days and days in the scorching sun. After three days I could barely stand up, I could hardly keep going, my feet were blistered and my whole body ached. But we kept walking and I cried for my wife and our life that was over. The old man, he said nothing, just kept on walking, but I noticed that the straps on his pack were cutting into his shoulders and he was bleeding, but still he said nothing. On the fifth day we stopped for a drink of water and he said to me, "Juan, I can see you are sad. I would like to give something to you." He reached into his pack and from it, he brought a big, juicy peach. "It is for you," he said. I couldn't believe my eyes! After five days of only maize and water, he brings out this beautiful peach! It was like a priceless jewel.'

Rachel and I nodded in empathy.

'So, I pull out my knife and I cut the peach in two and I give him one half. But he won't take it, he says to me, "Juan, you do not understand. This peach is for you." And I say, "but we must share it, we have walked the same distance, we are both tired and hungry," but he says, "No, it is a gift for you, because you are sad." I say to him, "But it is good to share, I want you to have half of the peach." Again, he refuses and again I insist. And for a moment, he is very quiet, staring at the ground and shaking his head. Then slowly he turns to me and he says, "Juan, if this is how you receive, I would hate to see how you give." '

Juan looked at us meaningfully.

'A lesson in the art of receiving gratefully,' I surmised.

'Exactly,' Juan smiled, 'now let us eat.'

We messed about on the bikes and enjoyed the high life of Valle de Bravo but soon, the day rolled around and it was adios, amiga. With a big hug, Rachel and I bid each other adieu, making plans to meet up again farther on down the road. Juan was also flying out of Mexico City the same day, on a business trip to Cuba, but ever generous, he let me stay on in his house while I finished some essential maintenance on my bike. The next day I changed the oil, replaced the speedo cable, which had snapped many miles ago in Canada, cleaned the oil and air filters, lubricated the clutch and throttle cables, changed the spark plug and gave everything else a quick check-over, relieved to see that Che's improvised oil seal was still holding up.

The Serow and I were in good shape for the road ahead. Before I packed up my belongings, I fished out a ten-dollar ring that I'd bought in San Francisco and slipped it onto the ring finger of my left hand. Now that I'd be travelling solo, it wouldn't do me any harm to have an imaginary husband to lend an air of respectability at the checkpoints. I shut the door behind me, leaving Juan a farewell note and a juicy peach on his kitchen table and took a last look through the orange trees across the lake to the mountains in the distance. Then I fired up the bike and headed off alone towards the highlands of southern Mexico and the Guatemalan border.

Eight

My bike and I were becoming nicely moulded to each other by now, fusing into one like some mythical creature—half woman, half motorcycle. Riding felt more normal than not riding, and each morning as I swung my leg over the saddle, fired up the engine and shifted into first gear, off on another adventure, never knowing what would happen that day, I was greeted with the gratifying sensation that there was nothing else in the world I'd rather be doing. Any uncertainties or qualms that may have taken root during the night would be left in the dust with the onset of motion, as the simple act of moving along became my only reality.

I was pleased with the way the Serow was holding up too. I'd endured a steady trickle of sarcastic and patronising comments about my choice of motorcycle, especially in America, where big bikes rule, and even though I rarely made it over fifty-five miles per hour, I didn't mind my leisurely pace. Considering the hit-or-miss driving habits of the locals and the sudden appearance of donkeys, dogs and *fútbol*-crazy kids, it seemed like a good idea to be taking it easy. The bike was really coming into its own on Mexico's unkempt, bumpy roads, and it blended in nicely too; it seemed like everyone rode tatty little trail bikes in this part of the world.

I calculated distances and percentages as I motored along, figuring I'd clocked up about six thousand miles, just over a third of the journey from Alaska to Ushuaia. But then, of course, there was the minor matter of another two thousand miles back up the east coast of Argentina to Buenos Aires once I'd made it to the bottom. And what with a bit of noodling here and there, I was probably looking at a total run of about twenty thousand miles. Rachel had found my focus on getting to the southernmost tip of South America rather silly; 'It's very Anglo Saxon, this goal-orientated, conquering approach to travel,' she would say with Gallic superiority. I could see her point but I liked having somewhere to aim for, and although I didn't have much idea what was involved in being an Anglo Saxon, if it meant motorcycling long distances to get to weird and wonderful places, it sounded like it might be fun.

After I left Juan's, my eight-hundred-mile ride to the Guatemalan border town of Mesilla saw me plunging back down to sea level through a landscape dominated by tequila plantations, passing miles upon miles of neatly sown fields filled with endless rows of the blue spiky plant unrolling across the country into the distance. With the drop in altitude, cool pine forests and mountain goats gave way to a more tropical backdrop of succulent cacti, chattering parrots and humid, sticky nights.

But no sooner had I made my descent than I was climbing up again into the highlands of Chiapas, the most southerly region of Mexico, its reputation now firmly on the world map as the centre of the Zapatista rebel movement, led by the enigmatic and mysterious Subcomandante Marcos. In the regional capital of San Cristóbal, a grand colonial town, an earnest and rather dowdy English couple queuing in front of me in the bank were complaining in affronted tones about the deluge of well-meaning European students that had gravitated towards the town in sympathy with the rebels, since the Zapatistas' uprising there in 1994.

'Of course, they don't know the first thing about the movement,' the man sniffed indignantly, 'they come here to learn Spanish, on their year out or gap year or whatever they call it now,' he spat the terms out in disgust, 'bankrolled by mummy and daddy, and all of a sudden they want to save the Mayan people. It's a down-right insult.'

'If it wasn't for Marcos, they wouldn't be interested,' his companion agreed, as they shuffled towards the front of the queue, 'but one has to admit, he is very charismatic, he's become a role model, like a Che Guevara for their generation. And he is quite handsome, I suppose.' She gave an embarrassed giggle.

'Oh, for God's sake,' huffed the man, 'you sound like one of them.'

A raucous buzzer summoned him to the cashier and he stalked off in disgust.

I was inclined to agree with the woman. Marcos had created quite an image for himself. A young leader of Spanish/Indian mix, his promo photos invariably showed him dressed for battle and smoking a pipe through his trademark black balaclava, his face always hidden. He communicated to the outside world via the Internet, spreading his revolutionary rhetoric about returning the land to the indigenous Mexican people and the perils of neo-liberalism. His 'post-modern revolution from cyberspace' had picked up such a following you could even buy Marcos dolls on the streets of San Cristobal.

The buzzer sounded again. My fellow countryman was already striding towards the exit, obviously irritated by some facet of Mexican banking bureaucracy.

'Bloody idiots won't accept my Amex card,' he ranted in his plummy voice to his hapless companion as she followed him out, attempting to placate him.

In the sunny cobbled square outside, a bunch of the gap-year types had taken over the outdoor seating area of a café, self-consciously sipping their mango milk shakes while studiously ignoring a deformed beggar. Two of the girls were braiding what looked like pieces of rags into each other's hair, while the boys, one of them wearing a Marcos T-shirt, competed loudly on the worst ever bus journey in the world, nastiest ever food poisoning in the world, cheapest ever hostel in the world and other high-scoring factors in the backpacking game. I wondered what would happen if they were rounded up and told they would now be spending their gap year in Belfast, where they could sympathise with the natives and buy Gerry Adams dolls. Somehow, I doubted they'd be so keen. On the opposite side of the square, I could see the earnest Brit couple storming another bank, flexing their Amex card, ready for battle.

Wondering if this was what being an Anglo Saxon was all about, I decided to leave them to it and get going. The time had come to say good-bye to Mexico. A final day's ride along the Pan-Am Highway through the rebel highlands would deliver me to the border with Guatemala, where my Central American adventure would begin.

When the policeman stepped out into the road and pulled me over, I wasn't too worried. I'd had a couple of brushes with the Mexican bobbies, and contrary to the popular horror stories put about in the USA, they hadn't roughed me up, squeezed a bribe out of me or attempted anything that could be considered in the slightest bit improper. In fact, one member of the force, stationed on a long lonely stretch of highway, had even bought me breakfast, finally putting to rest the image of the corrupt, greasy-palmed *policía*. This latest member of the constabulary was no different; he just wanted to impart some important information to me.

'*Hablas español?*' he enquired.

'No,' I replied. '*Hablas inglés?*'

'No.'

We both laughed at the futility of our exchange. But he spoke Spanish to me anyway, gesturing to get his message across, pointing down the road in the direction I was heading, shaking his head and waving his gloved hands in a manner that suggested there was trouble ahead. I nodded, pretending I understood, thanked him profusely and carried on. Whatever he'd been trying to tell me, I figured it couldn't be that serious.

After a while I wondered if I'd got the wrong end of the stick; there didn't seem to be anything on this road to impede my journey. What could he have meant? I rode for a mile or so along the empty two-lane highway, passing a few wizened old men ambling along on their donkeys and a farmer herding an unruly bunch of cows that, admittedly, did slow me down a bit, but I was certain that wasn't what the policeman had been talking about. After a couple of miles I put the whole thing down to a case of miscommunication and forgot all about it.

That was, until I came round a bend to discover the tail end of a lengthy traffic jam. Oh! So this is what he meant. There must be roadworks going on, I surmised, and with the motorcycle proving itself as the finest form of transport, I whizzed up the side of the mile-long line of stationary vehicles to the front, where to my utmost surprise, I found not the gang of swarthy, pickaxe-swinging workmen that I had envisaged, but instead, a heaving mob of rowdy protestors who, using a combination of themselves, rocks, tree trunks, branches, burnt-out vehicles and blazing bonfires, had brought the Pan-American Highway to a grinding halt.

Despite the impassioned activity of the demonstrators, the roadblock had something of a fiesta atmosphere, with a few entrepreneurial types selling barbecued corn and overpriced cans of drink to their captive market. The protestors were chanting and shouting; some of them had linked arms, creating a human barricade across the road. The entire blockade was a family affair, with everyone out in force, from granny and granddad down to babies slung on their mothers' backs. But although the atmosphere seemed reasonably good-natured, the message was coming across loud and clear: NOBODY'S GOING ANYWHERE. In typical laid-back fashion, none of the drivers of the trucks and cars seemed to object to the holdup; it was just another day in Chiapas. Some of the truckers were taking the opportunity to have a nap in their cabs, while others strolled up and down the queue, chatting to each other. Families sat outside their cars, enjoying an impromptu picnic, as if this was the most normal thing in the world. And maybe to them, it was.

As I pulled up to the frontline, the noisy crowd waved their arms at me, shouting, *'NO PASAR! NO PASAR!'* and glaring angrily. From the centre of the throng, their leader appeared, a man with twinkling eyes and a face that had seen it all, brown and lined from years of outdoor toil and strenuous roadblock organisation. I had to admire his tenacity.

'Qué pasa?' I asked him. What's happening?

The jeers of the crowd fell to an excitable hum when I spoke, all eyes turning to their head honcho, as he addressed this foreign *muchacha* on a motorcycle. As I had made my opening gambit in Spanish, the leader understandably assumed I could speak his lingo and launched into what I guessed to be a stirring, rebel-rousing piece of agitprop, if the raised fists and whooping cries of his supporters were anything to go by. I thought it best to put him straight.

'No entiendo, hablo un porquito español—solo un porquito' I explained apologetically—I only speak a little Spanish.

Undeterred, he continued to bombard me with more unintelligible propaganda.

After I'd listened and nodded for long enough not to be considered rude, I popped the million-peso question.

'Es posible . . . ?' I asked him, motioning my request to continue my journey.

His face opened up with a kindly, almost avuncular smile, which seemed at odds with the vigorous shaking of his head.

'No. No pasar.'

What is it with these people, I wondered, the way they deliver bad news in the nicest possible way? I'd encountered this phenomenon before when asking directions, often finding myself sent completely the wrong way, not maliciously, but because they'd rather say anything than 'I don't know.' It was the same thing with the fictitious restaurant menus. Nobody likes to disappoint, but to be honest, there were times when I'd have felt more comfortable with a good old-fashioned no. At least I'd know where I stood.

I surveyed the hostile crowd. But curiosity had got the better of them and, having dropped the offensive, they were now edging towards me, pointing and nudging each other excitedly. The protestors at the front gathered around me, gingerly touching the bike and staring at my map of Mexico. I pointed to our location, and seeing the name of their hometown, they gaped in astonishment, beckoning their fellow campaigners to take a look. I smiled at one of the women and when she smiled back shyly, I realised that this was the moment. I had them in the palm of my hand, and if I was going to get through this blockade, it was time to start playing the crowd.

With a beaming smile I addressed the leader and his followers again in my faltering Spanish.

'What's happening?' I cried. 'Please may I go through?'

The murmur of the rabble rose to an excited chatter and they stood transfixed as the twinkly eyed man once again refused my request.

'No pasar.' Another shake of the head, another dazzling flash of teeth.

The crowd, deferring to his command, began to ebb away, moving back to their positions.

Damn! I was losing my audience. It was now or never, and I had an idea. With an exaggerated flourish I whipped out my Spanish dictionary from my luggage and displayed it to the demonstrators, prompting peals of laughter and a hearty cheer. They stared at me, engrossed, murmuring to each other, as I quickly flicked through to the H section, where I found the translation for the magic word. OK, this was it, time for a bit of method acting. Clutching the dictionary to my heart, I imagined myself as the leading lady in a Shakespearean tragedy. I stood up on the foot pegs and, in what I hoped to be an anguished tone, dripping with longing, lost love and heartbreak, I delivered my plea to the crowd in their language.

'Ladies and gentlemen, please may I go through? My *husband* . . . he waits for me in the next town!'

For added effect I pulled off my left glove and raised my bare hand to the protestors, pointing to my fake wedding ring that glinted convincingly under the late afternoon sun. A gasp went up from the female members of the crowd. I turned to them, dewy eyed and pleading. But all eyes were on their leader, as they stood still and silent, awaiting his response.

In the hush I could hear the whirring of insects in the trees and the shriek of exotic birdcall high above me.

The leader looked at his people, then back at me. Our eyes met and I smiled wanly, still in character.

A dog was yapping somewhere in the queue of stationary vehicles. A tinny car radio played a wailing Spanish ballad.

The man turned again to his followers. They hadn't moved or uttered a sound, still waiting for his decision. I stared at him, steeling myself for the worst, imagining the forthcoming night, or days or weeks, even, camped out at the roadblock, hundreds of us drawing straws for the last piece of barbecued corn, starving and thirsty, forced to drink the water from the car radiators. . . .

But just as I was getting carried away with my survivalist nightmare, I was yanked back into reality by an almost imperceptible nod from the leader. A deafening roar erupted from the crowd! The magic sign had been given! I was free to go! The demonstrators leapt into action, cheering and clapping as they hurriedly cleared me a rough path through the debris, waving me on, patting me on the back as I bounced and bumped my way over the remaining rubble. Oh! The roar of the crowd, the smell of the . . . er . . . grease. My Oscar-winning performance had done the trick!

'*Muchas gracias! Muchas gracias!*' I shouted jubilantly, not daring to look back in case they changed their minds.

I gunned it down a deserted southbound Pan-American Highway, hoping to make it to the border before it shut for the night. My heart quickened as signs for *la frontera* appeared and, once again, I felt that stomach-churning excitement of a new country to discover and the thrill of the unknown ahead. 'Adios, Mexico!' I shouted out loud. 'It's been fun!'

Nine

I wondered what all the fuss was about as I glided through the Guatemala entry formalities. These Central American border crossings had a terrible reputation for bribe-hungry policemen, corrupt officials and hours of soul-destroying bureaucracy, but here I was in the customs office being processed in the most able fashion by an efficient, incorruptible young woman and surrounded by government notices encouraging their people to say NO! to bribery. Other than an entrepreneurial man hovering outside with a pressure washer, who halfheartedly sprayed the wheels of my bike in an unsuccessful attempt to charge me for *'fumigación'* services, I was pretty much left alone to wade undisturbed through the mayhem of Mesilla.

Never before had I encountered this concentrated number of humans per square foot; even the road itself was so jam-packed with bodies that I had to slow down to crawling pace until I was forced to put my feet on the ground and paddle my way through the throng. The border town reminded me of a mini-Tijuana, without the tourists, bustling with the air of an ancient trading post where folk from every neighbouring country would come to barter and haggle over each other's wares.

But my romantic image of exotic spices and hand-tooled leather saddles changing hands for gold bars or silver-handled pistols was dashed by the reality of knockoff Nike sneakers and mountains of cheap Tupperware.

Despite the abundance of bogus designer sportswear, it was an exciting entry into this new stage of my journey. As the crowd thinned out and the frenetic hustle of the town ebbed away, I followed the Pan-American Highway through a lush, verdant river valley that glowed luminous green with giant ferns and exotic plants boasting leaves big enough to sleep under. The skyline was dominated by a range of black volcanoes, jutting into the heavens like Jeffrey Archer's polygraph reading, their peaks obscured by the clouds that hovered patiently all day, waiting to deliver the rainy season's daily deluge.

All along the road, the people of Guatemala were going about their business, the women dressed in their traditional brightly patterned shawls and long skirts, while the men opted for a more sombre look in dark-coloured Western-style clothes. Children and old folk alike carried colossal bundles of firewood on their backs, women effortlessly bore baskets of fruit on their heads and the men tended the goats and sheep. I felt as though I'd been transported back to a bygone age, and for the first time since leaving England, I was acutely aware of being in a distant, faraway land. Even in Mexico, enough dribs and drabs of Western civilisation had seeped over the border from the USA to remind me it was still out there, and the long stretches of mountain scenery and pine trees had provided me with no big surprises. But here in this corner of Guatemala, there were absolutely no visible references to life as I knew it. Heading for the old colonial city of Antigua, the fairy-tale feel intensified as the road began to climb steeply towards the volcanoes, until I reached such an altitude that I was riding through the very clouds I had been gazing at earlier.

I'd always had this image of the Pan-American Highway as a grand slice of multilane, international motorway traversing half the globe, but I was quickly getting used to the idea that it was little more than a title given to a collection of major routes that linked up across the continent, and that what passed for a major route in the

*Hombre de
Guatemala*

USA or Canada was very different from those here in the Banana
Republics, with their legacies of civil war, earthquakes and scatterings of land mines to add to the fun. In Mexico, the highway was
known as the Inter-Americana, here it was the CA-1—*Centro Americana Uno,* but whatever its name, it was often no more than a narrow
rural road, and this leg was as rough going as a farm track, littered
with gaping potholes and long stretches where Mother Nature had
successfully beaten back her archenemy, the mighty blacktop.

I studied the map, examining my course through this isthmus of
tiny Central American countries: Guatemala, El Salvador, Hon-

duras, Nicaragua, Costa Rica, Panama. Some of them were so small, I'd be crossing a border every day or so. With the exception of Costa Rica, maybe, none of them jumped out at me as a popular holiday destination. I recalled some of the more memorable snippets from the Foreign Office travel advice Web site:

'*Travellers in smaller vehicles have been targeted by armed robbers after crossing the Honduran border.*'

Hmm . . . smaller vehicles? Well, I guess a motorcycle would fall into that category.

'*Dengue fever and malaria are endemic to Nicaragua; outbreaks tend to increase in the rainy season.*'

The rainy season, eh? Well, that'll be round about now.

'*You should be wary of persons presenting themselves as police officers. There have been instances of visitors becoming victims of theft, extortion or sexual assault by persons who may or may not be police officers.*'

So forget 'when in doubt ask a policeman'?

'*Stay alert and do not travel alone.*'

Oh dear.

But I knew by now there was no use in dwelling on these overly cautious warnings, and as usual, it didn't seem anything like as bad as they made out. In fact, Guatemala struck me as a gentle, amiable sort of place. That is, until I hit the sprawling, seething fleshpot that is Guatemala City with its wretched shantytowns in the garbage dumps, tooled-up security men in blacked-out Jeeps and hopeless, shoeless children selling flowers, lighters and anything else they could find at the traffic lights. I didn't mean to go there, but the concept of ring roads hadn't made it to this part of the world, thus the CA-1 dived straight in and out of the savage heart of every Central American capital city. The 'in' bit was easy enough, but getting out on the other side was another matter.

'Centro Americana Uno? The road to El Salvador?' I shouted to drivers of the cars beside me in the traffic jam, craning to hear their replies before the lights changed and they sped away with the combined roar of a hundred rotting exhausts, zigzagging across each other's lanes in a billow of black smoke, horns blasting at everyone and everything in sight. This scene was repeated at every red light and as usual, each of my enquiries elicited an array of fingers pointing in different directions, leading me on a distinctly unmerry dance around the city, searching helplessly for signs, clues, the casting of shadows, anything to guide me south through this hellish maze. The few road signs I saw referred to places that weren't even mentioned on my map and the infuriating one-way system sent me cavorting around the city centre in a dizzy spiral, fading fast under the tropical sun and the oppressive heat produced by the mobile metal prison of decrepit vehicles that penned me in on all sides.

'Uh-oh!' I groaned, feeling a little nudge to the back of the bike as one of my overstuffed pannier bags clipped the wing mirror of a car as I filtered through six lanes of stifling, gridlocked traffic. I stopped to apologise to the four women inside and was relieved to find I had escaped seven years of bad luck—no damage done, just a slight dislodging of the mirror. The driver reached out her window and readjusted its position.

'Disculpe,' I said to her. Sorry.

She turned to acknowledge me and with a sinking heart I watched her face change as our eyes met and she realised the Get Rich Quick scheme that had presented itself to her. Her passengers needed no prompting, they were on message, and raring to go.

Rolling down the windows, the four of them launched into an aggressive verbal attack, pointing at the mirror and waving their fists in a dramatic manner that would have been quite comical had they not been deadly serious. I attempted to pacify them, showing them that their mirror had survived unscathed, but they didn't care to hear my opinion—this was their lucky day! The dollar signs were twinkling in their eyes like a Las Vegas fruit machine, and Ding! Ding! Ding! they'd hit the jackpot. Their hysterical yelling knew no bounds, and although I couldn't make out what they were saying, the menacing tone told me all I needed to know.

'No entiendo,' I explained calmly. *'No hablo español.'*

But they continued to scream their furious diatribe at me.

'*No entiendo. Disculpe.*' I shrugged.

The discordant quartet turned more low and threatening, all the time shaking their heads in a slow, ominous fashion. Big trouble in Guatemala City.

'*No entiendo,*' I repeated, enjoying the benefit of our linguistic stalemate, but they weren't giving in that easily. An English translation was attempted.

'Broke!' one of them screeched, pointing at the mirror.

'*Sí, sí.* Broke! You broke,' another agreed.

'*Dólares!* Dollars!' came a shrieking demand from the backseat.

I patiently showed them once again that the mirror was in good shape, nothing broken, I explained, I'd just knocked it out of position and they couldn't ever possibly begin to imagine how darned sorry I was that I had ever tangled with their bloody mirror and for crying out loud, would they please pipe down now?

'Broke!' they howled, playing up to the other drivers who were leaning out their windows, watching the performance.

'*Disculpe!*' I protested through gritted teeth. I Am Sorry.

'Broke! Broke!' screamed the driver, her eyes slitty with rage.

I was confounded. The evidence was there for us all to see that the mirror was in full working order, but still they thought that if they screamed long enough and loud enough, their obviously false accusations would bear financial fruit. Their complete lack of rational thinking was quite bizarre. Upping the ante, they began motioning for me to pull over to the side of the road, I didn't know what they had in mind, maybe a hair-pulling contest or a spot of arm wrestling? One of the women in the backseat flung open the door and lunged out of the car, gesticulating manically and fussing over the mirror as if it were her firstborn child. I'd seen enough of their drama queen antics to realise that these chancers were nothing if not completely bonkers and that any argument based on reason would be totally lost on them.

'Broke! Money, fifty dollars!' the woman addressed me in menacing tones, her face inches away from mine, jabbing at my arm with a sharp red fingernail. This was it; I'd had enough of these have-a-go housewife extortionists. I surveyed the deadlock of snarled-up vehicles ahead of me and laughed inwardly at the obvious simplicity of the solution.

'Senoras . . .' I addressed them collectively with the biggest, friendliest smile I could muster. Their eyes settled on me with suspicious steely anticipation, awaiting my announcement.

'. . . UP YOURS!' And with a flick of the middle finger, I was out of there, throttle wide open, bombing it through the stationary cars, weaving in and out of the gaps to the front of the queue, running the red light, over the junction, through the tangle of buses and cars, through another red, horns blaring, down a side road, up a one-way street, never looking back. Once I was sure I'd shaken off the opportunist harridans, I allowed myself a sigh of relief and an affectionate pat for the nippy Serow.

'Now *that* is why you ride a motorcycle,' I said to myself with a grin.

I continued my tour of the city, now searching more avidly than ever for that southbound escape route.

Eventually I saw it: a road sign marked CA-1. Oh joy! Thank you, thank you, God of Motorcycling, get me out of this labyrinth of grot! But relief soon gave way to dread when I felt a strange sense of backwards déjà vu creeping up on me. Hadn't I passed that building with the fountains before, and that gas station looked awfully familiar . . . but weren't they on the other side of the road last time I saw them? My sense of direction had become so utterly addled that although I was indeed heading out of the city on the CA-1, it was back the way I'd come in. Now I had to start the nightmare all over again! I pulled into the gas station and looked up the word for 'lost' in my dictionary, completely frazzled by my geographical disorder.

'Zona 1, very dangerous, do not go there,' warned the gas station attendant, in response to my plea for directions.

'Yes,' I replied wearily, 'I've just spent an hour riding around there, now please, can you tell me—'

'Six people killed every day in Guatemala City,' he interrupted me in earnest tones.

'Yes, yes, jolly good,' I said impatiently, 'but I'm actually looking to get out of here—'

'They stop you, they want money, and bang bang!' he said, imitating a gun held up against his head.

'Yeah, I can believe it,' I replied.

The shelves of the little shop were crammed with bottles of oil, exhaust repair bandage and lots of other bits and bobs for the Guatemalan boy-racer. But there was a distinct lack of maps. Yet another idea, along with road signs and ring roads, that hadn't caught on in this neck of the woods.

After a while the realisation dawned on me that this man didn't actually have any of the answers, he was just idling away the day with his conversational horror stories, so none the wiser I returned to the fray for another gruelling lap. Once I'd established that I could now identify all the flags outside the embassy buildings, had translated and memorised the anti-USA graffiti in the underpass (BUSH GENOSIDA, ENEMIGO DE LA HUMANIDAD) and ridden past the same newspaper seller so many times that I was beginning to consider him a close friend, I was forced to consider the possibility that in fact, my trip had come to its end. Forget Ushuaia, forget South America, forget everything. This was it; there was no way out of Guatemala City. I was destined to spend the rest of my life riding round and round and round this infernal black hole.

Bzzzzzzzz went the sound of a tinted electric window retreating next to me.

'You need some help?' came the gentleman's voice from within the car in perfect, almost accentless English. Whatever he was driving was black, shiny and had personalised Guatemalan number plates. I peered inside to find an immaculately dressed man fixing me with a welcome, friendly smile. A rich bouquet of expensive aftershave and leather upholstery rushed out with a woosh of cool air-con. I felt very grubby and smelly all of a sudden.

'I'm trying to find the Centro Americana, towards the border with El Salvador,' I explained. How many times had I said these words today? I was sick of hearing them.

'Follow me,' he said, 'I will show you where the road leaves the city, then you just keep going, keep going and you come to the frontier.'

My guardian angel had arrived!

'And a piece of advice,' he added, 'if you ever need to ask for directions, you must stop the best cars, like this one.' He waved a gilded hand around the luxury interior. 'If someone in Guatemala is driving a car like this, they will certainly speak English, and may be a very important person, maybe someone who can help you, someone in a high position. Do you understand what I am saying?' He looked at me with a hint of a knowing smile.

'Er . . . right . . . thanks for the tip,' I said, totally confused by his subtlety.

'Or maybe . . . they are a drug dealer. . . . HA HA!' he roared with laughter. 'Now, follow me.' The window buzzed shut again as he disappeared behind the black glass.

I was past caring whether my mystery man was a coke baron or the president of Guatemala. Either way, I never found out. Good as his word, he left me on the edge of town with a glittering salute and disappeared back into the mean streets. The straggling outskirts of the city went on for miles in a blur of slums and industrial decay, before the highway finally broke away into open country and another international border loomed.

It pains me to say that I will always remember the Guatemala/El Salvador crossing with shame and self-loathing, the place where my morals unravelled, where I sold my principles like a cheap tart, just to get across the border. I knew some of these frontiers might involve cutting a few deals and when I was pounced upon by a bunch of teenage freelance 'fixers,' hustling to help with the paperwork, guard my bike and change my money, it was evident that my future was not in the hands of the customs and immigration officials, who merely sat around banging rubber stamps in their dingy offices. No, my key to a slick and successful border crossing lay with these wised-up, hard-nosed boys, who could make or break my entry into their homeland. They knew the ins and outs of the convoluted system better than anyone, and I had to keep in with them, trotting along in their wake and doing what I was told. They didn't do this for fun, though, oh no, their services came with a price. And I didn't mind. I didn't mind paying them to do the talking for me, I didn't begrudge the dollar tip for guarding the bike (which really amounted to paying them not to steal my kit). I didn't even mind them haggling over their fee, or trying to fob me off with a laughable exchange rate, or even the incessant flirting and the suggestive comments. But things went even further than that, I'm ashamed to say. I still can't believe that I sank to such depths in order to continue my journey across the Americas, but it's true, and I hope, dear reader, that you can find it in your heart to forgive me when I tell you the shameful, sickening truth of how I ingratiated myself with these young boys—I pretended to like football.

'*Inglésa!*' they exclaimed upon seeing my passport.

I nodded emphatically, indicating the Union Jack on the bike's front mudguard. I wasn't big on flag waving, but it was always a good idea to make it clear you weren't a member of the Bush Genosida gang.

The boys crowded round to look.

'*Inglaterra?*' said one with a broad grin 'Aaaaaaah . . . David Beckham.'

'David Beckham, David Beckham,' they hollered excitedly, running around, scoring fantasy goals and generally displaying their admiration for our sarong-sporting soccer star.

'You like David Beckham?' they enquired.

With the welfare of my motorcycle and passport in their hands, common sense told me that this wouldn't be the best time to announce my antipathy, verging on loathing, for the revolting Becks and anything to do with the so-called beautiful game. So I swallowed my pride and joined in: 'Aaah, yes! David Beckham. *Excelente!'*

'*Sí, sí, David Beckham, increíble! El mejor,'* they agreed. The best!

'*Sí,* Manchester United, *mi favorito!'* I enthused.

They stared at me blankly and exchanged quizzical glances.

'No,' said one, 'Real Madrid.'

'No!' I laughed. 'Manchester United.'

'No,' the others chimed in, shaking their heads. 'Real Madrid.'

Didn't these idiots know anything about football? Everyone knew Becks played for Manchester United. Even I knew that.

'No,' said the oldest boy with authority. 'No more Manchester United. Now Real Madrid.'

He seemed to know what he was talking about.

'Oh really?' I said somewhat sheepishly. 'Um . . . when?'

'*Junio,'* said the boy, regarding me with deep suspicion. June. Three months ago.

I garbled something about having been away travelling for a long time . . . I'd been out of touch . . . but they weren't listening. I'd been caught out good and proper. They'd rumbled me for the footie fraud that I was.

The diminutive size of El Salvador meant that the next border, with Honduras, was only a couple of hundred miles away, but despite these Central American countries being so small and tight knit, each one felt noticeably different from the other. My first impression of El Salvador was how much more Americanised it was in comparison to Guatemala. The U.S. dollar was now the official currency here and MTV, CNN, Discovery, Fox News and the Entertainment Channel had taken hold of every hotel, café and bar like a virulent cable-transmitted disease. Even U.S.-style supermarkets had crept into the bigger towns, although a uniformed guard with an M16 in the fruit and veg department was enough to re-

Sleeping with the Serow. A motorcycle-friendly hotel in El Salvador.

mind me that some things would take a while to change in the Banana Republics.

While every Salvadorian I encountered had a welcoming smile and a friendly word, I didn't feel the urge to hang around for long, one reason being that it was the dirtiest country I have ever visited, and I feared that every lungful of air I breathed was rapidly decreasing my life expectancy. I didn't realise quite how bad it was, however, until I pulled into a café for lunch, causing a roomful of diners to pause mid-mouthful, dragging their eyes away from a Spanish-dubbed episode of *Happy Days* while the girls behind the counter burst into fits of giggles.

'*Qué?*' I asked. What? Trying not to feel too much like the paranoid foreigner.

The girls pointed at my face, laughing behind their hands. A trip to the loo revealed my new incarnation as the Al Jolson of the Pan-American Highway. Little did I know that I'd been running my very own Black and White Minstrel travelling show through El Salvador. The ambient dirt of the towns was unavoidable, with their crumbling, grime-coated buildings and streets choked with dilapidated buses belching clouds of black smoke so thick you could almost chew them, but I couldn't believe the layer of soot that had collected on my face in just one morning's riding. As I scrubbed away with the standard Central American washroom facilities of a trickle of cold water and most definitely no soap or a towel, it occurred to me that I could have avoided all this, had I not elected to set off on this journey with an open-face helmet and a bike with no mirrors.

It wasn't until I reached the border with Honduras a couple of days later that I really learnt how Central America got its reputation. Before I'd even made it to the ragtag sprawl of tatty portacabins and lumpen breeze-block buildings that signified the end of El Salvador, the gang of hopeful fixers descended on me like flesh-hungry vultures swooping onto a fresh carcass. I had spied them from a distance, waiting at the side of the road, milling about ominously, hoping some hapless foreigner would turn up who couldn't speak Spanish and had no idea how to negotiate the gargantuan amount of baffling paperwork required to enter Honduras. And lo and behold, their luck was in—here I was! My spirits dived as they legged it towards me, as if I were a long-lost (and very rich) relative. I didn't stop to chat but they ran alongside me anyway, howling out their services, competing against each other for my trade.

'Change money! Good rate!'

'I help you. Much papers. Very difficult!'

'I speak English!'

'You sexy, lady!'

'I help with papers!'

'My brother, he watch the moto.'

'Where is your husband?'

'Honduras very dangerous, I help you.'

'I show you where to go.'

Despite the smouldering cigarettes permanently fused to their lips and fingers, they showed no sign of fatigue as they galloped along beside the bike, and as I came to a halt at the metal barrier that indicated the frontier, they moved in, crowding around in front of me, beside me, behind me, all the while jabbering and pushing their deals like a gaggle of wannabe city traders, closing in on me in a claustrophobic sea of brown faces, gold teeth, bushy black mustaches, cowboy hats, baseball caps and counterfeit sportswear. Never letting their sales pitch slip for one moment, they repeated their well-worn lines with more gusto than ever, only now they were grabbing my arm and tugging at the sleeve of my shirt while the younger contingent fiddled with the bike and the money changers waved thick wads of notes at me, thumbing through them like a paper fan, barking out exchange rates and thrusting calculators under my nose displaying a variety of figures that only added to the confusion.

Being surrounded by a bunch of swarthy men waving bundles of cash in my face might have held a certain appeal in a different situation, but right now it was nothing but a big ol' pain in the *culo*. But if I was to continue my journey, I had to choose my fixer from this motley collection of unlikely suitors. I'm not really sure how or why I made my decision, but I ended up with a small, weasely chap with skin the texture of a sundried tomato and a mouth full of gold. He walked with something between a swagger and a limp and disconcertingly, avoided eye contact at all costs. I disliked him instantly.

The Weasel and I agreed on a price. 'Passport' he demanded, clicking his fingers impatiently. I handed it over resignedly, along with my driving licence and the registration documents for the bike. Then the circus began in earnest. Why does it have to be so complicated? I wondered in despair as we tramped in and out of unmarked offices, collecting a multitude of perplexing forms from an army of stony-faced officials, each of whom required between six and ten photocopies of every piece of paperwork, although I never found out why. The whole place had the air of a prison camp with its dirt roads, its depressing, windowless grey buildings, the cascades of barbed wire and the POW demeanour of its workers. Communication skills were not the Weasel's high point and as he scurried around, doing his Artful Dodger act, all I could do was tag along, smiling inanely, with very little idea what was going on. But when I plugged him for information—'What's this form for?' or 'Where are we going?'—he just flicked me off with a dismissive shake of his head and a wave of his hand, which I took to mean, 'Don't concern yourself with things you don't understand.' After the autonomy of life on the road, having my every move dictated by an incommunicative, shifty-eyed wide-boy was a frustrating experience, and I began to wonder if he was as sharp as he made out, but when he started spending my money, you'd think he'd graduated from the Anna Nicole Smith School of Gold Digging.

'Five hundred lempiras' he would demand before disappearing with my bundle of notes into one of the anonymous portacabins, returning a little while later with a faded computer printout to add to the burgeoning pile of papers. Then with a jerk of the head, we would fight our way across the road, through the rabble of sleeve-tugging money changers and lecherous travelling salesmen, to another office, running off a few more photocopies on the way. No explanations were offered, just more requests for cold hard cash, which I would hand over like a spineless businessman appeasing a demanding mistress.

'Three hundred and fifty lempiras . . . one hundred and twenty lempiras . . .' his hand outstretched, and another vanishing act would follow, leaving me hanging around outside, melting in the baking heat and wondering what he was spending my *dinero* on this time. In his defence, he did always return with a receipt and an official-looking piece of paper covered in inky stamps, but I was in no mood to trust anyone. In the end it became hard to keep up with the cash flow, and my brain sizzled with the constant arithmetic required to work out how the Honduran lempiras, with their oodles of zeros, transferred into U.S. dollars or British pounds.

The day was ebbing away, the sun had begun its move westwards and we were no nearer getting me and my bike into Honduras, despite now possessing a pile of paperwork so huge that I was genuinely concerned how I would squeeze it into my luggage. The Weasel was twitching impatiently, his eyes flicking, still not giving anything away. We were sitting in some gloomy premises that would surely qualify as a victim of Sick Building Syndrome, waiting for a stern woman in a military uniform to finish whatever important thing she was doing with my vehicle documents behind her closed door. But the clickety-clack of her ancient typewriter had ceased nearly thirty minutes ago, and since then, no progress report had been forthcoming. The poky waiting room did little to raise spirits, decorated with its one bare bulb, a wobbly ceiling fan that despite its noisy whirring failed to dissipate the muggy air, and most bizarrely, one of those so-called motivational posters featuring a school of dolphins leaping joyously through the ocean under the slogan THERE IS NO 'I' IN TEAM. It occurred to me that there was no 'I' in Honduras either. The poster's dog-eared, tattered appearance suggested that this office's days of inspirational leadership and seamless teamwork lay in the deep and distant fantasy of some SuperBri-type who had no doubt arrived from the city with big plans for 'modernisation' and left soon afterwards, having spectacularly failed to shake up the grinding treadmill of bureaucracy with his pictures of cooperative sea mammals.

The Weasel was pacing around the room, hovering at the closed door that had been slammed shut in his face half an hour earlier. When the boot-faced woman had refused to let him sit down and wasted no time in banishing him from her sacred office, I realised that there was a distinct pecking order here, with the officials holding the lowly fixers in utter contempt, only one notch above us scumbag gringos, and for a moment I almost felt a bit sorry for the Weasel. Eventually he plucked up the courage to knock on the door. I could hear him kowtowing to one of the woman's colleagues and when he emerged, his wheeling 'n' dealing savvy was showing its first signs of strain.

'*Qué pasa?*' I asked him. What's going on?

He slumped into the chair next to me and looking me in the eye for the first time, explained in resigned tones that the woman dealing with my case had gone off to brush her teeth.

'*Por treinta minutes?*' I exclaimed. For thirty minutes?

He nodded with a sigh.

I wished a curse of gum disease on the old cow and sat back staring at the dolphins. The poster was doing a good job—I was starting to feel very motivated—motivated to get the hell out of Honduras. The only problem was, I hadn't got in yet.

Despite my frustrations, I was strangely fascinated at the way these countries had allowed so much red tape to dictate their lives. Couldn't anyone see that there was only the need for two offices: customs for the vehicles, immigration for the humans, and maybe a bank, where you could change money without being pressed up into a dark corner by a greasy man wielding a bankroll as thick as his arm and a calculator that only works in his favour? It was obvious that the system was in shambles, but what did I know about the economics and politics of Central America? I was just here for the ride, and if there was one thing that would save my sanity amongst this madness, it was to remember that I just had to roll with it.

I walked over to the door for a change of scenery and watched a bunch of kids crawling all over my bike and a fat money changer roughing up a couple of German tourists in a Land Rover. Every doorway housed a group of three or four men, doing very little except smoking and escaping the late afternoon heat. A policeman was in the midst of a lively argument with one of the fixers, the stiff peak of his decorated hat bumping against his opponent's New York Yankees baseball cap as they exchanged face-to-face insults with typical Latin fervour. I returned to my seat and waited.

It was some four hours later that the Weasel uttered the immortal words: 'All finished. Now last thing, you pay policeman.'

'Oh yeah, and what's that for?' I asked, already knowing the answer.

'To make everything go smooth,' said the Weasel, his eighteen-carat smile overshadowed by his menacing tone.

We glared at each other, but I didn't have time to respond because a large outstretched hand was being thrust in my face. I looked up to discover it was attached to the long arm of the law. Fishing out a five-dollar note I placed it into the gnarled palm.

'*Más,*' muttered the Weasel. More.

Another fiver.

The policeman slipped the two notes into his pocket and walked away without a word. Now it was the Weasel's turn to demand his fee, souring our already curdled relationship with a figure far larger than we had agreed at the outset.

The blatancy! The lack of shame! The slipperiness of it all! But there was no use protesting. At that moment, surrounded by the filth and the haggling and the bitterness on everyone's faces, I longed for a bit of British fair play: a patient, orderly line in the post office, a handshake after a game of cricket on the green, giving up your seat on the bus to an old lady. Maybe I was being overly romantic about my distant homeland, maybe this green and pleasant land no longer existed, if it ever had, but I knew these things would never happen here, in this godforsaken dump in the middle of the jungle. The evening gloom was moving in and the sky loomed dark and threatening with storm clouds. I entered Honduras lighter of pocket and heavier of heart, and for the first time since leaving England I felt the miserable pangs of homesickness welling up inside me.

Ten

Less than twenty-four hours later, I was doing my best to get out of Honduras, but even that wasn't straightforward. I certainly had no desire to stick around, uninspired as I was by the miserable townships with their grubby shopfronts cowering behind steel grills, the routine power cuts and the packs of wild dogs that roamed the dirt streets. And now at the exit point I discovered that in addition to boasting the most expensive and time-consuming entry requirements, Honduras was also the only country that charged its visitors to leave!

'All the *turistas*, they say the same thing—they hate Honduras and they will never come back!' said the unusually sympathetic immigration official. He shrugged with the air of 'that's just the way it is.'

I shrugged back at him as he relieved me of my last handful of lempiras, and rode away across the barren mile of no-man's-land towards the Nicaraguan border, remembering the closing chapters of *The Mosquito Coast*. Wasn't it in Honduras that the boy's father had finally gone insane, coming to his sticky end in a sewage-infested swamp, pecked to death by seagulls? Now it all made sense.

I steeled myself for yet another round of frontier misery, making mental and emotional preparation for the onslaught of money-grabbing marauders and general mayhem, but Nicaragua seemed to have its act together a little more than its northerly neighbour. By this, I mean there were some signs dotted around, giving a vague suggestion of officialdom and order, as opposed to petty crime and racketeering. But nevertheless, the omnipresent fixers homed in, swarming all over the bike and mauling me relentlessly, causing me to come over all Barbara Windsor in the never-to-be-made classic, *Carry On Crossing Central American Borders.*

'Ooh I say! Steady on!' Swatting a young boy out of the way.

'Ooh cheeky! Less of that!' Shove!

'Excuse *me*!' A sharp stab with the elbow.

'Oi, Jose! Keep your hands to yourself!' Slap!

Casually indifferent to my rejections, they skulked away one by one, waiting for their next victim, and I wormed my way into Nicaragua, enlisting the help of the only female fixer in the gang. I was impressed by her snooty reserve and her barefaced gall in sporting an unauthorised uniform and a blatantly fake ID card, with which she tried to convince me she was a high-ranking official in customs, immigration and police—a busy lady indeed. All sweetness and light throughout the proceedings, she acted as though she were doing me a personal favour and waited until the very end before going in for the kill, hustling me venomously for a whacking great fee. These tactics once again grated on my innate sense of fair play, but I had to admit a grudging admiration for her ingenuity and lack of leisurewear.

This entry point provided me with a choice of routes across Nicaragua—the trusty CA-1 and the CA-3, marked as a thick red line on my map, indicating a major thoroughfare. For the sake of variety I opted for the latter, taking me down the western side of the country to León, a reputedly pleasant city with fine examples of colonial buildings still in existence. I'm no architecture buff but after miles and miles of shantytowns, jerry-built shacks and breeze-block huts, the sight of a grand town square in the Spanish style, or a crumbling old hotel complete with ornately tiled courtyard, lifted my Europhilic spirits no end. The need to witness man-made

beauty hadn't seemed so important in the glorious natural surroundings of the Rocky Mountains or the Baja desert, but in Central America's dense and uninspiring landscape, packed solid with
profitable coffee and banana plantations and distinctly lacking in
breathtaking views, I regularly found myself craving something
more pleasing on which to rest my hungry traveller's eyes.

'Those colonial buildings had better be good,' I was muttering
half an hour later, up to my knees in mud, heaving the bike through
a quagmire stretch of the CA-3 where the thick red line had dis-
solved into a gloopy brown swamp. Any evidence that this road had
ever been treated to the services of a steamroller and a layer of tarmac was in scant supply, and I wondered when my map had last
been updated. Judging by the way nature had taken hold, I was
guessing around the time Columbus had nipped over for his first
recce. Or maybe the map, like the menus, was more hopeful than
factual—did a thick red line actually mean 'We'd like to surface this
road . . . one day'? Whatever its history, it was now just a muddy
track, chewed up by tropical downpours and overloaded banana
trucks, and spat out as a mishmash of ruts and corrugations. Short
stretches of loose gravel would occasionally crop up amongst the
sludge, ravaged by the usual rash of potholes that spread like a violent cancer, ranging in diameter from a few inches to several feet,
but there was no use trying to swerve round them—they were
everywhere, in fact, there were more holes than there was road. All
I could do was to bang and bump my way across them, standing up
on the pegs to save my back from the spine-crushing jolts and listen
to the ominous clank and tinkle of unidentifiable bits of my possessions gradually falling apart inside my luggage. After a mile or so of
this gruelling exercise the gravel would peter out, as the road turned
to pure slop again, which almost came as a relief. But I soon tired of
the power-sapping suction of the mud, especially when the back
wheel got stuck in a deep trough, requiring a superhuman amount
of brute force to wrench it free. The alternating nature of the two
terrains at least meant I didn't get bored too quickly, but after a

while the novelty began to wear off and, upon consulting the map, I discovered that León was still over fifty miles away down this hellish highway.

'Oh Lordy!' I groaned out loud. 'Fifty miles of this!' It was London to Oxford, via a slice of the Congo Basin.

I was already knackered and filthy, doused in a pungent cocktail of sweat and stagnant water, and I'd barely covered six of these tortuous miles. I gazed at the steady line of the CA-1 on my map with the deep longing and regret of an unfaithful wife. Why, oh why, hadn't I stuck with it, why had I strayed? But the grass is always greener and the road always smoother. There were no towns marked on my route to break up the tedium, not even a hint of civilisation on the horizon, just endless fields of coffee, and not a drop to drink.

Cursed as I was with a steadfast stubbornness, verging on an unhealthy obsession about keeping on, keeping on, it never occurred to me to retrace my steps to the border and take the CA-1. No, I was in for the long haul and haul is what I did, experimenting with different methods to ease my travel. Was it best to ride along the edge of the road where the potholes were smaller, but the gravel deeper? Should I fly through the boggy sections as quickly as possible to prevent getting stuck, but risk a back-wheel slide-out and get a muddy splattering in the process? I felt as though I were ploughing my way through the remotest jungle backwoods, but the occasional reminder that this was in fact one of Nicaragua's main roads would appear in the form of a cloud of dust or shower of mud in the distance, growing larger and noisier, eventually revealing itself as a clapped-out vehicle bearing down on me. A friendly wave from the driver was a standard greeting but when it came to keeping the shiny side up and the dirty side down, it was every man (or woman) for himself. Any claim to 'my side of the road' was irrelevant as we dodged and weaved towards each other, swerving round the holes, both vying for the least bumpy course, the only rule being that the biggest guy gets his way, a rule which invariably saw me forced over to the left hand side to make room for a pickup full of farmworkers, or slamming into a mammoth pothole to avoid a lumbering ten-ton truck that issued an exfoliating spray of mud and gravel in its wake, sloughing off my epidermis in one fell swoop. If I had any business sense about me, I would have scooped it up and flogged it as an Authentic Tropical Facial Treatment to some swanky beauty salon back home, but my future entrepreneurial ventures were the last thing on my mind as I struggled to keep moving in a vaguely upright position.

I should have known better, but I couldn't help watching the agonising process of the miles ticking by on my speedo. There's nothing more dispiriting than this kind of clock watching, and if there was one thing I had learned by now, it was that a watched trip meter never turns. But the tedium was taking its toll. I yearned for something to happen, something to break up the monotony of the featureless plantations and the endless grind of this miserable ride. I don't know what I was hankering after, really, nothing particularly exciting, just a little village or a roadside café or even a gas station. Somewhere to stop, something to focus on, something other than potholes, potholes and more potholes. But when a little Honda 125, straining under the weight of two men dressed in an all too familiar garb, appeared out of the bushes into my path, forcing me to a skidding stop in the loose gravel, the expression 'Be careful what you wish for' raced through my mind. I'd wanted a distraction, and I'd got one: two grim-faced Nicaraguan policemen pacing around my bike was a dead cert to take my mind off the road ahead.

'Your licence!' demanded the older one. He had the corrupt-cop look down pat—a monstrous mustache grew from his cruel, unforgiving face, thriving despite the shade of his mammoth peaked cap. The crisply ironed charcoal uniform featured an array of impressive stripes and badges and his trousers were tucked into his boots in the military style. His identically dressed pillion-riding sidekick was some years younger and not quite as intimidating, lacking the necessary facial hair for the job. He greeted me with a hint of an apologetic smile. The good cop, bad cop thing must be a global police tactic, I surmised, or maybe it took a lifetime's service in the Nicaraguan force to get really grumpy. I couldn't say, but I had a feeling I was about to find out.

'Your licence,' barked the scary one again.

I had a momentary flashback to my run-in with the Canadian Mounties—a trip to a Nicaraguan vehicle pound was definitely an experience I could live without, but this pair didn't seem organised enough to pull off a stunt like that. Their own bike was a heap of junk; the tires were bald and the seat held together by gaffer tape. Could this really be a police vehicle? I wondered. God knows what the cops use to get around in a country as poor as this, but this little runabout hardly looked up to delivering pizzas, let alone transporting a couple of burly rozzers along this ramshackle highway. The two men were examining my licence, still stalking round my bike, pointing and talking between themselves in sinister muted tones.

'Motorcycle papers,' came the next demand, again in Spanish.

There was something funny about the whole situation. I couldn't put my finger on it, but then I remembered the Foreign Office travel department had already done the detective work for me. What was it again . . . ?

You should be wary of persons presenting themselves as police officers. There have been instances of visitors becoming victims of theft, extortion or sexual assault by persons who may or may not be police officers.

May or may not be police officers? How were you supposed to tell? These guys looked pretty convincing, with their matching uniforms and shiny badges. I stood there in silence while they muttered between themselves, until eventually they agreed on their tactic.

'*Prohibido,*' said bad cop, pointing at my headlight.

Prohibited?

'It is illegal to have your light on,' good cop explained.

Well, they were certainly imaginative, I'd give them that, but there wasn't much I could do about my felony; the headlight was wired into the ignition so it couldn't be turned off, but God knows how I was going to explain that. I went into my emergency default Spanish of adding o's and e's on the end of everything.

'*Es automatico con la ignicione,*' I said hopefully.

Amazingly they understood, but not to be defeated by technology they continued to circle the bike, homing in on my second heinous crime—my rolled-up sleeping bag, strapped on the front end above the headlight.

'*Prohibido,*' said my mustachioed *bandito/policía* man. He was deadly serious.

There was nothing to do but play along. I removed the bag and strapped it onto my top box instead.

'There we are, that's much better, isn't it?' I said with an inane grin.

Their muttering became more animated.

'*Prohibido,*' they tried again, pointing at my panniers.

'*Prohibido,*' my tent.

'*Prohibido,*' my jerry can.

My lawlessness knew no bounds, I was an out-and-out criminal, terrorising the poor people of Nicaragua with my felonious luggage system. It's a fair cop, chuck me in the slammer and throw away the key.

'*Prohibido, prohibido, prohibido . . .*'

But I had stopped listening and started laughing; the whole idea was so utterly fantastical. Here I was in a country where motorcycles tear around the streets loaded up with entire families, various livestock and multiple crates of bananas, but my neatly packed bags were suddenly a cause of great concern to these two conscientious coppers. Why didn't they just come out with it? How much did they want?

They must have been reading my mind.

'Monies,' said the older one.

Aha! That's more like it, and how funny that he can speak English all of a sudden, but I guess you've got to learn the most important words first. I'd set off on my journey with only the Spanish words for *caution* and *cheese,* but these chaps had definitely got their priorities right.

'Monies,' he repeated, my documents still tight in his grip. His tone was firm, but an underlying hint of menace was creeping in now.

'Monies.'

He might be speaking my lingo, but I was still going to try the dumb foreigner act, if only on grammatical grounds. Unless he could request his bribe in the singular, I wasn't prepared to play along.

'Monies.'

'No entiendo.'

'Monies.'

'No entiendo.' Sorry, still plural.

'Monies.'

'No entiendo.' Must try harder.

The sidekick spoiled our fun.

'You pay money,' he said quietly.

I told myself it wasn't personal. This kind of thing was going on all over the globe, right now. Palms were being greased, deals were being cut and the well-lubricated wheels of the Third World kept on turning. From Tijuana to Timbuktu, folk were being roughed up and shaken down by bent cops, jaded border guards and middle-ranking bureaucrats—I was just a tiny cog in a huge machine.

'How much?' I asked in Spanish.

'Fifty,' said the older cop, taking control of the proceedings again.

'Cordobas?' I enquired, hoping that we were talking Nicaraguan notes.

He responded with a sneering, nasty laugh. He was right. It was a stupid question—bribery only dealt in one currency. But I was damned if I was going to hand over fifty greenbacks to these jokers. We faced each other out for a while, not because I was feeling particularly cocky, I was just thinking about my next move. Good cop used the awkward silence to launch his charm offensive.

'Where are you from? What is the weather like there?' and most bafflingly, 'Do you like Nicaragua?'

'England. Cold. Not at the moment,' seemed the easiest, if slightly unimaginative, response.

'Fifty,' repeated bad cop.

We glared at each other for a bit longer, until it became painful.

'Fifty.' This time he handed me back the bike papers as some sort of negotiating chip, but his thumb and forefinger kept their tight grip on my driving licence.

I tucked the papers away in my luggage, and allowed myself a secret jubilant smile. He didn't know it, but he'd just blown it.

'I leave now,' I announced, climbing onto the bike. 'Good-bye.'

'No, no. Fifty dollars,' he demanded again, waving my licence in my face with a smug smirk.

'*No necesario.*' I wafted the licence away with a gloved hand. I don't need it.

'Yes! Licence. Fifty dollars.'

'No, thank you, I don't need it.' I flashed them a benevolent smile.

They looked at each other, confused. He thrust the licence under my nose.

'No, thank you, I don't want it,' I insisted.

I started the engine.

'Fifty dollars,' he repeated, annoyed.

'No, thank you.'

Of course, any British bobby would have spotted the laminated photocopy a mile off, but in the backwoods of Nicaragua, who's going to know the difference? And besides, I could afford to donate one of them; I had another three tucked away in my purse for any future brushes with the law.

'Adios!' I shouted, as I roared away down the bumpy road, leaving them staring after me and then back at the bogus licence with an air of utter confusion. I was half hoping to get involved in a motorcycle chase that I could easily win, but they showed no interest in pursuing me, confirming my hunch that their badges and uniforms were merely a front for a couple of desperadoes. I gave them a victorious wave as I disappeared in a haze of dirt and satisfaction. You don't get many proper 'Eat My Dust!' moments in life, but this was a real corker.

León turned out to be just the ticket, a town of crumbling colonial grandeur with an easy-going atmosphere and the best cup of coffee on the trip so far. The moment I arrived, filthy from head to toe, I was adopted by a taxi driver who despite having a paying passenger on board, insisted I follow him around town on a guided tour and even fixed me up with somewhere to stay, refusing all my offers of remuneration with a good-natured vehemence. I wasn't quite sure what sort of place he'd found for me to lay my weary head (and oh, was it weary) but I felt as though I'd stumbled onto the set of a Nicaraguan soap opera. Located down a quiet, shady side street a few blocks from the main town square, it definitely wasn't a hotel, more like a shared house that hosted the various comings and goings of a bunch of young, laid-back Nicaraguans who sat around watching TV, cooking and generally just hanging out. The young man who opened the door was as charming and welcoming as the policemen had been surly and intimidating. Thankfully, he was keen to practice his English, providing a welcome rest for my struggling bilingual brain.

'Come in, bring the moto into the house; he insisted, heaving my bike into his living room. I had encountered this in hotels all over Mexico and Central America, but still the novelty of parking my motorcycle next to my bed, or riding up a couple of steps into the hotel lobby, never failed to amaze and delight me. Where in England would you find any hostelry that positively encouraged the parking of motorcycles in their dining room? This Nicaraguan reception was far removed from the hostile glare and the hasty flip of the NO VACANCIES sign that the British two-wheeled wayfarer knows so well. As part of his English practice, my host quizzed me on the usual subjects and talked with heartfelt warmth about his country and the struggles of its past.

'Things are different now, the war is finished,' he explained. 'Nicaraguans have had enough violence. We just cannot take any more. Now we are thinking differently, we are looking to the future, we want to make Nicaragua a pleasant, peaceful country for everyone, for us and for visitors.'

A stroll around town confirmed his statement; for a start there was a distinct lack of guns, in stark contrast to Honduras and El Salvador. The general demeanour of the people of León was open and friendly, again a far cry from the guarded distrust I had encountered in Honduras. But most notable was the complete absence of harassment from the male population, not a single catcall, whistle or shout of *'guapa, guapa.'* Mind you, I did look a bit of a state, so that might have had something to do with it.

Back at the house, some awesome news was presented to me by one of the girls: 'We have a laundry room if you would like to wash your clothes.' A laundry room! Right here! I couldn't believe my ears! Within seconds I had stripped off my mud-splattered outfit, ready to bundle it into the machine and wash away all traces of the dreaded CA-3, while I relaxed with a bottle of the local brew and discovered the pleasures of Nicaraguan TV. Aaah . . . the thought of a lazy evening ahead, what a joy after the day I'd had.

Maybe I've got the wrong room, I thought as I pulled back the curtain to reveal a corrugated slab of stone next to a huge sink supplied by one cold tap. I scanned the small bare room for the washing machine but I couldn't see it anywhere, not a Whirlpool or Maytag in sight, not even a humble twin tub. I stood there clutching my bundle of begrimed duds and stared at the stone washboard with a mixture of dread and fascination as the truth sank in. My fantasy evening of Nicaraguan game shows and ice-cold beer dissipated like a sink full of soapsuds. There was no rest for the mucky motorcycle traveller—tonight I would be scrubbing, sloshing, rinsing and wringing as if my life depended on it.

The following morning, crispy clean inside and out, having re-alised that the bit of lead pipe sticking out of the bathroom wall was a shower, I set off for Costa Rica, passing the enormous Lago de Nicaragua and its surrounding volcanoes. Impressive lake that it was, it didn't succeed in quenching my nagging thirst for the ocean, exacerbated by thousands of miles of inland travel, and I couldn't help but stray down to the Pacific coast to pull over and relish the deserted beaches with their swaying palm trees and scatterings of exotic fruit and tiny red crabs that scuttled between my toes. I was in danger of allowing this tropical paradise to mellow me out, but it wasn't long before I was seeing signs for yet another *frontera* and it was time to toughen up and adopt my newfound border attitude—hard-nosed, guns blazing, don't mess with me. I'd got the measure of it by now; I wouldn't be intimidated, I would fix a price in advance, I'd take no nonsense from anyone. I approached the barrier with the frosty glare and pursed lips of a wronged suburban housewife.

But my aggressive front was immediately disarmed by a ravish-ing Costa Rican teenager who flashed his big chocolate eyes and a pearly smile, informing me in honey tones that it was he who was destined to be my helper today. I certainly had no objections to spending the next few hours in the company of this budding la-dykiller, but despite my rapidly melting heart and other parts of my anatomy, I stuck to my guns, insisting on him setting his fee before embarking on the familiar treadmill. But my silver-tongued aide was having none of it.

'No, no,' he protested, 'later, at the end. You pay from the heart.'

'What the hell does that mean?' I groaned, immediately wary of his hippie vernacular.

'I help you with the papers. At the end you decide. You pay what your heart tells you; if you don't like what I do—you pay nothing.' He placed his hands on his chest. 'Listen to your heart, pay from the heart.'

I could see this little charmer making a mint with his novel pricing system, but it all sounded a bit woolly to me. Still, I decided to succumb to his wiles and we set off on the paperwork trail while he bombarded me with a stream of incessant flattery and the usual questions about the whereabouts of my husband. But his company was engaging and his English good enough to turn his onslaught of flirting into a genial rapport.

'Why do you do this?' I asked him. 'Hanging around a grotty border town, hoping to make a few dollars? Isn't Costa Rica the richest, most advanced of the Central American countries? You seem pretty sharp, surely you could earn more money doing something else?'

'I hate doing it,' he admitted, his silky-smooth confidence dropping for a moment. 'I have done this for a year, but I'm going to college in San José to learn computers next year. Then I will never come back, you can make a lot of money with computers.'

I questioned him about his country and he warmed to the subject, pumping me full of facts with bright-eyed patriotic fervour.

'Costa Rica is the best country in Central America, you can do everything here, windsurfing, white-water rafting, trekking, we are leaders in ecotourism,' he announced as if he'd been swotting up on travel brochures, 'and it is the best country for wildlife, we have five percent of the world's biodiversity,' he added proudly. I had no idea what that meant so I just nodded.

'All the girls say Costa Rican men are the best,' he continued knowingly. 'We have the best clothes, we are the most romantic, the best-looking . . .' he fixed his melted Nutella eyes on me, '. . . and the best in bed.'

Crikey! These Latin lover boys start young! I was almost old enough to be his mother.

'I'll take your word for it,' I replied.

He gave me a sly wink.

Naturally, I tipped him generously when the time came to go our separate ways.

I don't know if he was right about the local men, but Costa Rica had certainly worked hard on its tourist appeal. There was even a patch of grass at the border with a sign proclaiming it to be the Park of Peace between two friends—Costa Rica and Nicaragua; it looked quite unkempt so I guessed there must be an ongoing dispute about whose turn it was to do the gardening. Being the only Central American country without an army undoubtedly liberated a fair amount of cash for Costa Rica to spend on more wholesome pursuits than the civil wars and military coups so popular with its neighbours, but there was something insipid about the place that left me cold. I couldn't fault it for its beautiful scenery, its spotless beaches or the abundance of exotic flora and fauna (including wild monkeys swinging in the trees) but I preferred the down-home earthiness of Nicaragua and Guatemala, even if you did have to watch your back a bit more. It felt as though Costa Rica was geared up to pleasing the Yanks, and if this was the case they were doing a good job of it. At every turn I stumbled across groups of painfully cool American kids holidaying under the misconception that they'd risked life and limb by flying into San José for a week of organised adventure, an oxymoron if there ever was one. Any social contact with these misguided folk inevitably involved them ramming horror stories down my throat about the dangers of solo travel south of the border, especially for a chick on her own, and especially if she's riding a motorcycle. Of course, this was nothing new, I'd been subjected to this kind of scare mongering from Anchorage to L.A., but one evening while tolerating a couple of California surfer dudettes drawling out third-hand tales of shootings in Mexico, rapes in Guatemala and robberies in Peru, it dawned on me that somewhere along the way, I'd stopped listening. There had been a time, not so long ago, that I would have gobbled up these tales of doom with an active paranoia, working myself into a frenzy of unfounded fear, but now I barely acknowledged them. After five months on the road, two of which had been spent crossing Mexico and most of Central America, I was beginning to realise that these horror-storytellers rarely spoke from personal experience, they just related old, exaggerated clichés and Foreign Office paranoia in an attempt at worldliness—and failed miserably.

I wasn't sorry to leave behind the adventure theme park of Costa Rica, and upon entering Panama, I celebrated my final Central American border crossing with one of the gastronomic highlights of the journey, a humble coconut bought from a sun-wizened but dapper old man who had turned his stock in trade into a precarious pyramid. 'Coco! Coco!' he hollered. I handed over twenty-five cents in return for a giant coconut complete with straw sticking out at a tantalising angle. 'Drink Me,' it urged, and for a moment I was Alice in my own tropical wonderland.

I slipped away from the bustle of the border offices and sat down in the quiet shade of a palm tree, sipping the ambrosial milk and savouring the moment. For once my mind was empty of motorcycle maintenance, police checkpoints, passports and paperwork or any of the other admin that can so easily overwhelm the simple pleasures of life on the road. A return visit to the coconut man for his after-sales service was essential, if only to watch his flamboyant smashing of the shell with his antique silver knife and the lightning speed at which he sliced and scooped out the white flesh for my second course, while simultaneously serving ten other customers. And who says men can't multitask?

I could have hung around all day, watching him juggling, smashing and slicing his wares, but there was work to be done. The Bridge of the Americas, spanning the Panama Canal, was calling me towards Panama City, where the biggest logistical headache of my trip awaited me—the crossing of the Darién Gap.

For reasons best known to the U.S. government there is no road linking Central and South America. The Pan-American Highway comes to an abrupt stop just forty miles short of the Panama/

Colombia border, possibly making it the longest cul-de sac in the world. It starts up again in northern Colombia, but despite the gap being just seventy miles, it's seventy miles of the Darién jungle—a lawless, roadless, impenetrable wilderness dominated by drug cartels and tropical disease. A few hardy souls have attempted to cross the Darién Gap by motorcycle, using two-wheel drive machines or dismantling the bike and transporting it by raft along the network of rivers. Fortunately for us mere mortals, there was an easier option, although as far as challenges go, the task of organising international air cargo in Spanish seemed demanding enough, especially when making advance enquiries from roadside phone booths. The first problem was finding one in working order, the second was that when I did get hold of an airfreight company, the staff and I were both so keen to communicate in our poorly executed version of each other's language that neither of us understood what the other one was on about.

'*Buenos días,* Panavia,' said a man's voice, followed by a double-speed onslaught of Spanish niceties.

I tripped off my well-practiced line: 'Er . . . *Hola!* I would like to fly my motorcycle from Panama City to Quito, Ecuador.' Silence.

'Er . . . hello? I would like to fly my motorcycle from Panama City to Quito, Ecuador,' I tried again, to be met with more incomprehensible yakking at the other end.

'No, no, a motorcycle . . . a moto . . .' I explained slowly.

'Yes, yes, *motocicleta.* You have a cargo flight to Ecuador? . . . Yes . . . yes . . . Quito, Ecuador . . . Yes, Quito . . . No, no . . . a motorcyle, *motocicleta* . . . Oh blimey, there go the pips . . . hang on . . .'

Shove more money in . . . no, not that stuff, that's Costa Rican, and what's this? Oh yikes, it's Canadian, why have I still got that? Oh, here we go . . . some cents . . .

'Hello, hello? *Hola?*'

Beeeeeeeeeep.

Bugger. Too late.

Start again.

'*Hola,* I was just talking to someone about . . . Yes, yes . . . a cargo plane. No, a motorcycle. No, no, from Panama to Ecuador . . . Yes, Quito. A moto, yes, yes, that's me . . . you have a cargo flight? . . . Yes? You fly twice a week? . . . Oh great, three times a week. What days? . . . Er, hang on . . . *Lunes* . . . *Miércoles* . . . *Viernes* . . .'

Translating on the hoof.

'Right. Monday, Wednesday and Friday . . . No? Oh, not Friday? *Jueves?* Thursday. Monday, Wednesday and Thursday . . . No? *Lunes,* Monday? *Miércoles* . . . ? Pardon. Oh, not Wednesday. Thursday? *Jueves?* Thursday? But not *Viernes?* Oh . . . sorry . . . pardon . . . *Viernes,* yes? OK, Friday . . .'

Pip pip pip . . .

Sod it.

'*Uno momento, por favor . . .*

More coins down the hole.

'Hello, hello . . . yes, where were we? So, it's Monday, Thursday and Friday, yes? . . . No? Erm . . . pardon . . . sorry, can you say that again, please? OK. You fly to Quito on Mondays and Thursdays? So that's *twice* a week then?'

The sound of the receiver being banged against my forehead.

'Hello . . . yes, yes, I'm still here. OK. So it's Mondays and Thursdays? *Lunes* and *Jueves?* Yes? . . . OK. Monday and Thursdays. *Muchas gracias. Adios.*

Click.

Aaaaaaaaarrrrrrrrrrrrrrrgh!!!!!

I pushed on down to Panama City, eager to get this monster dollop of admin out of the way, and maybe relax for a few days while my bike was winging its way to South America. After eight thousand miles on the road I was suddenly extremely tired. The last few months of solid riding, the constant brain ache of communicating in a foreign tongue and the remorseless sun that burned ever hotter as I neared the equator were all taking their toll. But my strangest symptom was a weird numbness of the senses; it was like nothing I had felt before, and I could only put it down to being encapsulated in my own little bubble for too long. Whilst this travelling across foreign lands provided me with all manner of sensations—from excitement and jubilance to curiosity and fear—it also removed a lot of life's core elements that until now I had taken for granted. No music, no socialising, no physical human contact and no banter or meaningful discourse in my mother tongue. It all made for a bizarre feeling of being removed from the world around me. My senses were crying out for some sort of stimulation, to the extent that I found myself lingering in a grocery shop for the sole purpose of listening to the entirety of 'Hotel California' on their tinny radio—and I don't even like that song.

And it wasn't just me—the bike was behaving oddly as well. One too many tankfuls of cheap 'n' nasty fuel had caused the dreaded *ring-a-ding-a-ding* sound of engine pinging, a condition caused by low-octane gas that could potentially burn a hole in the piston, and much of my Panamanian miles were spent ducking in and out of auto parts stores on a fruitless search for octane booster, while my nights were haunted with lurid, Technicolor dreams of hot, molten pistons. It was time for a rest.

A couple of days away from Panama City I found myself caught up in the typical thought process that can get you on a long straight road if you're not careful: '. . . that noise is getting worse, I hope the engine doesn't blow up, when am I going to get my hands on some decent gas? I've still got another twelve thousand miles ahead of me. . . .'

But some law of nature, or travel, or motorcycling dictates that it's at these moments that something or someone comes along to give you a little nudge, a reminder of exactly why riding a motorcycle halfway round the world is the best thing ever. On this occasion my timely reminder came in the incarnation of Edgardo, a Panamanian motorcyclist on his way home from work. I heard the purr of his BMW first, pulling up beside my bike at the side of the road.

'*Hola!*' he called out.

Unfortunately, I wasn't in a position to return his greeting, being hidden away behind a bush, answering the call of nature in that ungainly fashion that us ladies have to endure.

'*Hola!*' he called again.

Oh cripes! Where can a girl find a bit of peace round here? I quickly yanked up my clothes and sheepishly emerged. But Edgardo acted as if it were the most normal thing in the world to find an English girl on a motorcycle relieving herself by the side of the road on his way home.

Once we'd got the Alien Lands on Planet Earth preliminaries out of the way—Who are you? Where are you from?—Edgardo, in that chivalrous Latin fashion, took control of the situation. He would take me to the nearest town, show me around and find me somewhere to stay for the night. I'd been on the receiving end of this sort of gallantry before and I knew better than to protest; after all, I didn't have any big plans, and I'd long since learned to trust my judgement on these matters and he seemed like a particularly decent chap, so I followed along behind him for a couple of hours until we pulled up outside a house in the small town of Santiago. It was a reasonably tidy residence with a few motorcycles parked in the yard and a halfhearted sign advertising rooms for rent.

'This is where you will stay tonight,' Edgardo informed me, 'it is the house of a man named Pastor. All the motorcyclists in Panama stay here.'

Sounded good enough to me.

Prompted by the rumble of our engines, the front door opened and an elderly man stepped outside, greeting Edgardo warmly.

'Pastor, this is Lois from England,' introduced Edgardo.

'*Con mucho gusto!*' I declared, pleased to be able to use my favourite Spanish phrase, it seemed so much more enthusiastic than our own rather tame 'pleased to meet you.'

'Captain Miguel A. Pastor Ponce,' he announced formally, extending a wrinkled hand and a business card, advertising his services as a commercial pilot and a small-time hotelier.

'I am the oldest motorcyclist in Panama,' he declared with authority, 'everybody knows me. The police, the army, everyone. Anything to do with motorcycles, they come here first.'

This was delivered with no arrogance, it was plain fact, and I believed it.

'I have been divorced for twelve years,' he continued. 'Now my house is a hotel for motorcyclists.'

'Great!' I enthused. I liked this place already.

'I am eighty-two and I still ride my motorcycle every day.' He pointed at a massive Yamaha custom cruiser that would make even the most die-hard outlaw biker wince with embarrassment, complete with airbrushed naked women on the tank and leather tassels swinging from the handlebars.

'Very, er . . . nice,' I said.

'Now let me show you to your room.'

Edgardo bid us farewell and I thanked him heartily for his kindness. Pastor's guest room was living proof that men have no interest in soft furnishings. Each one of the three curtains, and I use that term loosely, for they were just bits of cloth nailed to the wall, were of eye-jarringly clashing fabrics. The bedclothes were a pile of unmatching blankets, sheets and counterpanes, and the entire room had the feel of a village jumble sale in its Everything Must Go! All Items Five Pence! stage. The vintage 1960s TV took ages to warm up and then showed two channels of migraine-inducing flickering, the loo didn't flush, the clock didn't work and part of the ceiling was falling down. But as I noted in my diary that night, *It's not much, but it's home for the night. And I kind of like it.*

However, what the oldest motorcyclist in Panama hadn't told me, and what I discovered at the crack of dawn, was that he had devoted his twilight years to domestic ornithology, and that my room was located right next to the aviary. Thus, I was up with the larks, the parakeets and the motmots for an alarmingly early start to my last day on the road in North America.

The streets of Panama City were a wild circus. The local buses, decked out like fairground rides with flashing neon lights and elaborate paint jobs, raced each other along the Avenida Centrale, the drivers exchanging raucous banter with each other as they ran red lights and took corners at breakneck speed, informing pedestrians of their presence with a deafening blast of *"La Cucuracha"* on their horns. The sight of their glittering decoration always raised my spirits and the sound of the horns became embedded in my head as the city's theme tune, but the noisy streets weren't the easiest place from which to finalise my airfreight arrangements with Jose at Panavia and I decided that this was an activity best left until the following morning. Instead I went out for dinner, enjoying a celebratory bottle of wine and a bowl of whelklike seafood that appeared as if from nowhere with the compliments of the chef. The next day, after much searching for Panama City's quietest pay phone, I checked in with Jose, relaxed in the knowledge that I had a couple of clear days before the next flight to Quito.

'No! No!' Jose cried, exasperated. 'The flight leaves in one hour. You must be here soon!'

'But, but . . . it's Tuesday,' I spluttered, 'aren't the flights on Mondays and Thursdays?'

'*No!* Only one flight a week to Quito, on Tuesday!'

What?! I relived our previous conversation in my head, still feeling the slight tenderness on my forehead where I had bashed the receiver in my frustration. Maybe I'd killed a few brain cells in the process.

'You must come now!' implored Jose.

There was no use in arguing. I flung the phone down with a promise that I would be there as quickly as the Mighty Serow could carry me. Rushing back into my hotel, I legged it up the three flights of stairs to my room and begun gathering my strewn belongings. What would I need over the next few days until I was reunited with my bike? Think quickly . . . toothbrush, Spanish dictionary, a book to read. Anything else? Leaving my few essential belongings in the room, I stuffed the rest of my kit into my panniers and jumped on the bike, bungees and straps flailing as I flew across Panama City, dodging the maniac buses and singing *"La Cucuracha"* at the top of my voice, buzzing on the adrenaline of being on a mission. I was quite enjoying the despatch rider feeling; it had been a while since I'd had to be anywhere at a certain time. I picked up signs to the airport, silently thanking Panama for being an organised sort of place, but when I arrived, it was a different story. The cargo terminal was nowhere near the main airport and nobody seemed to have any idea of its whereabouts.

'Cargo? Cargo? *Terminale cargoa?*' I shouted to cabbies and truckers, to be met with either a shake of the head or a vague pointing of the finger from the ones that couldn't bear to admit they didn't know. I looked at my watch. Twenty minutes to go. If I could only find the darned place I'd just make the flight. I whizzed around the airport complex, seeking signs for cargo or freight but there was nothing. Eventually I found myself in a run-down district of slummy warehouses and dirty streets where a gang of boys threw stones at me as I rode past. It reminded me of the industrial areas around Heathrow, so I guessed I must be close. In the end I broke the rule and asked a policeman, who sent me off with a slightly unnecessary pat on the backside, but at least it was in the right direction. I whizzed through the gates, ignoring the sentries who jumped out of their booths to flag me down. There was no time for idle chitchat or security checks. The plane was leaving in ten minutes. But the terminal itself was another labyrinth, a maze of cargo companies with no signs or a map to aid the uninformed. In a state of complete confusion I lapped and looped the terminal, slaloming around forklifts and piles of pallets, seeking out clues. I checked my watch. Four minutes to go. Then I spied a small dark man jumping up and down and waving his hands in the air.

'Excuse me, I'm looking for Panavia?' I cried, trying to keep the panic out of my voice.

'I *am* Panavia!' he burst out with an unintentional lack of modesty. 'I am Jose! Quickly, quickly, you must come now, the plane is leaving. They are waiting just for you!' and without warning he leapt on the back of the bike, sitting up on the top box, urging me on like a rodeo rider into the dark, cavernous hangar.

'Drain the tank,' he ordered, handing me a plastic can. I whipped off the fuel line with fumbling fingers, sending gas spraying all over the pair of us.

'No matter, no matter,' he insisted, as if this was a regular occurrence.

'OK!' he called out to a couple of swarthy men lurking in the shadows. Within seconds my bike was strapped down and cling-wrapped onto a pallet, zooming across the runway aboard a forklift. I could see the plane waiting at the far end, its engines roaring impatiently.

'Aaaaaah . . .' Jose sighed, turning to me with a broad smile, suddenly composed. *'Esta bien.* Now, you come with me and we do the paperwork.'

Ah yes, the paperwork.

The paperwork?

'Paperwork!' I yelped.

The forklift was in midair, the bike was almost in the plane.

'STOP! STOP!' I shouted, tearing down the runway.

The men turned to look at me, pegging it towards them, waving my arms and yelling as they loaded the bike into the hold.

'My papers . . . passport . . .' I gasped, 'they are on the bike.'

I was sure I was in big trouble, but the men burst out laughing.

'Tranquilo, chica, tranquilo,' they chuckled, lowering my motorcycle back to the ground.

I shuffled back across the runway towards Jose, feeling rather foolish, but he was very nice about it and made me a strong cup of coffee in his office as I stared out the window, watching the plane lift my bike into the clouds. Once coffee was out of the way, Jose handed me the bill and I handed him my Visa card. But he shook his head.

'No Visa. Cash only.'

What?! Had I stumbled across the only international airfreight company in the world that didn't take credit cards? But I suppose I should have checked first, I should have known by now not to take anything for granted. What an idiot I must appear. I cringed silently. First, I get all the days mixed up, then I almost delay the flight, then I leave my documents on the bike and now I can't even pay for all the trouble I've caused.

'I'll have to go to a bank and get some cash,' I said in apologetic tones.

'I will drive you,' offered Jose.

Thank God for the worldwide phenomenon of ATMs, thank God for Visa cards, I thought, temporarily enjoying a bit of globalisation as I tapped in my number. But of course, for the first time in my entire trip, the cashpoint wouldn't give me any money. Even in deepest Nicaragua and darkest Honduras, I'd managed to coax some *dinero* out of the machines, and here we were in organised Panama with its skyscrapers and supermarkets, but still, my flexible friend failed to work its magic.

'We will try another bank,' said Jose with saintly patience.

'And another one,' he said again, when that one failed to deliver.

'And another one.'

And another.

'I have *got* the money,' I promised Jose as we continued our tour of Panamanian financial institutions. I was sure he thought I was an evil con artist, flitting around the world, swindling airfreight companies out of millions. He was taking the whole debacle very calmly, but time was pressing on and at Bank Number Five, Jose stepped in and persuaded the glamorous but grumpy manager to get on the case. After what seemed like hours of faxing, phoning and photocopying, and of course masses of forms to sign, none of which I bothered reading, my embarrassment being so acute by now I would have agreed to anything to get my hands on the cash, our persistence was finally rewarded with a thick, juicy wad of dollar bills.

Minutes later I found myself sitting in a car on the outskirts of Panama City, counting out hundreds of dollars in cash to a dark, swarthy stranger that I had met only hours earlier. I imagined my mother choosing this moment to check my progress via some secret high-tech, SatNav video camera gadget. I'm sure she'd be rather perturbed at the sight of her daughter apparently cutting some dodgy deal with a mysterious man in a deserted car park in Central America. I looked up to the sky with a grin—Don't worry, Mum, it's not what it seems!

A rickety raucous bus dropped me back in the city centre and I ambled in the direction of my hotel, passing the financial district with its glittering New York skyline. I followed the sweep of the palm tree–lined bay and stopped in at a little café for a coffee, enjoying my new, gentle pedestrian pace. The sense of relief in having achieved the potentially troublesome task of freighting the bike was immense. A weight had been lifted from my shoulders; at last I could relax, knowing it was safely on its way to South America. All I had to do was get myself on a flight to Quito in a few days' time and meet my motorcycle at the airport, although liberating it from Ecuadorian customs would doubtless have its fair share of aggro, but I would worry about that later. It was at this moment I realised that in the fluster of sending the bike I had completely forgotten to ask Jose for the details of Panavia's office in Ecuador. I could see a pay phone across the road from the café. 'The admin never ends!' I groaned, but I'd better call him now and get it done, then maybe, just maybe I could finally have my day of relaxation.

I grabbed my coffee and nipped across the road, dodging the six lanes of rush hour traffic without spilling a drop. In the booth, I balanced the paper cup on the top of the phone, dug out the Panavia business card and, ramming my finger in my left ear to drown out the blare of horns and car radios, I dialled the number. A woman answered with the usual incomprehensible greeting.

'*Hola! Jose, por favor?*' I requested.

'*Uno momento.*'

I could hear the sounds of office activity in the background. I chucked in a few more coins and took a hearty gulp of coffee as Jose came to the phone.

'*Hola,*' he greeted me.

'*Hola, Jose,*' I said. 'Lois here, I was just calling because I need the—'

SLAM! It was like a punch in the stomach. I bent over double, contorted, collapsing against the side of the booth.

'Hello, hello . . . Lois?' said Jose

'Urrrrgghh . . .' I managed in reply.

Uh-oh, here it comes again. SLAM! Another red-hot poker in my guts, twisting and stabbing at my innards. The phone slipped from my hand as I sank to my knees, clutching my stomach, shaking and shivering.

Jose's voice crackled from the dangling receiver.

'Lois . . . hello. Hello, Lois?'

The sweat streamed down my face.

'Jose . . . Jose . . . I'll call you back,' I gasped into the phone. But it was too late. There had been no warning, and now I could feel the dreaded telltale signs.

I lay there, curled up on the floor of the phone box, listening to the dialling tone and cursing the chemical reaction of complimentary whelks and strong black coffee. Free seafood in Panama City, for crissakes! If that isn't the epitome of fishy, then I don't know what it is. What the hell had I been thinking? I slowly picked myself up, replaced the receiver and waddled the most unpleasant sixty yards of my life back to the café and straight into their loo for a full inspection.

The sight that greeted me was not for the fainthearted and shall be left, dear reader, to your imagination (assuming you're still with me). But try if you will to imagine the deepening of my despair as I noted a glaring absence in the toilet paper department. I scoured the room for a suitable substitute, but there was nothing, not even a scrap of newspaper or old rag. It was time to use my initiative and I could see only one solution. With the deftness of a bomb disposal expert, I gingerly removed my knickers and, employing the least soiled corner, embarked on Operation Mop-Up as best I could, but it soon became clear that the extent of my task was such that further back up was urgently required. With a heavy heart I kicked off my boots and enrolled my socks in the action. Mission finally accomplished, I chucked my besmirched undergarments in the bin and went to wash my hands in the little cracked basin, lamenting but not surprised by the lack of soap. However, the complete non-appearance of water from the open tap was the living end. I ran out of the café, into the street, my bare feet slapping around in my boots as I legged it back to my hotel as fast as my state of inordinate discomfort would allow, up the three flights of stairs, into my room and straight into the shower. I soaped and scrubbed with the unhealthy violence of a Catholic priest after an extracurricular session with a choirboy. At last, feeling suitably cleansed, I emerged a new, purer woman, but it wasn't until I went to get dressed that I realised every pair of socks and knickers I owned were packed away in my luggage, flying high above the Darién Gap on their way to South America. I cursed my bad planning, and imagined my next call to Jose—'Turn the plane round, I lost control of my bodily functions in a phone box and you've got all my spare underwear!' Somehow, I suspected he wouldn't be in the least bit surprised. But then a glimmer of a silver lining revealed itself to me.

'*Excelente!*' I said to myself. 'An excuse to go shopping.' And with a distinctly funny walk I set off for the swanky part of town, Visa card at the ready.

Eleven

I was gazing at a floor-to-ceiling map of the Americas in the air-conditioned bliss of a travel agency as I waited to book my flight to Ecuador. The familiar landmass felt like my second home, its shape forever burnt into my brain. I craned my neck, squinting north to Alaska, remembering the freezing blizzards and black bears; they seemed to belong to another lifetime. Back at eye level was the altogether sultrier Panama City and my imminent destination, Quito, the capital of Ecuador. But there was a glaring gap between these two cities in the form of a huge slab of South American soil, the most dangerous country in the world by all accounts. Colombia.

Locals and travellers alike had warned me off visiting Colombia for all the usual reasons, and even in the last week a group of backpackers had been kidnapped there, making headline news around the globe. But as I stood in the office with the whole of the continent laid before me, I bitterly regretted my lily-livered decision to avoid the kidnap capital of the world. My bike was already Ecuador bound, but there was no reason why I couldn't take in a whirlwind tour of Colombia on my way. After all, when would I be in this neck of the woods again?

'Next,' called the woman behind the desk.

She was dressed like an air stewardess, despite being shackled to a landlocked job, but they do love their uniforms in this part of the world. I took a seat in front of her. This was it, decision time.

'I'd like a one-way ticket to, er . . . Quito, please.'

'When are you flying?'

'Tomorrow . . .'

She tapped away on her keyboard.

'Um . . . would it be possible to make a couple of stopovers in Cartagena and Bogotá?'

'No problem, *senorita*.'

Done. I was on my way to Colombia.

Dusk was falling as I walked back through the steaming streets; the rainy season's regular afternoon downpour had ended as abruptly as it had started, and Panama City sizzled like a sauna in its aftermath. I was excited about my spontaneous change of itinerary. How bad could it be? I reasoned to myself. After all, if I'd listened to every warning, I'd never have left home. Remember, the doom merchants are everywhere and they must be ignored. And looking on the bright side; a kidnapping would save on hotel bills, and as for the torture and mock executions I'd heard about . . . well, there are people in London who pay good money for such services.

I was feeling quite chipper due to my impending adventure. Realising that this was my last day in Panama City, I took an explorative route back across town, wandering first through the busy shopping streets and then into a quiet residential district. It was here, tucked between two unassuming houses, that I spied a ramshackle little shop, its grubby windows promising a treasure trove of scratched records, yellowing books and other intriguing goodies, including an ancient piano accordion inlaid with shimmering mother-of-pearl. A handwritten sign proclaimed the place to be *abierto,* and never having been one to pass by a junk shop, I gave the door a creaky shove and slipped into a strange and wonderful world. Once my eyes had adjusted to the dim light, the first thing that caught my attention was the pile of faded orange paper packets featuring a topless Linda Lovelace lookalike simpering out from under an ill-advised seventies perm. *Delta Bust,* it said at the top, with the enticing subtitle *Bare Breasts . . . Supported!* I sneaked a look inside the packet to find four strips of flesh-coloured, sticky-backed plastic. A series of photos that verged on soft porn provided the necessary instructions on the back. With a price tag of fifty cents, how could I resist? But it was the bookshelves that really got me intrigued. Amongst the Spanish novels and the section for Panamanian authors were three shelves of books in English, devoted entirely to 1970s self-help paperbacks, the titles of which had me salivating with curiosity: *Doing It—How to Organise the Perfect Orgy; The Wife Swapping Scene—Exposed!; How to Find and Fascinate a Mistress; Sex in Prison; Can Drugs Improve Your Sex Life?; How to Find a Teenage Boy (and What to Do With Him Once You've Got Him).* I couldn't believe what I had stumbled upon. And what on earth were they doing here, in a dusty, back-street thrift store in Panama City? The only explanation I could think of was that these literary gems were the legacy of the bored wives of long-since-departed American troops. While their men were busy keeping Noriega and his cronies in check, these women were living out their own tropical *Abigail's Party*—up to their coked-up eyeballs in beige nylon and fondue sets, sharing orgy tips with fellow army wives and sleeping with each other's husbands to pass the long hot days in this faraway, foreign post.

Well, I thought, justifying my pile of purchases, I've been wanting to buy some sort of souvenir and I've never been big on ethnic weavings and whatnot, I'll post them home right away so I don't have to lug them around on the bike. But it was too late to get to the post office that evening and the following morning I was up bright and early for the first plane to Colombia.

Hence I found myself buckled up on the Cartagena flight laden with a bounty of fascinating reading matter, but it was a little hard to concentrate on the finer points of LSD-fuelled fornication when the woman next to me launched into a wailing prayer and repeatedly crossed herself as the plane prepared for takeoff. Not very encouraging for the atheists on board, but fortunately the Divine Powers were smiling on us, and believers and nonbelievers alike were safely deposited in Colombia an hour later. From the plane window I could see the aged fortifications of the old city and the locals kicking a football around on the beach under clusters of palm trees that swayed in the breeze. Just hours earlier I had woken up in grey, rainy Panama City; now here I was in sunny, exotic South America. The lure of a new country, and even more exciting, a new continent to explore, had me chomping at the bit, but the customs officials had other ideas. I was whisked away to a cell-like room, along with a couple of other shifty gringos, where my luggage was searched in meticulous detail and sniffed over by a team of panting hounds. I imagine the officers' suspicions were further aroused by the fact that I was carrying little more than a toothbrush, a selection of seedy paperbacks, a carrier bag full of brand-new frilly knickers and my highly prized packet of *Delta Bust*.

'Are you married?' said the officer as he emptied out my bag, barely hiding his scepticism. And I couldn't blame him; the contents of my luggage hardly suggested a well-balanced, eligible young woman.

'No,' I replied, momentarily forgetting my phoney wedding ring, and then hurriedly stuffing my left hand in my pocket.

He gave me a funny look.

'Are you carrying any drugs?'

Here we go again.

'No drugs.'

A blond California surfer type being frisked next to me shot a conspiratorial glance and a sideways smile in my direction.

'No husband, no drugs . . . no life,' he said under his breath with a cheeky wink.

As far as Cartagena goes, he wasn't far off the mark. If there was one place I could have done with a burly male escort it was here. And failing that, a line or two of Colombia's favourite export would have steeled me for what the guidebooks euphemistically refer to as 'unwanted male attention' in their "Advice for Women Travellers" section. As I strolled through Cartagena I was instantly enchanted by the crumbling grandeur of the ancient walled city with its colonial buildings, its twisty streets buzzing with noisy traders and the multicoloured explosions of flowers spilling from every balcony. I was eager to capture all this on my trusty Nikon but my efforts were constantly hampered by the onslaught of hombres that stalked my every step, touching me, grabbing me, lunging at me and, to my utmost horror, even planting an unsolicited slobbery kiss on my chops. It's all part of the Latin American experience, I kept telling myself through gritted teeth. I'd had several months' practice at brushing off amorous overtures from attentive Latino 'gentlemen,' but here it reached such an intensity that I found myself praying for a FARC rebel to jump out of a palm tree and kidnap me at gunpoint, just as long as he promised not to pinch my arse.

In the end I simply couldn't take any more mauling, and with a mixture of seething resentment and deep despondency, I gave in to the lecherous locals and retreated to a hotel with air-conditioning and cable TV, where I stockpiled a load of comfort food and locked myself in, scoffing my way through reruns of *Seinfeld*. Some adventure this is turning out to be, I sighed, cowering in my room like a hunted animal. And to make matters worse, I was stuck here for another two nights until my flight to Bogotá. I pined for the freedom and independence of my motorcycle and the wary respect generated by arriving in town leathered up and grubby faced after a long day's ride. Like it or not, a little bit of intimidation could be a very useful thing for a *chica solita* in the Land of Latin Lovers. But one thing was for sure—being a pedestrian was not my bag.

Seinfeld was followed by an American sitcom so unbearable that I was forced to watch the local version of MTV, and I soon discovered why Latin pop music had failed to expand beyond its home market. Young men who should know better were formation-dancing in the street, their hair permed and oiled, wearing white eighties suits with the sleeves rolled up and crooning along to a Stock, Aitken and Waterman meets (and maims) Perez Prado backing track.

'*Es número uno! Es magnífico!* . . . blah di blah blah!' enthused the presenter, dressed exactly like the offending number one artist. A young sprightly girl with enormous breasts bounced onto the screen, exchanging banter with her co-presenter, so trite that even I understood it. '*Y ahora* . . .' she squealed with great excitement, '*un exposé de Naomi Campbell! Ayeeeee!*'

Oh, *Dios mio!* Spare me the Naomi Campbell exposé, *por favor.* I thumbed the remote into life but the sitcom was still numbing brains on HBO and every other channel seemed to be discussing football. Failed by TV, I paced the room, examining the cupboards for interesting items left behind by the previous occupants. Nothing in the wardrobe. How about the bedside cabinet? Nope. What about the bathroom? Aha, what's this? *Seda Dental.* Dental floss! At last, a thrill-laden activity to indulge in. I set to work with the enthusiasm of someone who has been granted early release from a life sentence of solitary spinach eating. This is incredible! What a sensation! I thought, totally absorbed in the satisfying ritual. I forgot all about the horrible Cartagenan men and the terrible number one single and the Naomi Campbell exposé. In fact, I forgot about everything. I was living in the moment. 'Nobody can take this away from me!' I cried as I whipped off another length of *seda dental* with a cavalier flourish. The instructions said I only needed thirty centimetres, but I'd pulled off at least two and a half feet in my wild urgency. Damn the extravagance! You only live once! After all, when would I find myself incarcerated in a Colombian hotel with a gratis supply of dental floss again? Sometimes, you have to take what life throws at you, run with it—ask questions later; that's always been my motto.

Completely hooked, I found myself turning to the heady kicks of *seda dental* again and again over the next two days, desperate to re-create that first high. But it never came, and each time I succumbed to its lure, I would emerge from the bathroom, frustrated and dissatisfied, until one day I woke up and I knew it was over. I threw the confounded stuff in the bin and packed my bags. I'd hit rock bottom. It was time to move on.

Bogotá was another whistlestop, a flat-out crazy city where the populace was more concerned with staying alive than bothering the likes of me, and I could have happily hung around for a while longer. But a week without wheels anywhere in the world was enough, and I left Colombia's capital city for Quito and a welcome reunion with my trusty steed. As it turned out, it was a timely departure, as the following day a car bomb exploded in the centre of Bogotá, killing six people.

The gentle calm of Ecuador came as a welcome relief, as did Quito's cool climate, thanks to its lofty altitude of ten thousand feet above sea level. I was so keen to get back on two wheels that I didn't even mind the two-day bureaucratic headache of retrieving my motorcycle from the customs warehouse at Quito airport. After a morning of faffing around followed by an unfeasibly long lunch break, the little bespectacled, besuited agent man delivered the bad news.

'I am very sorry, senorita, but you will not get your moto today, the office closes at four o'clock.'

'But it's only two-thirty,' I pointed out.

He smiled at me as if I were a simple but harmless fool.

'But this is Ecuador,' he explained with a pitying shake of the head.

I'd heard tell of Ecuador's famously laid-back attitude to just about everything and my arrival coincided with the launch of the nation's *Campaña Contra la Impuntualidad*—Campaign Against Unpunctuality. Heaven knows how they work these things out, but according to official sources, Ecuador's legendary tardiness was costing the country $724 million a year. Even the president, who routinely turned up for meetings three hours late, had promised to mend his ways, but I didn't see any signs of the manana attitude getting a kick up the backside when I was there, and it was this relaxed approach that made it such a pleasant place to be, especially after the macho aggro of Colombia.

I'd been looking forward to the Ecuadorian leg for some time, as the international motorcycling community had once again worked its magic and I'd been tipped off with the contact details of an Ecuadorian biker boasting the porn star name of Ricardo Rocco. We'd been in communication by e-mail and he'd invited me to join in some sort of ride or rally that was happening while I was in the country. I was under instructions to turn up at a motorcycle shop in the centre of Quito the following Friday morning from where, as I understood it, a group of us would depart for a weekend of hearty partying at an unspecified location. To be honest, I wasn't really sure what the occasion was, or whom I was meeting, although I'd got the impression that I was joining some sort of annual off-road ride with a group of other dirt bikers. I was mightily excited by this prospect, partly for the opportunity to ride some long-distance trails in this beautiful country but I was also looking forward to hanging out with some like-minded souls. Motorcycling across Central America had been an unforgettable experience, but a testing and solitary one at times, and I was more than ready for a dose of social interaction.

At 7 A.M. on a chilly, drizzly morning I arrived at the shop and my heart sank as I watched a glistening formation of gleaming sports bikes appear, roaring up the street powered by huge, throbbing, multicylindered engines. The first thing I noted was that I most definitely wouldn't be riding any dirt with these street-biking folk, and second, how the hell was I going to keep up? Of the thirteen machines, the smallest number of cubic centimetres in sight was 750—over three times the power of my little Serow, and it occurred to me, not for the first time, that I might have got this power-to-weight malarkey the wrong way round. These guys were clearly from the upper echelons of Ecuadorian society, if in such a small developing country they could afford these flashy motorcycles, and with my now rather tatty luggage and mud-spattered waterproofs, I felt quite the poor relation to these immaculately dressed, shiny-biked folk. But they couldn't have been more accommodating and adopted me into their gang without question, treating me like a visiting dignitary.

'So, where are we going?' I eventually asked someone.

'To Cuenca,' came the reply. I looked at my map and gulped. Cuenca was three hundred miles away in the south of the country, via a route that scaled the Andes at passes of thirteen thousand feet. My bike was already struggling at Quito's altitude and any further elevation wasn't going to help matters. A comfortable day's ride for me was around two hundred miles with a leisurely break for lunch, but that was at sea level. The thin mountain air played havoc with my bike's carburation, slowing down the already gentle pace of the loaded little Serow. This journey was going to be a hard slog for my poor old bike, and had I been traversing Ecuador alone, I would have split it over two days.

'I will meet you there,' I insisted, not wanting to spoil the others' fun. But they wouldn't hear of it, and much to my embarrassment duly organized a rota in which they took turns to ride with me as I straggled along at the back, spluttering over the high mountain passes, the mighty Andes giving my carburetor hell. Eventually, once the 25-miles-per-hour hill climbs became too much to bear for my throttle-hungry hosts, a kindly man riding a black 750 Yamaha cruiser and dressed like a Hell's Angel gallantly offered himself as my escort, claiming, rather charitably, that he enjoyed riding slowly. He spoke perfect English too, which was a bonus, not that we got to chat much; there was no time for breaks—just one fuel stop and an unplanned halt due to an impressive landslide that had blocked the road with hundreds of giant boulders, forcing us to find a detour and further delaying our arrival. Ten hours after leaving Quito my patient companion and I finally rolled into Cuenca

On the road with the Rolling Stones in Ecuador

to find the town teeming with motorcycles, most of them emitting an ear-splitting V-twin rumble that I hadn't heard since I left the States. I stared at the scene in disbelief.

'What's the occasion?' I asked my chaperone.

'It is the Ecuadorian celebrations of one hundred years of Harley-Davidson.'

Admittedly, this was not a date I had marked in my diary, and as far as I was concerned it required about as much celebration as would one hundred years of McDonald's. But sod it, in for a peso, in for a pound, and I threw myself into the proceedings with a vengeance.

Amongst the rumble and roar of the assembled Hogs and their longhaired, leather-clad riders, I spotted a kindred spirit, a KLR650, laden with luggage and a spare tire, the telltale signs of a seasoned motorcycle traveller. Astride this expedition machine was a giant of a man who, upon spotting my equally out of place bike, greeted me with a rib-crushing bear hug and whisked me away for a much needed hot meal.

Enter Ricardo Rocco: rally racer, two-wheeled adventurer and Ecuadorian ambassador for motorcycling. Ricardo was something of a larger-than-life local hero renowned for his inventive good causes, the latest of which involved teaching nurses to ride motorcycles, enabling them to deliver medicines to remote regions of Ecuador. But his most ambitious project, Around the World for Peace, in which he rode all over the globe visiting schools to promote the benefits of pacifism and the perils of drug abuse, had recently seen him kidnapped by Colombian rebels just miles from the Ecuadorian border on his final run home.

'No way!' I exclaimed, stunned by this revelation. 'What happened?'

'I was on the Pan-American Highway, riding behind a truck, and it just stopped in front of me, in the middle of a town; a load of guys jumped out the back with guns and told me to get in. They took me off to the jungle and went through all my stuff, but when they found my leaflets about Around the World for Peace, they changed their tune. The leader said he was very impressed, he approved of what I was trying to achieve and he was going to let me go.'

I gaped at him. It was about the most nonchalant telling of a kidnapping by Colombian guerrillas as one could imagine.

'So, hang on, the Colombian guerrillas set you free because you were promoting peace and an end to drug abuse?'

'Ha-ha! Yes!' he roared out loud.

Clocking in at six feet four and filling the room with his infectious, bellowing laugh and gregarious nature, Ricardo thoroughly enjoyed living up to his reputation as the motorcycle guy about town and seemed to know everyone. The archetypal chivalrous chauvinist (a species of predatory but essentially harmless males commonly found throughout Latin America), he took me firmly under his wing but made no attempt to hide the fact that he fancied himself as a bit of a ladies' man, although he blamed this on his mixed Italian/Ecuadorian blood, as if such matters were entirely beyond his control. But his auto-flirt mode was more an old habit than anything to be taken seriously, and I knew I was in safe hands.

'OK, OK! *Vamonos!*' someone was shouting and the parking lot erupted into a whirl of action as leathers and helmets were donned and hundreds of engines roared into life.

'Where are we going?' I asked Ricardo, but over the racket I didn't quite get the explanation and at that moment I made the conscious decision that for the rest of the weekend, I would stop asking questions and just go with the flow. Our cavalcade left town and within minutes we were plunged into the pitch-black night, heading across country. This was real darkness, not the glittering gloom of a city, but solid blackness with no street lamps or cat's eye to aid navigation. I couldn't see a thing except hundreds of little red taillights ahead of me, but I quickly worked out that the road was lined with overhanging trees as the branches brushed my face and hands, and as I bounced over bumps I could tell we were on a rough, unsurfaced road. A sharp swing to the right took us out of the forest and onto a rickety wooden bridge over a wide river. Moonlight illuminated the scene now and the fast-flowing water appeared black and treacherous as it swirled past outcrops of jagged rocks. The bridge was slippery from recent rainfall and as I made my crossing, I could see the water churning below me where the planks had rotted away. In single file we gingerly picked our way across this makeshift structure, and I breathed a sigh of relief upon making it to the other side without mishap.

But as far as adventure goes, that was it for the night and our journey ended shortly after at the unlikely location of a luxury country club. I'd been expecting to arrive at some outpost in the mountains for a weekend of goat sacrifices and orgiastic rituals, or at least a wet-T-shirt competition, but admittedly this was based on an image concocted from old copies of *Back Street Heroes* and an unintentional foray into a Lincolnshire bike gang's party at age fifteen. The Ecuadorian motorcyclists were an altogether more civilised bunch and the ensuing scene of five hundred bikers checking in at reception to discover they were all double, triple and quadruple booked was as close to an all-out bacchanalia as it got all night.

'This is typical Ecuador,' explained Ricardo, as we elbowed our way through the throng to the reception desk in a futile attempt to get me a bed for the night.

'But why did they take the bookings if there weren't enough rooms?'

'They will never say no. They say yes to everybody, then they deal with the problem later; all the time this happens. Well, they have no rooms,' he confirmed, 'so you will have to stay with me. I am sharing with three other friends.'

It looked like my fate was sealed. I was spending the weekend at an Ecuadorian country club with four men I'd only just met, all in the name of Harley-Davidson.

Over the commotion at the check-in, I could hear a loud voice speaking English with a foreign accent that appeared to be doing a hard sell to a captive market. The piercing sales pitch belonged to a tall Dutchman with a long blond ponytail dressed in red and white racing leathers who was flogging postcards of himself to anyone who would listen.

'Aaah . . . this is Sjaak!' announced Ricardo. 'He is travelling the world on a 1000cc sports bike, he is one crazy guy! Come on, you must meet him.'

By the time the night was through, Ricardo, Sjaak and I had formed our own rebel splinter group and the following day we forsook the organised Harley riders' pig roast for a day out riding a stretch of the Ecuador National Rally course and generally hanging out and talking nonsense. With our Dutch, English and Ecuadorian number plates, we made an unlikely international trio: Ricardo, a swarthy giant on his big rally bike; Sjaak crouched low over his sports bike, blond hair dangling down the back of his skintight leathers; and me, spluttering along on my little dirt bike. But we were united by the joy of motorcycling, our apparent disparity being no barrier to us as we revelled in the beautiful Andean scenery and plenty of good-natured banter. Back at the country club, breeze shot and fat chewed, it was beers all round and a flick through Ricardo's digital camera to relive the highlights of our day.

'Look, this is a good one of you,' Ricardo was saying to Sjaak as they hunched over the camera, scrolling through the shots.

'Ha-ha, look, I didn't make it in time for the self-timer.' Sjaak laughed.

'Let's have a look through,' I said, picking up the camera from the table and browsing through the photos of us tearing around the mountain roads. But the pictures of our antics came to an end and to my surprise, I found myself staring at the image of a lithe young woman on all fours wearing nothing but a very skimpy G-string in what appeared to be the bland confines of a hotel room. I glanced at Ricardo, but he and Sjaak were deep in conversation about tires or something. I flicked on to the next picture. Two girls in G-strings on all fours. And the next one. Three girls in G-strings on all fours. Crikey, this was intriguing. Ricardo and Sjaak were on to the old chain-and-sprocket-versus-shaft-drive conundrum now. Great, that would keep them absorbed for a while. I flicked on. The girls were pawing at each other on the bed in a self-conscious manner. They all had a similar look—skinny with enormous breasts and attractive in a certain kind of way. I flicked on to the next picture and nearly choked on my beer. On the screen was Ricardo himself, sprawled on the bed, completely starkers with a huge smile on his face. Whether it was the camera angle or nature's blessing, suffice it to say it was extremely unlikely he'd be falling prey to the spam e-mails that tempt less fortunate males. Unfortunately, it was precisely at this moment, with my eyeballs popping out of their sockets, that my companions concluded their transmission debate and all eyes fell on Ricardo's tumescent member.

'Looks like a good night,' I ventured.

'HA-HA!' roared Ricardo with a devilish glimmer in his eye.

'You don't know what you're missing!' said Sjaak.

'I do now,' I replied.

Twelve

But the fun had to come to an end at some point, and on Monday morning, as the last die-hard party animals rumbled off back to reality and the hotel staff began the daunting task of cleaning up, and counting the missing towels (and don't think I wasn't tempted after six months with a manky pack towel), I had to face the harsh truth that all was not well with my motorcycle. The dodgy roads and even dodgier gas of Central America had taken their toll on the Serow, and although the poor thing was still starting, running and stopping when it was supposed to, it was also knocking, banging and vibrating like a DO NOT DISTURB sign on Ricardo Rocco's hotel room door.

The man himself had, of course, put me in touch with a motorcycle mechanic he knew in Cuenca named Augusto, handy with the spanners, according to Ricardo, but not a word of English had ever passed his lips. This didn't bother me when it came to gas pump attendants, waiters and hoteliers; I had all that stuff down pat by now, but discussing technical motorcycle matters was still something of a linguistic challenge. My pocket Spanish dictionary was no help when it came to cam chain, tappets or sprocket, so as I pulled into the back-street workshop, I decided, rather radically, I thought, to free myself from the rigid constraints of the spoken word and employ the art of mime as my means of communication.

Augusto's workshop was a scavenging motorcyclist's dream, and an obsessive-compulsive's nightmare. 'A place for nothing and nothing in its place' seemed to be the motto here, and I was pleased to see that my leaky, dirty, smoky bike blended in effortlessly amongst the jumble of half-formed motorcycles, quads, scooters, wheels, tires, spare parts and tools that spilled out from the big brick building into the yard.

'Lois?' enquired a small middle-aged man, emerging from behind a stripped-down trail bike and offering me an oily hand.

'Augusto?'

'*Hola!*'

'*Con mucho gusto!*'

I'd encountered plenty of greasy palms on this journey but never in such literal form.

'*La chica inglésa!*' announced Augusto to the bevy of boys tinkering away in the background. Whether it was sheer luck or a ploy to lure more girls into his workshop, I don't know, but it seemed Augusto operated a policy of employing only male models, and I felt as though I'd stepped into a living, breathing Athena poster as these hunky bronzed men, wearing grease-stained overalls open to the waist, immediately dropped their tools and converged on the Serow. They gathered round, examining the foreign plate and the stickers I'd acquired from locations along the way, asking questions about Alaska and the USA, which I tried to answer as best I could without too much visible drooling.

But it was time to banish the reader's wives'–type fantasies from my mind and get down to business. Business being fault diagnosis, Marcel Marceau style. Augusto watched patiently as I flitted around the bike, pointing out the trouble spots and describing the problems as best I could using a combination of hand signals, anguished facial expressions and cartoon sound effects straight out of a Marvel comic: "SPLAT!' went the oil leak. 'PING!' went the low-octane-gas problems. 'KERRUNCH!' for the grinding noise at high revs. Every now and then I would look hopefully at Augusto, seeking a response, but he just continued to stare, sometimes nodding, which was reassuring, and occasionally laughing, which wasn't. Nevertheless, I continued apace, entering into the vaudeville spirit of the occasion. *Engine mountings* was reasonably straightforward, *cam chain* and *tappets* proved a little tricky and *vibration* was simple, if verging on the burlesque. Finally, all mimed out, but having covered each and every one of my mechanical gremlins, I concluded my performance with the ultimate question.

'*Entiende?*'

I knew of Augusto's reputation as a wizard mechanic, but had never dared to dream of his secret life as grand master of charades.

'*Sí,*' replied Augusto, nodding slowly, '*entiendo.*'

He called over one of his rippling Adonises and a jabber of indecipherable Spanish followed between them.

'So . . .' said the Greek god to me in faultless English, 'you want us to check the tappets, you think the engine mounting bolts are loose, you might need a new cam chain and you're wondering if the chain and sprockets will last till you get to Lima?'

I gaped at him and then burst out laughing.

'Why didn't you say you could speak English?'

'It is much more fun this way,' he replied with a ravishing smile, while Augusto chuckled quietly.

A couple of days later, the Serow was back in action and the news wasn't so bad. And as an added bonus, it was delivered in my mother tongue by an Antonio Banderas look-alike.

'The engine bolts were very loose, that is what was causing the vibration. We have adjusted the valve clearances too. The cam chain is OK, but you should change the drive chain and sprockets soon.'

'I'm getting a new set sent to Lima, do you think it'll make it?' I asked. Peru's capital city was nearly one thousand miles away and the sprocket teeth were looking pretty worn.

'Yes, you will be OK, I think, but ride gently!'

To have a delectable English-speaking motorcycle mechanic at my disposal was a rare and valuable thing, so I made the most of it and quizzed the poor bloke to death on every technical matter I could think of, the most pressing being the ropey performance of the bike at high altitude.

'You need to change the main jet in the carburetor,' he explained, 'the thin air affects the mixture. At high altitude you have less air, so you need less fuel, yes?'

I nodded.

'And the main jet controls the amount of fuel, so you need to put in a smaller jet,' he concluded.

I nodded again but I groaned inwardly and he laughed at my worried face.

'*Tranquilo!* It is very easy—*muy fácil.*'

Muy fácil eh? It was easy for him to say. The truth was I'd been in denial about this whole business. I knew the skyscraping Andean roads were liable to slow the bike down a bit, but I was hoping I'd get away without having to rejet the carb. But judging by my pitiful spluttering on the ride from Quito to Cuenca, there was no avoiding it—if I was to take on the Andes again I was going to have to sort it out. The thing was, I didn't have a clue how to change a main jet and the whole thing sounded a bit technical and daunting. Stop trying to get out of it, I reprimanded myself. If I wanted to get up the mountains faster than a lame llama it was time to swap the Jackie Collins bonkbuster for my Haynes manual and get busy with the tools. Luckily I had plenty of time before I was up in the clouds again. My route would take me back to sea level in a couple of days' time followed by a good few hundred miles across the coastal desert of northern Peru to Lima, where I was meeting Amalia, who was flying in there from London with her Serow to join me for the ride south. Lima would be a natural pause in the proceedings; somewhere I could work on the bike and sort out this jet-changing business in preparation for the next leg—the ride inland to Machu Picchu and Bolivia, crossing the Andes at the highest altitude of the entire journey.

My healthy bike was a great boost to morale and I was itching to get back on the road. Over the last few weeks, my motorcycling adventure had turned into one long headache of flights, admin, repairs and the weary grind of one big city after another. Panama City, Cartagena, Bogotá, Quito. They'd all come and gone so fast and the chore of always getting my bearings in yet another frenzied metropolis had become tiresome. I was yearning for a long road ahead of me, some wide-open scenery and the chance to put a few miles on the clock after all the stopping and starting.

As I headed south out of Cuenca, climbing the Andes once again, the elation and relief that swept over me at being back on the road was overwhelming. And the sense of affirmation burned brighter than ever: This is what I'm meant to be doing, this is why I'm here! I remembered those evenings back home in London, avidly soaking up tales of other motorcyclists' adventures, hardly daring to think that I could ever do the same. And here I was, little ol' me, in South America, riding across the Andes, with twelve thousand miles of the Americas already under my belt! Sometimes, I could hardly believe it. I was totally unprepared for the Andes themselves, not the unfortunate effect they had on my carburetor, but the sheer size of them; I gazed in awe, eyes out on stalks, mouth hanging open at the monumental scale of my surroundings. How can *anything* be this big? I wondered. I couldn't have imagined such magnificence had I not seen it with my own eyes. The highway was just rough enough to infuse a sense of excitement into the ride but not so bad as to reduce it to a miserable slog. And what's more, I had the road to myself, save a farmer herding his cows and a few Indian women, dressed in their traditional shawls and black panama hats, collecting firewood by the side of the road, who raised a hand as I passed. At this high altitude, a cool, floaty mist hung in the air, giving the scene an ethereal feel, and when the evening sun moved around, flooding the giant moun-

Riding a mountain trail over the Ecuadorian Andes

tains with warm, golden light, it was as close to paradise as anything I had known. Just me, my motorcycle, and all this.

Soon the road was snaking its way down the mountains into a different kind of paradise, a warm, fragrant valley buzzing with hummingbirds, and I stopped for the night in the small town of Vilcabamba, where the inhabitants supposedly live longer than anywhere else in the world. I had a feeling this might be something of a marketing ploy, even the local bottled water featured pictures of happy, grinning old folk on the label, but the town certainly had a dreamy charm that found approval with the international backpacking community that congregated there. I happened upon a gaggle of them in a café the next morning, male and female dressed identically in their asexual uniform of Velcro sandals and zip-off trousers. They were chewing little mouthfuls of muesli and complaining to one another about the food and how much everything cost.

'I'm not paying six dollars for another night in that dump!' whined one bloke with a wispy beard and a bead necklace.

'Yeah, fuck that, man. Asia is like *sooooo* much cheaper than South America. Asia is like really cool, you can get a room for like a dollar,' said his worldly friend.

I shrank at the sight of them. Not only did they all dress the same, they spoke the same too: in a tone and vernacular that exuded a world of university rag week wackiness and a tragically pre-dictable collection of books and CDs. I knew what they would be-come once their dismal gap year was over; they were the successors to SuperBri, coming up through the ranks; the very people I had come here to get away from. I've got to get out of here, I thought, before they start quoting the 'funny' bits from *Withnail and I*. I headed for the door as another troop arrived.

'Uh-oh, they'd better not give me Nescafé,' bleated one of the girls as they took their seats, 'it's just like *so* totally shite when you ask for a coffee and you get Nescafé.'

'Yeah, what's that all about?' her companion groaned. 'Like to-tally random, Nescafé in Ecuador. Duh!'

Disproportionately depressed by this fleeting contact with my fellow countrymen, I made a hasty exit and set off for the Peruvian border on an empty stomach.

A squiggly grey line on the map caught my eye; a thirty-mile shortcut over the mountains that would knock about a hundred miles off the route by road to the frontier town of Macara. The map legend revealed that squiggly grey lines were, rather quaintly, 'carriage ways,' but whatever it said didn't count for much. As I well knew, even thick red lines had been known to dissolve into muddy swamps and sometimes there were roads marked that didn't even exist.

Sod it, I thought, I didn't choose to ride a dirt bike for nothing, and I set off for the edge of town, seeking the start of the track. On the outskirts I passed a few smallholdings and tumble-down shacks where goats and chickens nibbled and pecked amongst each other's feet, and I stopped to ask a man tending his animals about the state of the road ahead; his tanned face was lined and toothless beneath his battered panama hat and I presumed he must be one of the famed long-livers of Vilcabamba.

'*Es malo,*' came his reply—it is bad. 'But on this,' he continued, patting my bike reassuringly, 'no problem.'

His knowing assurance made my heart soar, and I beamed a grateful smile at him. He flashed his gums in return. Ahead of me towered the Andean peaks, mammoth slabs of rock, not to be messed with. I could see the trail snaking off into the distance and I accelerated away, waving farewell to my confidence-boosting sage. The midday heat raged with a new fierceness, and I realised this was as close as I would ever get to the sun, high up in the Andes, just twenty degrees south of the equator. Although my black trousers and shirt were of thin cotton, they soaked up the heat like a sponge and the breeze from riding only served to blast hot air in my face like a hair dryer. The track was flat and stony to start with, nothing too daunting, but as civilization ebbed away and wilderness took hold, it became steeper and more twisty, winding up the mountainside with a sheer drop to my right, then down again into the valleys, splashing through small streams as my arms brushed against the spiky leaves of huge succulent cacti. After a few miles the going got rockier and the sense of remoteness more palpable than ever. My back wheel was sliding around in the loose surface and a couple of sharp uphill bends with jagged rocks sticking out of the ground had me gritting my teeth and reciting my mantra: *Just keep going, keep going!* In my enthusiasm for a spot of off-road action, I had forgotten all about my rear sprocket, and as I bounced over the bigger rocks I could feel the chain jumping on the worn teeth. 'Ride gently,' the mechanic in Cuenca had said when I asked him if I would make it to Lima; somehow I doubted if this was what he'd meant. I forced myself to banish the 'what if?' thoughts from my mind and instead concentrated on the mind-boggling scenery stretching out around me. The rocks and earth were a rich rusty red, a striking contrast to the cloudless azure sky and the dusky green of the steep-sided valleys. I could see for miles across the mountains, and there was nothing here, not a house or another vehicle in sight, not a soul except me! But compared to road riding, the going was slow and I began to wonder if I would make it to the Peruvian border that day, but the last few miles of the track descended from the rugged mountain scenery into more pastoral surroundings and the track turned to hard-baked mud. The grassy lowlands were dotted with cows living an enviable free-range life and the streams I had happily splashed through before were now crossed with makeshift wooden bridges, evidence of the human hand at work. Civilisation was once again in sight and although the excitement of a new country beckoned, I was sad to bid farewell to peaceful, gentle Ecuador.

What a difference! was my first thought as I arrived at the border crossing. I'd been dreading this moment, based on my experiences in Central America, but this sleepy, dusty little settlement, nestling around a bridge over the Macara River that created the natural divide between the two countries, was about as unlike my previous frontier experiences as I could imagine. No hustlers, no fixers, no street traders, no moneychangers, no grubby-faced kids grabbing at my clothes. Just a few vehicles making the crossing and a couple of guards lolling about in the shade, who went into genial hosting overdrive as soon as I pulled up at the exit from Ecuador.

'Please senorita, come this way, please follow me. Where are you from? Aah, *Inglaterra! Inglésa! Muy bien!*' Please sit down, you would like coffee, yes?'

'Er, thank you, yes, please,' I replied, bemused by this onslaught of hospitality; surely there must be a catch? More soldiers were arriving now, shaking my hand reverentially. Through the window I could see yet more uniformed men examining the bike with great interest.

'Please, senorita,' said the soldier bearing my coffee, 'the commander wishes for you to see him in his office.'

OK, whatever you say. I gathered up my paperwork and entered the adjoining room, a spacious affair with views over the river. A line of obedient troops marched in behind me, stationing themselves around the walls, standing to attention, hands behind their backs. On the other side of a big wooden desk was a large man in an impressive uniform, decorated with an array of badges and gold braid. He stood up as I entered the room.

'Good afternoon, please sit down,' he spoke to me in English, clasping my hand in a suitably sturdy grip. 'I hope you have enjoyed your visit to our country. This is a very beautiful part of the world and there is much to see and do in Peru also.'

I smiled and nodded, assuring him, genuinely, that Ecuador had been a highlight of my journey.

'Where are you going?' he asked.

'I'm heading for Lima now,' I said.

'Please, come look at the map, I will show you the way.' He beckoned me behind his desk.

I didn't feel this was the moment to point out that I did in fact own a map, and that I'd been studying the route to Lima for the last week. So I made polite noises and nodded a lot while he pointed out the familiar names of towns along the way. The sound of the door opening stirred us from our cartographical reverie and had the soldiers spinning round, quick off the mark. But it was only a small boy of about nine or ten, carrying a silver tray piled high with slices of watermelon for the troops.

'*Chico!* Our foreign visitor first,' growled the commander in Spanish, and the little boy duly trotted behind the desk, lowering the tray in front of me.

'*Muchas gracias.*' I thanked him and he met my eyes shyly, his face half hidden behind the pile of fruit. *'Muchas gracias,'* I said again, this time to the soldiers and the commander, thanking them collectively for this spontaneous show of hospitality. They nodded politely in response, silently watching me. I lifted the melon to my lips and took a generous bite from the middle, feeling the sweet juice dribble onto my tongue. But as my teeth sank into the succulent flesh, a bite-size chunk broke away and plummeted earthwards, landing with a resounding *SPLAT!* To my horror I felt the sensation of sticky fruit against warm flesh and glancing down, I confirmed my worst fears. The piece of melon had come to rest slap-bang in my cleavage and was lying there for all to see, pink, glistening, and firmly wedged in position.

The silence that followed was excruciating, broken only by the stifled snigger of one of the more callow soldiers. A few melon jokes passed quickly through my mind, but I was unsure how the Benny Hill humour would translate into Spanish, and embarrassment won out in the end. I could feel my face turning as pink as the fruit itself, and desperately refusing to meet the eyes of the tittering troops, I stared with a newfound enthusiasm at the map, aware that I was studying the contours of their country with the same intensity as they were bestowing on my own topography.

'Good-bye, senorita, it has been a pleasure, we have all enjoyed meeting you,' said the commander later on, once my paperwork had been completed, 'it is not often we see an English lady on a motorcycle . . .'

Yeah, who drops bits of fruit down her knockers in front of half the Ecuadorian army, I thought to myself, finishing his unspoken sentence. But I just smiled idiotically, bid him adios and scampered into Peru. Safely across the border, I fished out the offending piece of melon and tossed it away into the desert, wondering if I'd broken any ancient laws regarding the crossing of an international frontier with fresh fruit secreted on my person.

I was on a mission now. Destination, Lima; twelve hundred kilometres through the desert on the Pan-American Highway. The road hugged the Pacific coast all the way and the ocean breeze blasted sand into my eyes, face and hair. But I was glad to be back in the desert, relishing the almost monotonous routine of each day's ride. The road seemed to go on forever, a straight strip of hot black tarmac, shimmering with distant mirages under the glaring sun.

There were just two vistas along this stretch depending on which way I turned my head. To my right—immaculate sculpted sand dunes and the waves of the Pacific Ocean breaking in the distance. To my left—sand. Miles and miles of sand, and the peaks of the Andes occasionally visible, like gnarled grey fingers clawing up out of the haze. The highway was lined with small towns straight out of a spaghetti Western, where shirtless horsemen, their cowboy hats pushed back on their heads, trotted through the dusty, unpaved streets, past the sun-bleached doors of the liquor stores with their grimy bottles of unidentifiable spirits behind barred windows. At the rare stream or river, groups of women and children gathered to wash bundles of clothes, laying them out on the hot rocks, where they dried in minutes. Animals, both alive and dead, appeared routinely along the highway too, mostly black hairy pigs, snuffling for food, but occasionally I would have to swerve round the carcass of a cow or donkey, lying flat on its back, legs straight and stiff as planks.

And every mile or so, just to remind me that I was still in the twenty-first century, huge billboards appeared advertising Inca Kola, the national drink of Peru; a sickly bubblegum-flavoured, carbonated libation, appropriately coloured gold in keeping with the riches of the nation's ancient tribe.

I couldn't linger on these sights for too long, though, as my concentration was required to operate at maximum efficiency just to deal with the sheer insanity of the Peruvian driving tactics. Never had I seen such wild recklessness! The boy-racers of Guatemala City paled in insignificance next to these maniacs, and their harassment wasn't confined to the vehicular variety. As they flew past me

with inches to spare, a torrent of lascivious suggestions, corny compliments and piercing wolf whistles accompanyed each near-death
experience. I soon learnt to keep my head down and carry on moving at all costs; stopping only seemed to encourage them more. Just
pulling over to take a photo was tantamount to stripping naked by
the roadside and offering free oral sex, judging by the hysterical
yelling, swerving and blaring of horns that met each of my attempts
to take a snap of my bike next to a sand dune. And as if this wasn't
enough to contend with, the Serow had sprung a new oil leak from
the base gasket, the rear sprocket's teeth had all but worn away and
the chain was ready to curl up and die.

Irksome as all this was, nothing that occurred on this stretch of
the Panamericana could have prepared me for the outright lunacy
that awaited me in Lima.

My badly timed arrival coincided not only with afternoon rush
hour but also a political demonstration involving thousands of protestors with placards demanding *'UN VASO DE LECHE! UN
VASO DE LECHE!'*—A glass of milk! A glass of milk! 'Just get out
of the bloody way and I'll buy you a whole cow!' I cried as I
plunged into the mayhem. Admittedly, I was in at the deep end, but
it felt as if the city's eight million inhabitants were out on the road
that day—and out to get me. The heat of the city was thick and
poisonous, and the sweat dribbled down my face, stinging my eyes
and soaking my hair and clothes. I had no idea where I was heading, only that I had to find somewhere to sleep, and hide, in this
crazy city.

Lima must be where American scrap yards sent their wrecks to
die. It was as if I had unwittingly entered a South American demo-
lition derby. Built-to-last prewar trucks battled it out with 1970s
muscle cars in this game, where cracked windscreens were a must-
have accessory, bumpers and doors were held on with gaffer tape
and every vehicle belched plumes of filthy black smoke.

But to join in the banger racing, it was necessary to know the
regs. First, I had to understand that an awful lot of white paint had

been wasted creating lane markings on Lima's roads. Second, where traffic lights were concerned, red and green were one and the same. Third, I mustn't use my indicators, it only confused the natives. Finally, and most important, I must sound my horn at all times.

It took me a little while to work out these basic rules and initially my heart was in my mouth as I tentatively weaved my way through the madness. It was only when I reached the centre of the city to discover four square miles of twisty, narrow streets snarled up in furious solid gridlock that I realised if I was going to get anywhere I had to start acting like a local.

With my left hand alternating between two positions, namely thumb on the horn or middle finger in the air, I was suddenly riding as if possessed by El Diablo himself. 'Get out of the way!' I yelled as I rode up onto the pavement, pedestrians flattening themselves against the walls as I tore past. Running a red light. Up along the central reservation. Through the park. Across a manicured garden. I was enjoying every minute and the great thing was, nobody batted an eyelid, it was all considered to be perfectly normal behaviour. At last I spied the welcome sight of a flashing hotel sign, and with a swift U-turn and a blast of my horn to the oncoming traffic, I peeled across the road, pulling into the parking lot unscathed but slightly frazzled and in need of something a little stronger than Inca Kola. With the bike tucked away under a sickly palm tree, locked up and dripping hot black oil into the dusty ground, I staggered to my room and flopped onto the bed in a state of collapse, praying that my internal organs would one day resume normal working practice.

Darkness and hunger reared their ugly heads, but I couldn't bring myself to move and I spent the rest of the night lying there in the sticky heat, listening to a woman in a room across the courtyard enjoying the benefit of a Lima man doing what he does best. I flicked on the telly and found the Playboy channel. The image was scrambled, but I watched it anyway. I already had the sound track.

Once I felt ready to brave the outside world again, which seemed to take several days, I tackled the changing of the main jet, which, as predicted by the Ecuadorian Adonis, was a cinch, and left me wondering why I'd got in such a tizz about it. Later that evening it was time to jump in a cab to the airport to meet Amalia. She arrived off the plane from London looking immaculate in a coordinated outfit, hair accessories and makeup, and I realised what six months on the road had done to my sartorial standards. I hadn't slipped when it came to hair dyeing, and my toenails remained red and shiny, if a little chipped at times, but there was only so much a girl could do with one set of clothes.

I was excited by the prospect of having a riding companion again, and although I only knew Amalia vaguely, through our mutual friends back in London, she represented the familiar face of home—a welcome change after so many months spent amongst strangers. I was looking forward to having some female company too. Since Rachel and I had gone our separate ways in Mexico, girl talk had been a bit thin on the ground. It was no surprise then that Amalia and I spent the first night yakking until sunup, catching up on the minute details of each other's love life—in a strange parallel, she too had met the man of her dreams just before she left—gossiping about mutual friends back in London and plotting our South American adventure.

'I'm planning on flying home from Buenos Aires, probably in January or February,' I told her.

'Well, I've got a return ticket from Lima in March, so when you go home I'll carry on up through Brazil on my own, and then head back to Peru.'

'I wonder where we'll be for Christmas,' I mused, looking at the map.

'What's that, about seven weeks away? Probably down here somewhere,' she said, pointing at southern Chile.

'Excellent! It's all lakes and snowcapped mountains down there, it looks beautiful, like Switzerland.'

'So, we're going to head for Cusco and go to Machu Picchu next, are we?' she asked.

'Yeah, fine, I'm easy on the route, if you want to go somewhere or see something, just say. As long as I make it to Ushuaia in the end, that's what matters! Anyway, when does your bike get here?' I asked.

'In a couple of days' time.'

'Oh good,'cause I'm waiting for some parts to arrive, a chain and sprocket and a few other bits. They're coming by DHL, but they seem to be held up at the airport, problem with customs, I expect. We've got all that to look forward to with your bike too, it'll probably be a load of hassle getting it out of customs.'

'Yeah, well, I'll go prepared with plenty of dollar bills.' She raised her eyebrows knowingly.

'That's the spirit! Oh yeah, the other thing is, if we're going up in the Andes you might have to fit a smaller main jet in the carb.' I relayed my tales of sluggish woe in Ecuador. She looked at me blankly.

'To be honest, I don't even know where the carburetor is, or what it is,' she said with a shrug. 'I never work on my bikes, I just pay someone to do all that stuff.'

'Well, OK, fair enough. I'd never done it before but I had a look at the manual and it was all pretty straightforward. I thought it was going to be aggro but it's just a matter of undoing a few screws.'

'Oh good, you've got a manual.'

'Haven't you?'

'No, I assumed you'd have one.'

'Have you got any spares? Y'know, cables, brake pads and stuff?'

'No, but my bike is practically brand new,' she said gaily. 'And anyway,' she added in a defiant tone, 'I've decided there are two things that aren't going to happen on this trip—my bike isn't going to break down, and I'm not going to get sick.'

And with that optimistic statement, we rolled over to our respective sides of the double bed and sank into a long-overdue sleep while dawn broke over Lima, warming up the city for another day of heat-crazed chaos.

Thirteen

As predicted, releasing Amalia's bike from the airport was the usual bureaucratic farce, featuring all the lovable characters one had come to expect at such an event—the brutish policeman, the slimy customs agent, the stuck-up glamorous office girl and the collection of hangers-on we picked up en route, all willing to run around in return for a few dollars at the end of the day. By the time we left, Amalia was handing out greenbacks like sweets. Back at the hotel, parked next to my bike, her gleaming Serow with its gold wheels and luggage specially matched to the paint job looked pretty flash. My tired old hack was not so much the poor relation, as the poverty-stricken impostor making a spurious claim to the family lineage. Amalia gave it a pitying look.

'Don't worry, once those parts arrive from DHL, I'll get a few things sorted out on the bike and we'll get going,' I said as we lugged her belongings up the stairs to our room.

'How much longer are they going to be?'

'They've arrived in Peru, apparently, but customs won't release them to DHL for some reason.'

'Well, maybe you should start hassling them.'

'Yeah, I'll call them tomorrow, see what's happening.'

'Well, I hope they don't take much longer, I want to get going now.'

'Same here. Crikey! What have you got in these bags?' I asked as we heaved another bulging pannier onto the bed.

My question was soon answered as she began to unpack her luggage. Before long the room was covered in an array of beauty products, several coordinated outfits complete with matching hair accessories that looked more suited to a five-year-old girl than a thirty-eight-year-old woman embarking on a Third World motorcycle expedition, and last but not least, five pairs of footwear.

'Well, you're quite the motorcycling Imelda Marcos, aren't you!' I exclaimed.

As well as the boots she was wearing, I spied a pair of high-heeled sandals, a pair of trainers, some flip-flops and another pair of motorcycle boots.

'Well, you never know what you might need in the Amazon!' she replied flippantly.

While Amalia arranged her selection of T-shirts, a distant memory from my school days floated up to the surface, the annoying catchphrase of my old form teacher: 'Girls, this is *not* a fashion parade!' she used to squawk as we turned up for class in our pencil skirts and winkle-pickers. Of course, we just dismissed her as a bitter old crone and applied another coat of Twilight Teaser to our teenage pouts. Much as I hated to admit it, her slogan seemed woefully apt in this situation, but I decided to keep the recollection to myself.

The next morning Amalia kicked me out of bed.

'Come on, call DHL,' she was saying. Not being much of an early riser, it took me a while to get my befuddled brain into gear, by which time she was up, dressed and pacing the room. My phone call returned only bad news.

'Um . . . the customs people want to know exactly what part is what and which part number is for what thing.' I wasn't explaining myself very well but it was still a bit early for lucidity.

'What?!' cried Amalia.

'Yes, they're going to fax a photocopy of the parts over to the hotel and I have to send it back with the details of what they are.'

'Oh Jesus!' She groaned.

'Well, that's the way it goes with these customs people. There's no point in arguing with them, believe me.'

'Well, tell them to get a move on, I don't want to be stuck in Lima for another week.'

'Neither do I,' I assured her. 'Anyway, it looks like we've got another day to kill, what d'you fancy doing?'

'Let's go into the old part of town, wander around and take some photos,' Amalia suggested.

We took a crammed *collectivo* into the city centre, a sort of minibus/taxi affair that picked up and dropped off passengers in only the most hazardous of situations. No 'Sorry, love, I can only open the door at bus stops' nonsense that you get from the bus drivers back home. Here, the approach to passenger safety was more along the lines of 'Sorry, love, I can only open the door when there's a truck hurtling towards you up the outside lane.' This was a proper free-for-all with the people of Lima, young and old, hanging off the sides and out the door while the driver tore up the main drag like a rally racer; and if you got hurt, it was your own fault.

Lima was hardly my idea of the perfect Citybreak destination and I was as keen as Amalia to get on the road. It was bad enough when I'd been here on my own but at least I could dress like a tramp and skulk around in dark glasses to avoid the incessant harassment and persistent street hawkers. But two pale-skinned gringas were a little harder to ignore, especially with Amalia's penchant for skintight skirts, strappy vests and lashings of bright red lipstick. It started the minute we left the hotel with the two men permanently hanging around on the corner, who despite having received a daily knock-back from myself still insisted on sidling up to us and offering their dodgy wares in a suspicious mumble. *'No, gracias,'* we de-

clared, walking briskly and avoiding eye contact. But once we hit
the city centre, the unwanted attention reached fever pitch.

Amalia's flesh was too much for Lima man and he was too much
for her. He whistled and pinched and slavered. She yelled and
screamed and swore, which of course only encouraged him further.

'Amalia, don't rise to the bait,' I pleaded. 'I know they're horrible lecherous bastards, but it just makes it worse.'

'I just want to fucking walk around without being molested,'
she shouted.

'Yes, I know, I know. It's a nightmare, but just try to ignore them.'

But my words fell on deaf ears and the next hapless male to mess
with Amalia got her full bottle of Evian thrown squarely in his face.
He was not amused.

'Amalia, please,' I groaned, 'please, that is not a good idea.'

'But they're driving me mad!'

'Well, maybe you should put your cardigan on; the less white
flesh on show, the better.'

She flounced off in frustration, teetering across the cobbled
square.

A cup of coffee calmed things down a bit and we continued our
tour of Lima's grand buildings and ancient streets.

'Wow! Look at him!' I said, pointing at a man sprayed gold from
head to toe and dressed in Inca-style tunic and sandals. He was selling snacks to the queuing car drivers. 'I wonder if he'd mind if I
took a photo of him.

'Probably not.'

'I think I should ask first.'

'Oh, he won't mind, just take it.'

'I don't know, they get a bit funny sometimes.'

'Well, whatever . . .'

'Hmm . . . I'd better ask him,' I dithered.

'Jesus Christ, Lois! If you want to take a photo, just fucking take
it!' she snapped, glaring at me furiously.

I didn't take the photo.

The journey back to the hotel was somewhat muted but I hoped that Amalia would settle into the swing of things soon enough. She'd been here less than a week and it took a little while to get used to being away from home. I knew what it was like; these places could drive you mad if you let them. It was difficult to drop hard-won principles, but sometimes it was the only way to stay sane. Back in our room I broached the subject.

'Are you all right? You seem a bit pissed off with everything.'

'Oh, I dunno, I'm just frustrated, I suppose. I want to get going, and hanging around for your bike parts to arrive and all that, it's just annoying me.'

'Yeah, I understand. I guess we're at different stages of our trips; you've just started and I'm six months in. I know it's annoying, I got held up in Alaska right at the beginning too, before I'd even got going.'

'I'm not annoyed with you, I'm just annoyed with the situation. That's just the way I am, I'm really impatient. I blow up quickly, but then I calm down quickly too.'

My heart sank at this revelation. How about not blowing up at all? I wanted to say, but I kept quiet.

'I'm sorry. I'll be fine once we get on the road.'

'Yeah, I know,' I agreed, 'once we get out of Lima and get going, it'll be great. Come on, let's go out for some food.'

'OK.' She offered me a conciliatory smile.

'Promise you won't attack the two blokes on the corner,' I said with a pleading grin and she laughed.

'I promise. What are they trying to flog us anyway?'

'I don't know, drugs probably.'

We braved the hawkers and their shifty sales pitch without mishap and set off for dinner.

But Peruvian customs didn't care that I was incarcerated in a hotel room with a temperamental travelling companion. Nope, rules is rules, and they had plenty more hoops for me to jump through before I would be united with my package, which had now taken on Holy Grail status. Naturally, Amalia didn't take to this news well and I spent the next few days juggling endless faxes, e-mails and phone calls among myself, DHL and the customs office while desperately trying to keep her spirits up. Her face was now frozen into a permanent scowl and the grumpier she became, the more I tried to compensate with effusive apologies and displays of exaggerated cheerfulness until I was performing an exhausting act that alternated between a grovelling Indian waiter and a Butlins Red Coat. It wasn't working, but I didn't know what else to do. In the end, I came up with a plan.

'Amalia, I've been thinking. There's no use you hanging around here while I get all this sorted out. Why don't you get going and I'll catch up in a few days. There's plenty of things you can visit on the way, y'know, Inca sites and stuff.

'No, no,' she muttered from the bed in a wretched monotone. 'I might as well wait for you. After all, we're in this together, aren't we?' She uttered the last sentence as if we were on death row.

'Well, it's up to you, but I don't want to spoil your fun, that's all. If you want to get going, it's fine by me.'

'No, no . . .'

'Well, OK. I promise, we'll be on the road soon enough and we'll have forgotten all about this.'

Sure enough, when the call came in from the hotel reception— 'A package has arrived'—the mood in room 403 lifted considerably. Looking for the quickest option, I chatted up the local motorcycle shop and begged them to do the work as fast as was humanly possible. I would pay good *dinero,* was the underlying message, our mental health depended on it. The boys in the workshop came up trumps and Amalia and I went out to celebrate our last night in Lima, tackling our street corner pushermen for the last time. Maybe it was out of simple curiosity, but this time, instead of taking my usual stance, I slowed down, trying to catch the words they whispered each time we passed.

' 'arry Potter?' they mumbled. ' 'arry Potter? 'arry Potter?'

I stopped in disbelief, but I had heard it right. With a furtive glance up and down the street they opened their jackets to reveal bootleg copies of J. K. Rowling's best seller.

'Lima's making us paranoid,' I said to Amalia.

'Well, it's lucky we're leaving first thing tomorrow,' she replied.

Over the main course, Amalia announced the schedule for the following morning's departure.

'We're setting the alarm for six, leaving no later than seven,' she informed me, adding in pointed tones, 'And no faffing.'

'Er, do you really think we need to get up that early? How about alarm at seven?' I ventured tentatively, trying to keep the terror out of my voice. Six o'clock? What was this, Motorcycling Boot Camp?

She rolled her eyes.

'Six-thirty,' she said in a tone of voice that meant the discussion was over.

We were on the road by eight, after *mucho* faffing, mainly caused by Amalia's bike falling over due to its gargantuan amount of luggage. But as soon as we squirmed our way out of town and onto the Pan-Am, the irritations of *la vida* Lima slipped away into a dim and distant past life. The empty desert unfolded before us, a warm salty breeze blew in off the Pacific and all was well with the world again. God, I love this! I thought, and I had to admit, I was glad to have some time to myself again, time for my own thoughts. That's the joy of motorcycling, I mused silently, all the thrills of movement, travel and adventure, *and* the simple, idle pleasures of just sitting and thinking in the great outdoors. You can't beat it!

Amalia's morale appeared to have received a welcome boost too, despite her bike regularly toppling over, but we didn't mention that. Instead our conversation matter returned to our original subjects of route planning interspersed with X-rated girlie chats. Maybe things would be OK, I hoped, now we were on the road, and I put her mood swings down to a mixture of frustration, culture shock, homesickness and all the other demons that lurk in the shadows of a faraway foreign land.

'Let's spend the night in Nasca, and have a look at the Nasca lines,' Amalia said over an afternoon coffee break in a roadside café. We'd been on the road for a couple of days now and things seemed to be working out.

'Are those the drawings on the desert floor?'

'Yeah, I'd really like to see them, they're quite a mystery, massive pictures of animals and shapes etched into the ground.'

'Does anyone know where they came from?'

Amalia consulted her guidebook.

'It says some people think they might be an ancient form of calendar or something to do with the constellations . . . there's a viewing tower on the Pan-American or you can take a flight in a light plane from Nasca.'

The viewing tower soon appeared, jutting out of the flat brown landscape, an alien man-made structure in the vast empty desert. We pulled off the highway and waited for a coachload of Peruvian schoolkids to make their way up and down the steps, two at a time. But they were far more interested in our bikes than in some boring line drawings in the sand, and after staring at us warily from the other side of the road, one of the braver boys dared to come over for a closer inspection. The level of my Spanish was pitched perfectly for conversing with small children and soon my schoolboy friend and I were deep in conversation. Seeing that their classmate had made his move and survived, a couple of the others edged their way over, then a few more gathered round, and a few more, until the entire class surrounded me and the excited jabbering reached a deafening level. They took turns to sit on the bike, to rev the throttle, beep the horn. 'Where are you from? Where have you been? Where are you going? What is England like?' they asked. Their rapid transformation from timid spectators to excitable, inquisitive kids was a sight to behold. The teachers rushed over, worried they were bothering me, but as soon as they realised all was well, they too began asking questions and taking photos of their squealing flock crawling all over the Serow. I looked around for Amalia, assuming she was entertaining some of them in a similar fashion, but although her bike was parked just a few feet from mine, she was standing next to it, alone, with a grim expression on her face. I tried to send some of the kids over to play with her but she glared at them and they backed away nervously. Clad from head to toe in tight black leather with her square jaw jutting out defiantly from her black helmet, a heavy chrome key chain dangling from her hip and eyes hidden behind black sunglasses, her tall frame cut quite an imposing figure, especially to a small Peruvian schoolboy. One of the teachers attempted to bring her into the conversation, but without fluent English she struggled for a suitable opening gambit. Instead, she pointed at Amalia and uttered the first thought that entered her head.

'Arnold Schwarzenegger!' she declared and burst into a fit of giggles.

Amalia's face contorted in pure fury, and despite the dark shades I could feel her venomous glare burning like the desert sun onto the tactless schoolmarm.

'God, I hate children,' Amalia spat, once the bus had pulled away, the back window full of squashed noses and waving hands.

'Oh, they were fine,' I said; 'compared to the little oiks you get in London, they were nice.'

'When I was at art college,' she said, 'I made this sculpture of an enormous fat woman covered in insects and children, crawling all over her, eating her flesh. It was a statement about how motherhood is like having a load of parasites feeding off you'.

We climbed to the top of the viewing tower where the overtly gay guide looked at Amalia's outfit and asked her if she was into S&M. By the resulting scowl, I got the impression that Amalia wasn't very taken with the level of Peruvian social skills so far, so to lighten the mood I suggested we go and mess about on the bikes in the desert. This started out as good clean fun, but in a run up a dune I got my motorcycle stuck in a patch of deep sand and had to enlist Amalia's help to heave it out, sending her into another grumpy sulk and eliciting more Indian waiter impressions from me. In my last-ditch attempt to enjoy myself, I proposed a photo session.

'Let's take some pictures of us on the bikes. I'll take some of you on your camera if you want.'

Thankfully, this was met with approval.

'OK. Smile!' I shouted out.

'I don't smile in photos, it makes my face look strange,' she said.

'OK, whatever you want. Ready?'

'No! Wait!' she yelled. 'I only have my photo taken from my left side.'

I waited until she had adopted her seductive pose and sulky pout, and clicked away from the correct angle. This is what it must be like being on the road with Mariah Carey or J. Lo, I thought wearily.

My attempts to scatter a modicum of fun into our day had fallen like seeds on the desert floor, and by the time we got to the town of Nasca, the atmosphere was as heavy as my riding companion's luggage. The hotel receptionist got it first.

'Jesus Christ, why the fuck do I have to fill in all this crap?' muttered Amalia as she scribbled on the standard hotel booking form. She was extra annoyed because we'd had to wait while a Swiss couple in front of us went through the same rigmarole.

'I'm not telling them my marital status or my surname,' she fumed, 'and why do they need to know what I do for a job. Ha! I'm going to put down 'guidebook writer,' that'll make them think twice!'

I doubted very much whether a cheapo fleapit in the Peruvian desert cared one way or the other what she did for a living, but I attempted to placate her.

'Oh, don't worry about it, it's just the law over here, they don't take any notice of it.'

She slammed down the pen on the counter and sighed and tutted impatiently while I went through the same motions. Next on her hit list was the moneychanger, whose rule of only accepting crisp, new dollar notes provoked a torrent of abuse. And finally, it was the Internet café that received the full onslaught of her temper: the computer had crashed just as she was completing a lengthy e-mail home. I found her outside in the street, red in the face, shrieking, tears of frustration brimming from her eyes, literally stamping her feet in an outpouring of uncontained rage.

'Fuck! Fuck! Fuck! I'm sick of it all, God, I just want to change some money and send a fucking e-mail. Nothing fucking works in this shithole country!'

I whisked her off to the fanciest restaurant in town, where tinkling water features calmed her furious mood and attentive waiters soothed her fragile ego.

'Look, Amalia, are you OK?' I asked, desperate to get to the bottom of all this and create some sort of bearable environment for us to travel in together.

Like a child after a temper tantrum, she had become all worn out and mopey.

'Oh, I don't know. Sometimes I wonder to myself what I'm doing here. I mean, I don't really have any particular desire to be in Peru, or travelling around South America at all,' she said sadly. 'Sometimes, it all just seems so pointless.'

I had some sympathy for her. Once the initial excitement and novelty wore off, it was easy to be left wondering what it was all about. But as far as I could see, we had a lot of fun, adventure and beautiful places to look forward to—that was the point. And whatever happened, it was always preferable to being at work in rainy England.

'Well, I think the thing is that once you've realised there's no actual purpose, then you can start enjoying yourself. Y'know, was it Robert Louis Stevenson who said, 'The great affair is to move'?'

She stared at me blankly.

'Or maybe you need a goal. I mean, it really helps me to think I'm aiming to get to the very tip of South America, it keeps me going when it's raining, or the bike's playing up or whatever.'

She sighed.

'Y'know, I'm really sorry but I don't think I want to go all the way down there,' she said. 'It'll be cold and I don't like riding in the cold. You don't mind, do you?'

'Not at all,' I assured her.

The waiter moved in with some well-used lines and Amalia perked up considerably, simpering and flirting with him in Spanish.

'And what would you like, senorita?' He turned to me with come-to-bed-or-give-me-a-whopping-great-tip eyes.

'I'll have the Tacu Tacu, please.'

'Ah yes, a very good choice, a local dish, very traditional Peruvian,' he declared.

'What's Tacu Tacu?' asked Amalia after the waiter had left our table with a cheeky wink.

'It says it's a fried patty type thing made from beans.'

That's exactly what it turned out to be, although the menu description hadn't mentioned the additional chewy lumps of gristle.

'Anyway,' said Amalia, seeming a bit more cheerful now, 'I've been thinking, I'd like to take a flight in one of the light planes tomorrow to see the Nasca lines from the air.'

Sadly, I didn't feel my budget would stretch to such an extravagance and I explained this to Amalia, encouraging her to go without me.

'Well, I'll pay for both of us,' she suggested, and despite my remonstrations, she wouldn't back down.

'After all, I can afford it,' she said with a knowing look. She had recently inherited her late father's estate, which included a flat in Barcelona and a sum of money that meant she would never have to work again, a topic she alluded to frequently and celebrated by wearing a ring in the shape of a crown, featuring the word HEIRESS in block capitals.

'No, no,' I protested, 'I've seen the lines from the viewing tower, I don't need to go up in a plane, you go without me, it's only for an hour or so.'

But she wouldn't have it and the next morning we were sitting in a portacabin in a small airfield, watching an informative video about the mystery of the Nasca lines prior to our flight. The film looked like it might be quite interesting, but I missed most of it due to making regular dashes to the airport facilities. Tacu Tacu had taken its revenge, and it wasn't sweet. Up in the air, the situation took a turn for the worse. The plane was a cosy affair, just enough room for the two of us, the pilot and a young French chap twenty-six years old, sixty-eight kilos, according to the form we had to fill in. Within minutes of taking off, I was vomiting violently into the translucent plastic bags that had been provided for such an eventuality. The pilot took the professional approach to my predicament and continued to shout out his commentary over the roar of the engine, insisting on each of us confirming that we had seen every line drawing he pointed out:

'MONKEY ON THE LEFT.'

Lurch. Puke. Groan.

'Yes!'

'HUMMINGBIRD ON THE RIGHT.'

Lurch. More puke.

'Yeeees.'

'TRAPEZOID BELOW.'

Puke. Puke.

'Urggghhh . . . yeah.'

Half an hour later I staggered out of the cockpit, pale, sweating and shaking, holding three full quivering plastic bags.

'It's like carrying goldfish home from the fair,' I observed to Amalia, but she didn't say anything.

The pilot, who had proclaimed us to be *'muy bonita'* before take-off, wasn't so enamoured now, well, not with me anyway, and my formal apology to the French bloke failed to elicit any response at all. With international and personal relations at an all-time low, Amalia and I returned to the hotel in silence. I locked myself in the bathroom and Amalia stationed herself by the pool, entering our fetid room only if strictly necessary, and then with an exaggeratedly wrinkled nose.

'Is it safe to go in there?' she asked after a couple of hours, motioning towards the bathroom, distaste oozing from her every pore.

'Er, well, I just produced a rather impressive Lichtenstein-style SPLAT! so it's probably best avoided for a while.'

She sighed and raised her eyebrows, stalking off to find alternative conveniences. Her bedside manner owed more to Cruella De Vil than Florence Nightingale and her enquiries regarding my well-being were unconvincing in the extreme.

'Are you getting any better yet?' she demanded from the other side of the bathroom door a little while later.

'Well, about the same, really, although it's more Jackson Pollock now.' What with her art college background, I hoped the combination of toilet humour and art references might cheer her up but this was clearly a misjudgment on my part.

'I wanted to visit an Inca burial ground nearby this afternoon, but I guess that idea's gone out of the window,' she said in a tone of voice that suggested I'd spoilt everything . . . again.

'Well, I'm sorry,' I called back in between retches, 'but I don't think I'll be going anywhere today, but why don't you go without me, it's not far, is it?'

But this idea was rejected for the far more enjoyable option of an afternoon of guilt-inducing sulking. I suppose I could see it from her point of view; so far our trip had been held up first by my bike troubles and now by me getting sick, the two things she had vowed wouldn't happen to her. But all I could do was take a philosophical approach; 'These things happen' was my only excuse, but it wasn't worth uttering.

The pressure was on to get moving the next morning and fortunately, by the time Amalia's alarm interrupted our slumber, I had just about said tata to Tacu Tacu. I was back on the bike, in a slightly weakened state, but ready to take on the thirteen-thousand-feet-high passes of the Andes.

The road out of Nasca was an exceptional ride, climbing up from the desert on the tightest hairpins, snaking through the mountains and rising thousands of feet every hour. But my bike was faring no better than before, despite the new main jet I'd fitted in Lima, and to make matters even worse, my steering head bearings chose this most zigzaggy of roads to pack in. Coaxing the bike round the sharp bends and with the dreaded spluttering making its unwelcome return, it didn't take long for Amalia to leave me in the dust and it was a good couple of hours before I caught up with her, high up in the mountains, where she had stopped to photograph a pack of llamas ambling across the road.

'Oh, there you are,' she said. 'I was wondering where you'd got to.'

'Sorry, the bike's still having trouble and I'm feeling a bit ropey, probably a combination of Tacu Tacu and the altitude.'

'I think it's a load of nonsense, this altitude sickness,' she snorted, 'it's all in the mind, I'm feeling fine.'

A quick gulp of water and we were off again, but after a few bends Amalia had disappeared from sight and I was riding alone, winding my way up the empty Andean road across a landscape of sheer desolation. The air was becoming noticeably thinner, the temperature dropped a degree at every turn, and then the rain came down. But it didn't last long. Soon it turned to painful icy pellets, hammering into my face, and then to thick, heavy snow that wove a white tunnel in front of my eyes, reducing visibility to a matter of inches.

A desert storm in Peru

'How can this be? How can I be roasting under the desert sun in the morning and freezing in ice and snow by midafternoon?' I said aloud to myself, almost in disbelief. After so many months in the tropics, I was totally unprepared, both physically and mentally, for these arctic conditions. 'This is a nightmare!' I shouted but there was nobody else to hear me, just another flock of llamas casually strolling along the side of the road, looking smug in their woolly coats, knowing full well they were the only living creatures that could hack it up here in this godforsaken land. I wiped away the snow from my map case and sure enough there wasn't a town marked for over a hundred miles. I wondered how far ahead Amalia was; I guessed I would catch up with her at some point. All I could do now was keep going and hope that the snowstorm would pass or that the road would descend into milder climes.

Two hours later, the blizzard was still raging and I was back to the frozen fingers and toes I thought I'd left behind in Alaska. I bounced up and down on the foot pegs to keep my circulation in action and rode for miles at a time bent over with my left hand grasping the engine block, desperate for its warmth. I was beginning to give up all hope of ever feeling my feet again, when through the white haze I spied a hint of something, I wasn't sure what it was, but it was most definitely something. Something other than miles and miles of bleak, barren scrubland. As I approached, hastily scraping the ice off my goggles, I made out a small stone building with a motorcycle parked outside, and when I pulled up I saw a hand-painted sign bearing the most welcome word in my Spanish dictionary: RESTAURANTE. Next to it stood Amalia, covered from head to toe in snow, shivering and speechless.

I staggered off the bike and nearly fell over. I was utterly frozen through and almost paralysed by the cold. Amalia and I stood in front of each other, hardly able to move or speak. Please don't be in a bad mood, I begged silently, I just couldn't be doing with it, not now.

And as if she could read my mind she burst into hysterical laughter. I was so relieved that I did the same.

'Oh my God,' was all she could say, 'oh my God.' I could barely manage a response but we were united by our misery. We stumbled into the little building through a tiny door so low we had to stoop down to avoid banging our heads, to find a group of Indian women dressed in their customary shawls and hats sitting in near darkness. The room was constructed of bare stone with just a couple of tables and chairs scattered around, and in the corner a man was communicating with the outside world on a shortwave radio. There was no heating but at least the ambient temperature was slightly above what we had just endured for the past two hours. 'We have no electricity,' explained one of the women in Spanish. We nodded. We still couldn't form any words so we just sat there, rivers of melted snow pouring from our clothes onto the dirt floor, our whole bodies shaking and our teeth chattering uncontrollably. The woman brought us over two cups of pale green hot water with leaves floating in it.

'Maté' she said.

Maté tea, made from coca leaves. The local drink and supposedly an antidote to altitude sickness. I remembered Che Guevara raving about it in the book of his motorcycle travels around South America. We gulped it down, chewed the leaves and asked for a second round. Then we ordered everything off the menu and ate like savages. The restaurateurs were quietly amused by our snowy predicament, but sympathetic too, and offered to put us up for the night. We would just be sleeping on the floor with no power or heating, they explained.

'I'm up for it,' I said to Amalia. The thought of continuing in these conditions was unbearable and I would have done anything to lie down on a dirt floor at that moment, but Amalia was keen to press on to civilisation.

'I thought you didn't like riding in the cold,' I said, surprised.

'Tonight, I want hot water and a bed,' she declared. I knew better than to argue.

'The next town with a hotel is Chalhuanca, fifty miles away,' the man with the radio told us.

'Let's go,' said Amalia.

I groaned inwardly and asked the man if I could make use of the loo before putting on my soaking gear again. He pointed to a door-size hole in the wall, barely covered by a ragged curtain. On the other side a scramble over a pile of rubble took me to a derelict outhouse containing a hole in the ground and a dog with his face buried in a bucket of used toilet paper. Claridges, it ain't, I thought, wincing, as I took up position and watched the snow drift through the holes in the roof. I didn't mind the grot, the icy wind or even the stench of raw sewage, but I just couldn't get down to business with a canine washroom attendant on hand.

'Sorry, Rover, you're putting me off,' I told him, and shooed him back into the house. When I returned to finish off my maté tea, he had made a new friend in Amalia.

'I wouldn't do that if I were you,' I said as she rubbed his nose.

Amalia was ready to move so I pulled on a dry pair of socks and we returned to the bitter hostilities of the outside world. But my bike was as reluctant as I was to carry on and as we set off up a steep hill, it choked and spluttered, struggling to pull up the incline. With a very gentle easing on of the throttle in first gear I urged it forward, kicking and screaming, white smoke billowing from the exhaust, the speedo nudging six miles an hour—an all-time, soul-crushing low. I wobbled towards Chalhuanca, picking up a little more speed but never making it over twenty-five miles an hour. This bike needs some serious attention, I admitted to myself, but I could hardly bear the thought of breaking this news to Amalia.

By the time we arrived at the hotel, I had discovered what it meant to be truly frozen to the core. No matter what I did, I simply couldn't warm up. My head was pounding and I collapsed into bed fully clothed, and shivered my way through a night of hallucinatory dreams involving a rabid Andrex puppy chasing miles of soiled loo roll across the Andes, with me in hot pursuit.

Fourteen

Much to my surprise, I didn't die in the night, and woke up feeling surprisingly normal. I had slept for twelve hours, Amalia pointed out, also remarking on how she had restrained herself from waking me with her usual sergeant major–style reveille.

We were now just a day's ride from Cusco, the ancient Inca capital, high up in the Andes and a big tourist destination due to its proximity to Machu Picchu. For us two-wheeled travellers, Cusco held extra appeal in the form of Norton Rat's, an infamous biker bar located on the main square and a mecca for motorcycle voyagers in South America. Owned by American ex-pat Jeffrey, a well-travelled biker of yore with a soft spot for a warm beer and a lump of Brit Iron, Norton's was where everyone stopped in for a night, or a week, or a month, whether heading north, south, east or west across the continent. Amalia was fairly itching to get there, but we had a couple more hundred miles of twisty Andean roads before the twinkling lights of Cusco appeared amongst the mountains. Mercifully the sun had been blazing that morning and the road descended into a warm, sultry valley, following the route of a crystal clear river, swollen by the snowfall, which flowed easily through the foothills of the mountains. In the town of Abancay we stopped to refuel ourselves and the bikes in preparation for another long mountainous ride ahead.

The road to Cuzco, Peru, climbs 12,000 feet from the desert to the mountains.

'I can hardly believe yesterday ever happened,' I commented as we perused the menu, pondering the sudden change in our fortunes; 'isn't it strange to be in a country where the weather's dictated by altitude, rather than the season? And what about that gorgeous valley this morning? What an amazing ride.'

But the camaraderie brought on by yesterday's tribulations had melted away like the snow itself.

'I dunno, I didn't really notice it, I never take notice of that sort of thing,' Amalia muttered in a miserable voice and my heart sank at her return to form.

Not content with just me as a sounding board, the unwitting residents of Abancay were also treated to the brunt of her bad mood and it didn't take much to unleash the old demons again. The menu that failed to live up to its claims provoked an attack of rage in the restaurant and then the girl pumping gas at the gas station got it in the neck when the supply of 95 octane ran dry.

'Oh for fuck's sake! What is wrong with this country?' screeched Amalia. She was straddling her bike, hands on hips and yelling at the top of her voice. 'How do you idiots get anything done in this place? God, I am so fucking sick of useless fucking Peru!'

But as usual, the laid-back locals found her outburst highly entertaining and the gas station girls dropped tools to gather round, giggling at the spectacle. I could have seen the funny side myself, if the thought of another three months of this hadn't been hanging over me like the world's worst community service sentence.

'Amalia, Amalia, don't worry, low-octane gas is fine at altitude,' I assured her; this had reluctantly become my specialist subject due to my bike's plight, 'or there's another gas station round the corner if you want—'

But she wasn't listening; instead she was screaming obscenities at the girls, who just laughed even harder. Now all the drivers in the gas station were staring at her with amused expressions on their faces. I couldn't bear to watch anymore and I rode out into the street and waited round the corner, cringing with embarrassment at the whole affair.

'Amalia, you can't keep doing this,' I said, pleading, when she appeared red in the face and spitting blood. 'You're just ruining your own trip, and we'll give a bad rep to motorcyclists and other English people coming through here.'

'I don't give a fuck what they think!' she yelled. 'I don't represent England, I hate England anyway, the only good thing about it is the Archers!'

I think it was this display of all-out, head-spinning fury that forced me to admit that my Thelma-and-Louise-on-motorcycles vision was rapidly metamorphosing into *The Evil Dead*.

The last leg to Cusco was somewhat strained but fortunately, the steep winding road with its blind corners, long stretches of gravel, and the thrill of a rocky river to ford kept us concentrating on more imminent matters, but I was beginning to dread each time we stopped for a break. Every conversation was peppered with *tut*s, sighs, sarcastic comments and withering looks, until it finally degenerated into those sullen exchanges that men complain of having with their premenstrual girlfriends:

'What's wrong?'

'Nothing.'

'Are you sure? You seem a bit pissed off.'

'I said, there's nothing wrong.'

'OK, I was just asking.'

'Yeah, well, it's all right for you, isn't it?'

'What d'you mean?'

'Oh, nothing.'

'Look, what's the matter?'

'NOTHING!'

'OK, don't get angry.'

'I'M NOT ANGRY!'

Thankfully, as we arrived in the centre of Cusco, we were immediately collared by two fellow motorcycle travellers, providing us with a welcome distraction.

'Are you Lois?' said one of them, a big American guy with a goatee.

'Yes!' I said, surprised. 'How did you know?'

'Frank in Bolivia told me you were heading this way, I stayed with him in La Paz a few months ago, and he's here in Cusco at the moment.'

It turned out the overland bikers' grapevine had been at work again. I had exchanged a few e-mails with Frank, a German rider now living in the Bolivian capital, with plans of meeting up with him when we passed through the city.

'I'm Robb,' he said, offering a hand, 'this is Dieter from Switzerland.'

*Wet feet in the
Peruvian Andes*

Robb was heading south, Dieter north, but like us they were planning to visit Machu Picchu and party hearty in Norton's for a few days.

'This is Amalia,' I said.

The thunderous cloud of grumpiness evaporated before my very eyes to reveal the Simpering Temptress lying in wait.

'Hiiiiiiii,' she breathed, extending a floppy hand.

Meanwhile Dieter was examining our bikes with interest.

'Well, oh dear,' he said to me in his Swiss accent with a slightly cheeky smile, 'your bike looks like you have been on the road for six months and yours,' he turned to Amalia, 'looks like you have just started.'

'Yeah, but, but, her bike was old when she got it,' protested

Amalia. But the guys were busy making plans for the night's revelries.

'There's quite a few motorcyclists in town,' said Robb, listing the all-important info—their nationality and their bikes. 'Like I said, Frank's here on his Africa Twin, then there's a Mexican guy on an F650, a German couple on KTMs and an Austrian guy riding an R80GS.'

'Excellent. Well, we're going to find somewhere to stay and we'll see you in there later.'

Their hotel was full but Robb sent us in the direction of an alternative, with courtyard parking for the bikes. It was pretty shabby, but cheap and close to the centre of town.

'Oh God, this is horrible,' groaned Amalia as she entered the room. 'I'm getting a bit sick of staying in these grotty places. I mean, I can actually afford somewhere decent, but I know it's a bit different for you.'

'Well, it's got a toilet seat and a whole loo roll!' I pointed out, but these trappings of civilisation failed to convince her and she dumped her bags down on her bed with a noisy sigh.

'I suppose it'll have to do,' she declared in resigned tones.

'We can go somewhere else if you want.'

'No, no, it doesn't matter.'

Fortunately the excitement of a night out took her mind off our immediate surroundings and the dowdy room became a temporary beauty salon as we attempted to transform ourselves into something that didn't look like it had been dragged over the Andes. While Amalia was trying on different outfits and arranging her hair, I jumped in the shower and attempted to scrape out the dirt from under my fingernails. I might as well get clean even if I would be putting the same clothes back on.

When I emerged a while later, Amalia turned from the mirror and looked me up and down with the detached, appraising eye of a racehorse breeder.

'Y'know what,' she said, 'you'd have the perfect hour-glass figure . . .'

There was a slight pause.

'. . . if you lost a few pounds,' she added as she returned to her reflection.

In Norton's the beer and conversation flowed in equally bounteous measures. Jeffrey was the perfect host, providing us with the landlord's greatest gift, a lock-in and a steady supply of booze. The joint was jumpin', fragrant cigarettes were doing the rounds and even the hard-faced woman who, when I'd seated myself alongside her earlier had said in chilly tones, 'I am from Germany, do you still want to sit next to me?' appeared to have defrosted and even tried a smile on occasion. I discovered Jeffrey's CDs and took the opportunity to crank up some Little Feat, Hendrix and Stones, much to my delight. Robb and Dieter were in the midst of a lively BMW discussion (if there is such a thing), Jeffrey was sloshing pints of Peruvian lager in everyone's direction faster than we could drink it, Frank was overheard saying, 'Who is the woman with Lois who looks like she has smoked too many Gauloise?' the German couple made futile attempts to strike up serious conversations about world affairs (while everyone else made successful attempts to avoid them), and an English backpacker girl kept us all entertained by flashing her sizeable, if rather pendulous, breasts at every opportunity. The Mexican with the F650 just sipped his beer slowly and smiled easily, as if he were culturally incapable of joining in the Anglo-Saxon leisure pursuit of getting mindlessly drunk as quickly as possible. Amalia, being of good, Archers-listening English stock, had no such problems. She whooped and shrieked and giggled and flung herself around the room like she was out on day release. It was a relief to see her enjoying herself at last and I realised that she would never be happy travelling with me, or indeed, by herself. She needed the audience and I just wasn't appreciative enough. By three o'clock the backpacker was groping Amalia's breasts, who gamely entered into the Sapphic spirit of the moment. Then it was my turn to be mauled.

'Have you ever slept with a woman?' slurred the backpacker in my ear.

I quickly turned to the Germans and launched into an urgent conversation about Third World debt.

As is the nature of the drunk, stoned, thirty-something party-goer, Amalia suddenly, desperately, violently needed to leave. Right now. We staggered out of the door with Robb and Dieter, making foolish, inebriated, unfeasible plans to meet up for a ride the following morning. But the following morning never materialised on our calendar and, in fact, slipped clean out of our lives altogether. When I awoke trembling and gasping for water at midday, I looked over at Amalia to find her flat on her back on the bed, eyes tightly shut, but with the demeanour of someone in a state of denial rather than blissful slumber.

'Are you awake?' I whispered.

'Mmmmmm,' she groaned.

'How are you feeling?'

This elicited another long weary groan.

'Hmm, same here,' I agreed

There was a long pause. Then she spoke in a slow deathly tone.

'I can't face opening my eyes and seeing this hideous hotel room,' she said. If this had been a horror film, her voice would have belonged to an evil rotting corpse rising from a grave, and when she spoke it did seem as though the temperature in the room dropped a few degrees, sending a shiver through my body. Or maybe I just had a bad case of the DTs.

'Well, shall we get up and go out for breakfast?' I suggested.

But this was too much effort, considering the circumstances, and neither of us moved. She had a point; the room was poky, grubby and with the added misery of a hangover, could be considered depressing. A few shards of sunlight sneaked in on either side of the threadbare curtain, taunting us with the lovely day we were wasting. If only we were hearty wholesome types that had the strength of character to say no to free booze and jumped out of bed at 6 A.M. to engage in cultural pursuits. But not for us the life of the teetotal museum goer; instead our afternoon's activities took a different turn. It was never our intention, but on our first day in one of the world's most fascinating and culturally rich cities we lay in semidarkness in our beds, alcohol coursing through our veins, and discussed the cheery subjects of depression, mental illness and suicide. By the time the early evening gloom had swamped our room, I was in the full swing of the first topic, heading for the second and seriously considering the third. I dragged myself into the bathroom and stood shakily under the feeble shower, washing away the crawling grime of my hangover and wondering where it had all gone wrong. I thought about the early thrills of battling the snow in Alaska, the freewheelin' fun of California, the naive excitement of entering Mexico, the adventure of crossing the Andes off-road in Ecuador, even the ducking 'n' diving of Central America had plenty of good memories. What had happened to my Trip of a Lifetime™?

We managed to drag ourselves out to meet up with Robb later that evening, and over an alcohol-free dinner the three of us hatched a plan to ride together for a while, seeing as we were all heading into Bolivia and then southwards. The suggestion was made to leave Cusco in a few days' time, once we'd done Machu Picchu, and when Robb had returned from a three-day hike. I was pleased with this arrangement and the time it bought me to hopefully get my motorcycle sorted out. On the way back I brought up this thorny subject with Amalia.

'I think my bike needs some work done, maybe on the top end, it's burning loads of oil and leaking it as well, and I want to get to the bottom of this jet thing.'

'Well, it had better not take ages, I don't want to be hanging around, waiting again.'

'Jeffrey's going to take me to a mechanic he knows tomorrow, so we'll see what he reckons. But in the meantime let's visit Machu Picchu, that'll take a couple of days, and anyway, we've got to wait for Robb to get back from his hiking trip before we can leave. Unless you want to get going on your own? I don't mind if you do.'

'No, no, I'll wait for you. I'm glad we're going to travel with Robb for a bit, though, I'm looking forward to riding with other people. No offence or anything,' she added with a tinkly little laugh.

My visit to Antonio the mechanic's workshop was not the start of a happy period in my motorcycle's life. With a combination of Jeffrey on translation duty, my patchy Spanish and Antonio's equally patchy English, we compiled the list of doom: new cam chain, new piston rings, new valve guides, new steering head bearings, and a whole host of oil leaks to attend to. But after twelve thousand miles across every terrain and condition imaginable, I wasn't surprised. It was only a little bike and I had always expected some sort of scenario like this. For somewhere to be stuck for a while, Cusco was a pretty good location. Things could be a lot worse. At least, this was the upbeat propaganda I fed to Amalia on our way to Machu Picchu, but nonetheless the mood descended steadily as the train made its climb out of Cusco, dragging itself up the sheer mountainside, groaning and screeching back and forth along the zigzag tracks.

It was four hours before we reached the small station of Aguas Calientes, the nearest village to Machu Picchu, and we still had a five-mile trek up the mountain before we would lay eyes on the ancient city. Amalia steamed ahead up the path and soon I was walking alone, in awe of the giant mountains and impenetrable jungle that surrounded me, and enjoying the peace and quiet. After six months of sitting on a bike all day I relished the physical challenge of the steep climb, despite the blistering heat, thin air and clouds of vicious biting insects scattergunning my exposed skin with little red bites.

Much to my shame, I was overtaken by an elderly local man

who didn't seem in the least bit out of breath. He swatted at the insects and uttered an unintelligible word as he wafted them away from his leathery face.

'*Pumahuacachi,*' he repeated, realising my lack of comprehension. 'Makes the puma cry,' he translated.

'Really? That's what they're called?' I said, charmed at such a poetic title for this unpleasant creature.

'It is Quechuan, the Indian name,' he explained.

With that he was gone, pacing up the narrow rocky trail, lithe and sure as a big cat himself.

I thought the trek would never end, so when I finally caught a glimpse of the ancient stone walls through the trees, my heart leapt with a mixture of excitement and utter relief. Machu Picchu! I can see it, at last! I'm really here! I decided to mark this momentous occasion with a photo and whipped out the camera, carefully framing up my first sighting of the legendary Inca city. It wasn't until I turned the corner and approached the ticket booth that I realised I had in fact been photographing the café that had been built in an appropriately sympathetic style.

The real thing was even more remarkable than the café. A genuinely awe-inspiring and humbling experience and much to my relief, not the overcommercialised 'World Heritage Site' swamped with tacky souvenir stands that I'd been expecting. The Peruvian powers might not be too fussed about their present-day conurbations, but at least they look after their ancient lost cities. The sheer vastness of Machu Picchu and its highly developed architecture and irrigation systems were beyond impressive, especially considering its wildly remote location. The view down into the valley, where the gushing river I had crossed an hour before now appeared as a little trickle on the ground, gave the sense that the world was carrying on somewhere else without me, as if I were looking down from outer space. Eight thousand feet above sea level in a treeless mountain saddle, teetering above a cloud forest, it was almost inconceivable that Machu Picchu's granite stones had been carved with the most basic of tools. And even more astounding that these hundreds of buildings were created without the use of mortar, but with such workmanship that not even the thinnest knife blade could be squeezed between the blocks. I could hardly imagine the buzz of hundreds of Inca people going about their daily business here, all those centuries ago, tending their llamas, cultivating the terraces and swatting the dratted *Pumahuacachi*. But for someone whose love of all things abandoned has burnt brightly since my childhood explorations into derelict buildings, the thought of Hiram Bingham stumbling across this virtually intact but forgotten city four hundred years later thrilled me no end. I remembered the famous photo of him, from an era when explorers wore waistcoats and knee-high socks, leaning on a pole outside his camp, his face gaunt, clearly exhausted from the punishing trek across these mountains, and how it must have all been worthwhile when he hacked back the undergrowth and shouted the 1911 equivalent of 'RESULT! CHECK THIS OUT!'

My visit to Machu Picchu had the desired effect: it took my mind off the petty subjects that had been troubling me of late. It sharpened my senses, put things in order and for a while I stopped brooding about oil leaks, rejetting carburetors and replacing steering head bearings. It was a most welcome injection of tranquillity, and I felt incredibly lucky to be there. A trip to a mountain hot springs, the *aguas calientes* that gave the village its name, was an added bonus, particularly for Amalia. Lazing in the bubbly sulphurous water, she scanned the surrounding scene in slow motion, her head turning from side to side in a robotic fashion, checking out the other bathers with that horse breeder's eye of hers and a faint smile on her lips. After several minutes, she turned to me with a satisfied expression.

'Well,' she announced, 'I've had a good look around, and I have to say, I've got the best body here.'

Back in Cusco the next morning, Antonio was still tinkering away on the Serow and over the next couple of days I fell into a pleasant routine, dropping into the workshop each afternoon, hanging out with other mechanically troubled riders from around the globe and then heading back to Norton's for the evening session. However, this didn't fit in with Amalia's plan. She was chomping at the bit, and her frustration was understandable. When Robb arrived back in town and my motorcycle still wasn't ready I called an emergency meeting in the usual watering hole.

'Antonio reckons my bike will be done the day after tomorrow—'

A long and noisy sigh came from Amalia's corner.

'But,' I continued, 'as I suggested before, why don't you go ahead, visit a few places, y'know, Lake Titicaca or whatever, and I'll catch up with you in a couple of days.'

She turned to Robb and fixed beseeching eyes on him.

'Will you come with me?' she pleaded in a little girl's voice.

Robb shrugged his shoulders with Californian nonchalance.

'Yeah, I guess so. I'm sure Lois doesn't mind riding on her own, do you?'

I assured him in the affirmative. The next morning I lay in bed and listened to the sound of Amalia's bike rumbling away out of the courtyard.

Antonio was true to his word and twenty-four hours later, after farewells to Dieter and Jeffrey, I too was on my way towards Bolivia, heading first for the Peruvian town of Puno on the banks of Lake Titicaca, where I'd arranged to meet the others. All those old feelings I'd been missing came rushing back to me as soon as I hit the road. The old excitement was there again and the nervous tension was gone. There had been roadblock protests in this area the day before and although the road was deserted of traffic, the evidence was still scattered across the highway: burnt-out cars, broken glass, tree trunks, burning tires still smouldering. These hazards robbed me of the usual idle thoughts that were my luxury on a long empty road, but I couldn't help noticing that despite Antonio's handiwork, my bike didn't seem much better than before. The oil leaks and clouds of white smoke had thankfully been cured, but the high altitude was still playing its usual tricks on the carburetor, despite an even smaller main jet. It seemed that whatever I tried, my bike just didn't like teetering this high above sea level. In the end I had to force my brain from going round in circles over the problem, and accept my own official, if technically deficient, analysis of my motorcycle's woes—it's knackered.

In Puno I picked up an e-mail from Amalia with details of her and Robb's whereabouts and tracked them down easily enough. The town was small but jam-packed with both tourists and locals jostling for space in the narrow streets, respectively buying and selling various overpriced trinkets. Amalia was full of the previous day's adventures of tackling the roadblocks, her negotiations with the protestors and the precarious detours around the blockades.

'About time I had some excitement,' she declared. 'I never realised before I came out here that it would be so dull, just riding along every day.'

'It's what you make it,' said Robb in the controlled, flat tone of a henpecked husband about to commit uxoricide.

'So Bolivia tomorrow,' I said, changing the subject.

'Yeah, thank God, I can't wait to get out of Peru. I've been here too long,' said Amalia pointedly.

With three of us on the road, it didn't take us long to work out our riding positions. Robb on his 1000cc BMW was out in front, Amalia on her newer, nippier Serow kept a close second and I brought up the rear, rolling into every rest stop to find my companions' engines already cooling down.

'What's going on with your bike then?' asked Robb.

'Oh, I don't know,' I said despairingly, 'I've tried different jets but they don't seem to make any difference.'

'I'll take a look at it tomorrow if you want, maybe give it a little test ride,' he offered.

'What gear are you riding in for cruising?' interjected Amalia.

'It depends. Fifth usually, sometimes fourth if it's really bad,' I replied.

She rolled her eyes in exasperation and tutted loudly.

'Well, that explains it! I mean, my bike's not doing too bad at this altitude, but that's because I'm not trying to ride it in top gear.'

'Well, no, neither am I.'

'You just said you were riding in fifth,' she said, raising her voice as if she were addressing a naughty child.

'Um . . . yeah . . .'

'Well then.' She glared at me triumphantly.

'But, our bikes have six gears.'

There was a moment's silence.

'Oh,' she said huffily.

Our crossing into Bolivia was smooth, despite its status as the poorest, least developed country in South America. A new country is always a thrill, the heady expectation of the unknown, the slight variances in the language, a new currency to get to grips with, the subtle changes in the look and dress of the local people. It was these thoughts that kept me occupied as we took a winding road round the shores of Lake Titicaca. The huge body of water was more like a small ocean, straddling the border between the two Andean countries, and it was easy to see why in this otherwise bleak terrain, nearly thirteen thousand feet above the sea, the native Indian population considered the lake to be sacred. The startling blueness of the water had been enough to convince the Incas that the sun and moon were created here, and even now the folk that relied on the lake for their living still made offerings to its cobalt waters. A man dressed in the typical Bolivian trilby hat and a faded T-shirt bearing the novel slogan FIZY WIZY AZTEC TRIBE was hiring out sailing

A rustic gas station in Bolivia

dinghies on a slipway in the small town of Copacabana. He informed me as part of his sales pitch that when a person falls in the lake it is traditional not to rescue him but to let him drown as an offering to the Earth Goddess. True or not, I did question his business sense in revealing this morsel of mythology to a potential customer.

We spent the night in Copacabana and I couldn't help but hum the dreaded Barry Manilow number as I packed the bike the next morning,

'Well, at last we're in Bolivia!' I said to Amalia, elated at the prospect. But despite the excitement at being here after what seemed like an eternity in Peru, her spirits were still at a resolutely low altitude. I had hoped that Robb's presence would help matters but despite Amalia's suggestion that they share a room in Puno 'to keep costs down,' he had opted for separate rooms and apparently spent the evening reading and playing Patience on his laptop.

'OK,' announced Robb, taking charge of the itinerary as we prepared to leave, 'follow me, I know a good route out of town, I came through here before.'

'So what's the plan?' I asked.

'Head for La Paz first off, I guess, that's about a hundred miles. Then from there we'll head south and cut across the Salar into Chile.'

I was excited by this prospect. The Salar de Uyuni—a huge salt flat crisscrossed with nothing but deep sandy tracks—had always been on my list of things to do and was set to be a highlight of the trip, not to mention a challenging ride.

'Frank lives in La Paz, he said we could stay with him,' Robb added.

'Excellent!'

Amalia emitted a loud violent sigh and squared up to me, fixing furious eyes on mine.

'Right,' she announced with feeling. 'I'm telling you some-thing, we are *not* hanging around La Paz, OK? I'm not spending an-other bloody week in some dump. I'm serious.'

'Er, yeah, fine,' I agreed hastily. 'I don't particularly want to hang around there either, but we might as well visit Frank, seeing as we're there anyway?'

She rolled her eyes.

'As long as we only stay one night,' she said and climbed on her bike, staring straight ahead, her jaw set in defiance.

Robb's secret exit involved bumping over piles of rubble and bouncing in and out of ditches, but soon we were out of town and on a dramatic road cut into the mountainside around Lake Titicaca, with steep drops to our right and sheer jagged cliffs rising skyward on our left. The usual South American booby traps of ankle-hungry dogs and wheel-swallowing potholes appeared sporadically but not enough to detract from the beautiful views across the lake and the waving hands and eager smiles of the barefoot kids by the roadside.

As usual, the highway was empty, apart from the odd dishevelled pickup, so I was surprised by the appearance of a small group of animated locals waving their arms, trying to flag me down. They were standing next to their stationary car, but I knew better than to fall for these old tricks and I kept going without slowing down. If there was one rule of the road to be adhered to in this part of the world, this was it. Around the corner I saw Robb pulled over on his own, taking photos from a particularly spectacular cliff top. The sun's reflection scattered flecks of white gold across the electric blue ripples, providing a perfect snapshot of the lake, complete with snowcapped mountains in the distance.

'Hi,' I greeted him. 'You OK?'

'Yeah, fine. Beautiful, isn't it? Where's Amalia?'

'I don't know, hasn't she gone ahead? I thought she was behind you.'

'No, I haven't seen her, I just stopped to look at the view and wait for you guys, but—'

'Oh no!' I burst out, a horrible thought dawning on me, and I told Robb about the people trying to flag me down before the bend.

'This isn't good,' he said and we jumped on our bikes and swung a fast U-turn back up the road.

Robb arrived at the scene first. More people had gathered now and as I approached he began riding back towards me. He face was white with shock.

'It's not good, it's not good,' he was saying. 'I'm going to get help,' he shouted over his shoulder, roaring away at top speed.

The crowd had started to swell and I frantically pushed my way through. I didn't know what to expect but nothing could have prepared me for the horrific scene that met my eyes. At the centre of the throng was the most gruesome sight I have ever witnessed outside the movies. Amalia lay motionless in a pool of blood that poured from her mouth, nose and ears, her front teeth were smashed out, her chin was gashed open, her nose appeared to be broken and her right arm dangled limply at an agonizingly unnatural angle. Her leather jacket hung in shredded tatters, the visor of her helmet lay in the road, smashed and bloodstained, her luggage was scattered across the highway and twenty feet away, wedged vertically in a ditch between the road and the mountainside, was her motorcycle. Amalia had crashed.

Fifteen

I knelt down and took her hand. I could feel a pulse. She was alive.

'Amalia. Can you hear me?'

She let out a small moan in response. She was barely conscious. The blood and gore was stomach churning.

I'm not trained for this, I thought. What the hell do I do?

'Do you know your name?'

'Am . . . a . . . li . . . a.' She struggled to say it; even moving her lips was causing her obvious pain and more blood trickled from her mouth when she spoke.

'Do you know who I am?'

'Lo . . . is.' Her voice was so faint, I could barely hear her, but at least this was promising.

'Do you know where you are?'

She managed a weak no.

'Do you remember what happened?'

Again, no.

Her eyes closed and she lapsed into unconsciousness.

What on earth had caused her to wipe out like this? The road wasn't anything particularly demanding, a winding mountain route, but we'd ridden much tougher stuff than this. What had made Amalia veer across the road and crash face-first into the mountainside?

'Don't worry, you're going to be fine,' I said, trying to keep my voice calm. 'Don't worry about a thing, everything's going to be OK.' And I sat there, holding her hand, repeating this mantra over and over again, with nothing but blind optimism to back up my statement.

The people that had found her were gabbling their version of events at me in Spanish. They hadn't seen it happen, they saw the crashed bike first, and then found her, lying in the ditch; they had pulled her out and laid her on the roadside. The men were staring at the scene, shaking their heads, while the women rummaged in their bags for tissues and water to mop the blood from Amalia's face. I dug my first aid kit out from the depth of my luggage and set to work with some antiseptic wipes. I didn't know if this was the right thing to do, but it seemed better than doing nothing.

The sound of a bike caught my attention and I was glad to see Robb was back with good news.

'There's a naval base in Taquina, about twenty miles away.' He was visibly wired, still fired up on the adrenaline of his mission. 'They're going to send an ambulance, but I'm telling you, getting these Catholics to do anything on a Sunday is damn hard work.'

'Well done for sorting it out.'

'How's she doing?'

'Well, she's alive, thank God. But it's not looking good, drifting in and out of consciousness, she can't remember what happened.'

'What a mess,' he said, shaking his head.

The crowd of concerned onlookers was increasing by the minute and incredibly now included a doctor who happened to be passing with his family on a day trip. He was urgently trying to call for help on his mobile phone but there was no reception. Meanwhile, a matronly type with a kindly face and some basic English was taking charge of Amalia's comfort, but she had failed to grasp a fundamental piece of information about her patient.

'Please, I put this blanket on him,' she said, producing a heavy woven shawl from her car.

'We must support his head,' she told me, 'you have something for under his head?'

Amalia stirred and began moaning.

Oh no! I thought. Please don't wake up now.

'He must not move,' the matron was saying.

Amalia moaned again and tried to speak.

'We must support his head,' said the matron again.

I looked at Amalia; she was groaning in a painful effort to communicate. Oh God, maybe she can hear this. I whispered the all-important fact in the matron's ear, but the shock of my revelation shattered her efficient composure. She let out a cry of disbelief.

'DIOS MIO! ES UNA MUJER!' she wailed to the assembled crowd, sweeping a plump forearm across her brow and falling to her knees in shock.

Oh Amalia, I prayed, I really hope you can't hear this.

The feeling of helplessness was the worst thing. Once we'd made Amalia as comfortable as possible and mopped up some of the blood, all we could do was wait for the ambulance. But when an hour had passed and there was still no sign of it, my mantra of hope was sounding less and less convincing. Robb and a couple of men from the crowd used the hiatus to pull her motorcycle out of the ditch and gather up her strewn belongings.

'Well, the bike's come out of this a lot better than she has,' reported Robb. 'The handlebars are bent, some of the controls are broken, but that's about it. I guess the bike bottomed out in the ditch and she went forward into the cliff.'

'What are we going to do with it?'

'I'll sort out the bikes, you stay with her and go in the ambulance to the naval base. I've got a phone number for Frank in La Paz. I'm going to see if he can get a truck out here and I'll get all the bikes to his place.'

'OK, I'll get her to La Paz, to a proper hospital.'

Robb was writing out Frank's phone number when the ambulance finally showed up. At first I didn't realise that it was the ambulance, it could have been any old beat-up van stopping to see what the fuss was about. But two men in military garb stepped out carrying a stretcher, looking decidedly unimpressed about having to rescue a smashed-up gringa on the Lord's Day. They promptly scooped up Amalia and deposited her in the back of the vehicle without a word. Inside was a seat and little else. I took my place next to her and continued with my repetitious reassurances as we drove the twenty miles to Taquina, leaving the fate of our bikes and possessions in Robb's capable hands.

The troops at the naval base were standing by and leapt into action as soon as we arrived. Maybe they were just glad to get out of going to church, but they seemed a lot more obliging than the ambulance men. Within seconds, the stretcher was carried aloft by eight camouflage-clad soldiers, Amalia high on their shoulders like the Queen of Sheba. I couldn't help but smile to myself, thinking how much she would have enjoyed this moment. An outbuilding with a broken window and a crudely painted red cross on the door suggested itself as the medical wing. The room was sparse but clean, and an efficient young nurse began busying herself with syringes, swabs and painkillers in a reassuring manner. Amalia was coming back to consciousness now and calling my name in a pained low moan.

'Don't worry, you're at a hospital now,' I whispered as the nurse peeled away Amalia's shredded layers of clothing to reveal open wounds on her rib cage. An attempt to move her right arm increased the volume of the moans by several hundred decibels, but it was the nurse's decision to cut the sleeve off her jacket that caused the biggest howls. She even managed to string a few words of heated protestation together. But the nurse was having none of it and the crisp snipping of leather was drowned out by Amalia's semiconscious accusations of sartorial sabotage.

A shot of morphine, mighty enough to send even the most

hardened junkie running for cover, sent her off into what I hoped was a state of blissful oblivion, and I commandeered another ambulance to take her to the capital, posthaste.

'What is the best hospital in La Paz?' I asked the nurse.

'Hospital de Clinicas,' she said, adding, 'this is where tourists and embassy people go.'

'Please, you have money for diesel?' requested the ambulance driver, a middle-aged man with sad brown eyes. I handed over a pocketful of bolivianos and climbed in the back.

Thank God she doesn't know what's going on, I thought, as we approached our first obstacle. The main road in Taquina petered out at the edge of the lake and an ancient wooden ferry lay bobbing and idle. It wasn't much more than a few planks of wood lashed together, big enough for only a couple of cars. We were ushered on first and the ambulance banged and creaked up the shaky ramp onto the boat. A pickup truck, a few pedestrians and goats squeezed alongside us before the ferryman cast off and poled us across the water. It would have been a lovely experience under different circumstances, but the bright sunshine and striking beauty of the lake seemed cruelly out of sync with the horrific turn of events.

Still clutching Amalia's hand and whispering positive nothings, I thought about us packing the bikes this morning, planning the next leg of our ride and how innocently we had set off for yet another day on the road. And I thought about how you never know what's going to happen, and about how that was what I'd wanted—the uncertain unfolding of every day. *But not this! This isn't what I meant!* I scolded the God of Motorcycling silently. I thought about the number of times I'd been asked, 'Don't you get scared?' but you only get scared if you think about scary things. No motorcyclist wakes up every morning wondering if this will be the day of the big crash, it barely crosses your mind. You can't allow it to cross your mind, because if you did, you would never ride again.

The second we bumped back onto dry land, the ambulance driver, having clearly made this journey before, stepped on the gas with a startling ferocity in order to gain enough momentum to make it up the steep dirt track in front of us. The surface was dry, dusty mud, grooved by rain washouts and studded with rocks. It would have been fun on the bike but attempting it in a vintage ambulance carrying a comatose crash victim turned a spot of off-road action into a white-knuckle scramble. Amalia's stretcher pitched forward at the moment of acceleration, then rolled into the far wall as the ambulance negotiated an adverse camber. I grabbed hold of the stretcher, steadying it with one hand, legs braced, my other hand gripping my chair for support. Amalia began moaning again.

'Don't worry, we're going to the hospital,' I said for the umpteenth time that day, trying to sound calm as we screamed up the track in first gear, bumping over rocks to a sound track of metallic clanking noises beneath us.

We made our final lurch at the brow of the hill, landing on smooth tarmac in a billow of brown dust. Breathing a huge sigh of relief, I secured the runaway stretcher and settled in for the three-hour ride.

On the outskirts of La Paz the traffic thickened and the familiar shrieking horns and dastardly driving of a South American capital city closed in on us. The driver switched to rally mode again and I feared for Amalia's second accident of the day as we overtook trucks on blind corners, drove down the wrong side of the road and shot straight across junctions at breakneck speed. The city flew past the window, sucking us in, a claustrophobic swarm of people, clapped-out cars, ragged dogs and sweeping dishevelment. And then we were at the hospital and Amalia was being rushed into intensive care and the ambulance had gone and I was filling in hospital forms and phoning her travel insurance company in England and calling her mum and trying to track down her boyfriend's number.

The latter proved tricky, as all I knew about him was that his name was Ziggy. The other facts that Amalia had shared with me, while revealing in many ways, were not very useful to my detective work. Eventually, I called Austin to see if he could phone around our friends in London to seek out Ziggy, but also as an excuse to hear his calm, reassuring voice in this nightmare. As soon as he answered the phone I blurted out the whole horrific story.

'OK, don't worry,' he said with knee-weakening authority. 'I'll find Ziggy and call him. You get on with what you've got to do there.'

When I called back an hour later Austin had tracked Ziggy down, broken the news to him and booked him a flight to La Paz.

And that was it: I'd done everything I had to do. With no more tasks and responsibilities to keep me occupied, the horror of the day swept over me, knocking me down like a tidal wave. Night was falling, and I was suddenly aware of being alone in a strange dark city. I sat in the waiting area and noticed I was shaking.

'Senorita,' said a voice.

The doctor had stepped silently out of the intensive care room and was standing in front of me. He was young, with a serious but kind face.

'How is she?' I asked in Spanish.

He shook his head slowly and in a solemn voice delivered his verdict: *'Muy grave, muy grave.'* Very serious.

'I can speak English to you,' he said with a gentle smile, 'I trained at medical school in Manchester.'

For some reason, this passing reference to my homeland had a strangely calming effect.

'There is a serious problem,' he continued. 'The skull is fractured.'

I gulped.

'Around here, above the ear.' He traced a line on the side of his head. 'She took the impact on her jaw; the jawbone was pushed back into the skull, causing the fracture.' He had a strangely formal, textbook style of speaking, like a Japanese businessman.

I nodded, wincing inwardly.

'The jaw is broken, of course, the nose too. She has lost some teeth. Her right arm is quite badly damaged, it is dislocated at the shoulder and elbow. She may have broken ribs . . . what is wrong? Are you all right?'

I was suddenly overcome by the severity of the situation, the physical wreckage involved and its implications. I tried to explain this to him but I couldn't make myself clear. I could hardly process my thoughts, let alone verbalise them.

'You are in shock,' he said authoritatively, 'but do not worry, she will recover and we can perform reconstructive surgery on her face.'

'Are you going to send her back to England?'

'No, she must not be moved. She will be here for several weeks, maybe longer.'

I nodded again.

'You can leave now, she is under sedation. You can come again in the morning.'

What happens now? I thought. Where am I going? I dug out Frank's phone number. Maybe Robb would be there by now. Frank's wife, Ann, answered the phone and was so kind it choked me up. Frank had got hold of a truck, she said, he'd driven out to meet Robb and the bikes in Taquina, they were on their way back now.

'Come and stay with us,' she said without hesitation, 'stay as long as you need.'

Ann's work was linked to the German embassy and their house was in an exclusive suburb of the city, where diplomats and embassy folk lived in comparative luxury, on quiet streets, safe behind locked steel gates and complex alarm systems. Robb and Frank arrived shortly after I did, in the hired pickup, full of our bikes and our luggage. The warm welcome and cosy security of a real home was just what I needed and I was immensely grateful not to be alone on this night. We were ushered into the house, where wine and food appeared before us, and Robb and I spent the evening spewing garbled versions of the day's events, reliving every moment, comparing notes, theorizing and speculating wildly, all in some urgent cathartic attempt to make sense of what had happened.

It took me hours to fall asleep that night. Every time I shut my eyes, the image of Amalia's bloodied face floated before me. I passed the dreaded hour between three and four writing a long rambling entry in my diary, finally dropping off as dawn broke.

The following morning's visit to the hospital found Amalia in her own private room, heavily bandaged with an array of drips plugged into her arms. She was conscious, hopped up on morphine but more lucid than I had expected. According to the hovering nurses, she wasn't allowed to speak, but as soon as Robb and I walked in, she couldn't help herself.

'What happened? What happened?' she said in an unrecognisable croaky slur.

It was a plaintive, desperate appeal and the change in her voice was bizarre.

'We don't know,' we said helplessly. 'Can you remember anything at all?'

She shook her head as best she could. Her lack of memory was driving her crazy, and she couldn't bear the idea that she would never know what had caused her to have such a terrible crash. She kept repeating herself and forgetting our conversations of just minutes earlier. Over and over again she asked us, 'What happened? Do you know what happened?' and each time we gave her the same answer. The nurses gave us a sharp ticking-off for breaking the no-speaking rule, and for the remainder of our visit we communicated with notebook and pen.

I sought out the doctor for a full report in preparation for the phone call to Amalia's mother, a task weighing heavy on my shoulders.

'She will be having the reconstructive surgery tonight,' he said. 'We will rebuild the nose and set the broken bones in her face. Overall, she is doing fine. However, there is some swelling of the brain; we are monitoring it, but we may have to drill holes in her skull to drain the fluid and blood if the pressure becomes too much. But we need your permission to go ahead with this.'

My permission? Drilling holes in her head!

In the absence of a family member, it seemed the buck was stopping with me, not a situation I was entirely comfortable with, especially when it came to skull-drilling decisions. I was going to have to run this one past Mum back in England. I went to speak to Amalia, but she seemed more distant than before and only vaguely aware of what I was saying.

'They're going to operate on you today,' I told her, trying to suggest that this was something to look forward to, 'they're going to rebuild your nose.'

This piece of news seemed to resonate.

'Give them a photo,' she said in her newfound gurgle.

'No speak!' squawked the sister, a rotund Bolivian woman.

'A photo? Of what?'

'Me . . . my nose.'

'Er, OK . . .'

'No speak! You no speak!' said the Sister, annoyed.

'Don't want a Bolivian nose . . .' slurred Amalia as the nurses homed in, shooing us away.

'We've got to leave now, Amalia, we'll be back tomorrow,' I said, as they began fiddling with her various drips and dressings.

'What happened? Do you know what happened?' she was still saying as we bid our farewells.

Our visits continued along these lines for several days. We would go to the hospital every morning and evening, and after a while there were definite signs of recovery, with Amalia becoming slightly more coherent and staying awake for longer each time. After each morning visit, I would pitch up at the Cheap International Calls shop, settle into a booth that smelled of cigarette smoke and stale sweat, and call Amalia's mother with regular updates on her daughter's condition. Next on the list was the travel insurance company, whose demands for information and minutiae about the crash seemed endless. And eventually I got hold of Amalia's boyfriend,

Ziggy, to be greeted with the good news that he would be flying out in a few days' time.

It seemed likely that Amalia would be able to return to England in the near future, so the next job was to get her bike back home too. Frank came to the rescue on this count and began the tediously laborious process of researching international shipping options. Robb, meanwhile, being a technical-type guy, had set up a dedicated e-mail account on his Web site for messages of support to Amalia, which he would print off each day and bring to the hospital. Meanwhile, back in the ward, the doctor informed me that the pressure behind Amalia's skull was reaching a dangerous level, and with her mother's blessing, the drilling would go ahead. It was all hands to the pump.

The rest of the time Robb and I whiled away roaming around La Paz, occasionally hooking up with passing motorcycle travellers for a few beers and an exchange of crash horror stories, or we kicked our heels around Frank's place, the three of us drinking nerve-jangling amounts of coffee in the garden or fiddling with the bikes while Frank broke national stereotypes, entertaining us with hilarious tittle-tattle of Bolivian life, gossiping with the fervour of a bored housewife and punctuating every monologue with a deafening shriek of laughter. However, his Germanic roots betrayed him once inside the house, and particularly in the neatly ordered kitchen. With Ann bringing home the bratwurst, the traditional roles had been reversed and this was most definitely Frank's domain.

'Nooooo!' he screeched at Robb. 'That's not how you chop an onion! Look, watch this. . . .'

THWACK! THWACK! THWACK!

We'd offered to cook dinner for him and Ann, but he couldn't resist watching us at work.

'What are you boiling water for? Don't use that pan, you American idiot! What are you doing? No wonder the rest of the world hates the Yanks! Too many herbs! Who put the blender in here?! *Mein Gott!* What is this doing in the fridge? Who are these philistines in my kitchen? Get out, get out! All of you!'

He leapt around the room, restoring order to the chaos in a blur of OCD, and although his Teutonic tongue was firmly in his cheek, we stuck to takeaway pizzas after that.

I met Ziggy at the airport the following day. I didn't know what to expect or even what he looked like, and I was curious to see what sort of man had softened Amalia's heart. The taxi ride across La Paz at six-thirty in the morning provided me with a grim view of the city's dispossessed, a world away from the clean streets and Range Rovers of the diplomatic district. The wide, brown river running through the middle of the city was home to hundreds of people, scattered along its banks under makeshift shelters, surrounded by litter, animal carcasses and human waste. But Ziggy beamed a ray of sunshine into an otherwise bleak morning, and although this was our first meeting, by the time our cab was speeding towards the hospital, I knew Amalia would be in good hands. As one of very few gringos in the airport lounge, he was easy to pick out: a tall, slim denim-clad figure with tousled brown hair, seventies Elvis sideburns and a typically English rosy complexion. He looked fresh-faced, smiley and relaxed despite his mammoth twenty-four-hour journey from London.

'It's all a bit strange,' he confided once we were in the cab heading back into town, 'we'd only been together for a month before she left, and here I am doing the knight in shining armour bit.'

'Well, I think her mum's too old to come out. Have you spoken to her at all?'

'Yeah, I said I'd call her every day like you've been doing. She's a really sweet woman, she said she'd sort me out for all the costs involved too, which was nice of her.'

'Yeah, she said that to me too, and for Robb; it's not much, though, just hiring the truck and the phone calls to England. Actually, I owe Amalia some money from when I lost my cash card in Peru, so it might be easier to knock it off that.'

The taxi pulled up outside the hospital.

'You're in for a bit of a shock,' I warned him, 'she looks quite different from the last time you saw her.'

Amalia was recovering from the skull-drilling operation and was still knocked out. Her head was completely bandaged and her face was covered in dressings from her nose rebuild. Two plastic tubes appeared to be growing out of her forehead through the bandages.

'She was worried she'd get a Bolivian nose,' I whispered to Ziggy.

'What? You mean with one nostril? What's that coming out of her head?' he asked.

I explained about the hole drilling.

'So, those tubes let the fluid out?'

'I guess so. All a bit gruesome, isn't it?'

'But what's on the end of them?' he said, leaning forward.

I looked closer and had to stifle my laughter. A transparent latex glove had been attached to the end of each tube to collect the fluid. They lay floppy and empty on each side of Amalia's head, except for a small amount of pink liquid in the fingertips. Ziggy was laughing too, incredulous.

'They're certainly resourceful, these Bolivians, you've got to give 'em that.'

When we returned with Robb that evening, the latex gloves were bulging with the pink liquid and sticking off the sides of her head like a pair of cartoon antlers. Even Amalia found it amusing, which was surely a good sign.

Over the next few days Amalia made good progress and seemed to be in better shape at each visit, although her memory still failed her on occasion. With Ziggy around she was beginning to return to her old self and he was running about, patiently attending to her every need. Robb and I hadn't given much thought to our respective trips over the last couple of weeks, but with Ziggy now stationed in La Paz, we broached the subject of moving on with Amalia.

'Yes, yes, you get going,' she croaked from her bed, then to my utmost surprise she said to me, 'I know I made such a fuss about not hanging around in La Paz, and now you've been here for ages, all because of me.'

'It doesn't matter a bit,' I told her. And I meant it.

'It's been quite an eventful day,' said Ziggy, 'we had a visit from the British ambassador this afternoon.'

'Oh really! Was he any help, or was it just a social call?'

'He was a bit of a funny character, really,' said Ziggy with an amused expression, 'he just talked about what a lonely life it is being an ambassador, and how he only gets to meet British people when they're about to die.'

Robb and I made our final visit to the Hospital de Clinicas the following evening. We uttered awkward farewells and halfhearted promises for the future. Ziggy came downstairs to see us off.

'I mentioned to Amalia about the money,' he said, 'y'know, that her mum was going to reimburse you. I said it might be easier to knock it off what you owed her. . . .' He was looking slightly uncomfortable.

'Oh yeah, right?'

'Erm, well, Her Ladyship,' he jerked his head in the direction of Amalia's room, 'says she wants to see receipts. . . .'

'Receipts?'

'Er, yeah, y'know, for the costs involved over the last couple of weeks.'

Ziggy shuffled around sheepishly.

'Don't worry about it,' I told him, 'I'll just put the full amount in her bank account, it's easier.'

'Her mum will sort you both out,' said Ziggy. 'I'm sorry. . . .'

'Don't worry, it's only about a hundred quid,' I assured him.

Ziggy managed a wan smile, wished us good luck and good-bye, and disappeared up the stairs, back to his duties. Robb and I returned to Frank and Ann for our last night in La Paz. The nervous excitement of getting back on the road was palpable, but there was something different about it this time.

Sixteen

Robb and I decided to ride together for a while, despite our bikes occupying opposite ends of the power spectrum, but I assured him that if the overleisurely pace of the Serow became too much to bear, he could roar off into the sunset with no hard feelings. As we shimmied through morning rush hour in La Paz, a steep-hill start in the city centre served up the final insult to the struggling Serow. Red light turned to green but the bike simply refused to budge, stalling every time I tried to pull away. The honking horns and bellowing suggestions from the impatient motorists in my wake didn't help matters, and eventually I was forced to dismount and push the bike over the brow of the hill. But with La Paz nestling in a deep chasm, flanked by mountains on all sides, the only way out was up, and by the time I reached the city limits Robb was gathering dust. Thankfully he seemed more amused than annoyed by my predicament, but it did beg questions about our proposed route.

'I don't think you're going to make it over the Salar on your bike,' he said. 'Four hundred miles of deep gravel tracks, it just doesn't have the power at this altitude. Also, the rainy season has started now and I don't want to put my bike through all that salt water.'

I knew he was right but I was bitterly disappointed about missing out on riding across the giant salt flats. But there was no point

in forcing the issue; the Salar de Uyuni was an inhospitable and potentially dangerous stretch, and much as it hurt me to admit it, the
air-starved Serow just wasn't up to the challenge. It was the one and
only time I cursed my choice of machine.

'I reckon we should head into Chile and get back to the coast,' he
suggested, 'it'll be hot and sunny and I could do with some of that.'

A quick glance at the map confirmed that the quickest route to
the Pacific Ocean was a three-hundred-mile ride west into Chile
over the Bolivian altiplano, the high plane. I noticed a few ominous
altitude figures on the map, hovering around the fifteen-thousand-
feet mark, and I groaned audibly.

'It's gonna take me a while,' I warned Robb.

It's true to say that the pair of us were feeling a bit strange, being back on the road after the events of the last few weeks. Amalia's
accident was still raw in our memories and the inevitable thought,
'It could have been me . . . it still could be me,' lay at the forefront
of our minds. When we happened upon a detour around some
roadworks, taking us along a rough track with patches of deep sand,
the two of us went to pieces, creeping along at walking pace, wob-
bling through the sand and gripping the bars in mortal fear, like a
couple of kids riding their bicycles without training wheels for the
first time.

'What the hell is wrong with me? Man, I am spooked!' exclaimed Robb, dismayed at his shaken nerves, and I must admit I felt
a bit of a wimp too. Every stretch of dirt road or gravelly corner
prompted a nervous deceleration, as Amalia's bloodied visage travelled with us across the Bolivian altiplano.

The eerie expanse lived up to its name of high plain, leaving us
in no doubt we were way up in the ether. The bleak, windswept
flatland gave way to high desert and we found ourselves riding
through a vast rocky landscape as cold as Alaska and as barren as the
moon. Reddish rock formations broke up the otherwise flat emptiness and the only sign of the human hand at work was the occasional yellow, diamond-shaped warning sign featuring a silhouette

of a llama, prompting the 'I'm in Bolivia!' photo opportunity. The moose that had graced similar signs in Alaska, and the warnings about migrating Mexican families in Tijuana, seemed to belong to a past life, as if they were part of a fanciful road-hazards dream I'd once had.

As I mused over the remainder of my journey, I realised with a mixture of relief and sadness that this would be my final crossing of the Andes, those mountains that had instilled so much awe in me, but caused me so much aggravation too. After months at altitude, the very words *sea level* had acquired an almost mythical quality, a Garden of Eden, a promised land where I could breathe easily again, where my shampoo bottle didn't explode on opening and where I could ride my motorcycle at the exhilarating speed of, woohoo, fifty-five miles an hour!

Due to my relaxed pace it took us all day to reach the border and we rolled into the Chilean entry point tired and cold. But our spirits soared instantly thanks to a gob-smacking travel brochure scene of snowcapped mountains, reflected in deep blue lakes, themselves brimming with pink flamingos.

But there was no time for bird-watching, it was down to business with the border guards, and soon Robb and I were hunched over a couple of exhaustive customs declaration forms, scratching our heads and chewing our pens in rapt concentration.

'Have you got to question nine yet?' I asked.

'No, what's that?'

'Are you carrying about your person, or does your luggage contain, any animal semen?' I quoted.

'Er, not the last time I checked,' Robb assured me.

'Are you sure? Frank's dog was rather fond of you.'

The difference in the two countries was immediately apparent. The Chilean offices were clean, smart and spacious, in comparison to the breeze-block shack at the Bolivian exit. Here they even had computers, not that it speeded up the process much, but maybe the

The difference between North and South America can be boiled down to their caution signs.

system was overloaded with top secret reports of illegal semen smuggling.

With night falling fast and the temperature following suit, we decided to call it a day. The tiny hamlet of Parinacota, an ancient Aymara Indian community with a population of just six families, was our nearest port of call. Tucked away in the mountains down a dirt track and cowering in the shadow of the enormous, and perfectly symmetrical, Parinacota volcano, the village consisted of a few dusty streets surrounding a sixteenth-century church, lined with rows of single-storey dwellings, all of whitewashed mud and stone construction.

'This place is cool, like an abandoned spaghetti Western set,' remarked Robb.

'Yeah, it's amazing, but it doesn't look like it'll have anywhere to

Robb and my bikes in the sixteenth-century Aymaran village of Parinacota, Chile

stay, maybe we'll have to camp.' But a passing elderly villager, recognising two tired travellers, led us to a small stone shack, empty except for a wood-burning stove and a couple of wooden beds, piled high with heavy blankets for the freezing night ahead. Our refuge had a dirt floor and no running water or electricity, but we didn't mind, we were delighted with our find, and it seemed a fitting return to the simplicity of life on the road after the high-octane intensity of the past few weeks. The temperature dropped below freezing outside, but indoors the stove blazed with a hunger, steadily eating away at the woodpile as we tucked into our own welcome if nutrient-deficient supper of potato crisps and biscuits.

'This is so fuckin' cool,' said Robb vehemently, taking photos of our humble but cosy surroundings, and I had to agree with him.

In the morning, the fire had died but it was warmer outdoors than in and the sun was already glaring high in the sky, bleaching out the white-painted walls of the village and the snowy peak of the volcano. Our backyard was still in shade and when I stepped outside, toothbrush and towel in hand, I discovered the water barrel had frozen over during the night. With a deep breath, I broke the layer of ice for a wash that took my understanding of the word *invigorating* to a deeper level.

Somehow, Robb had persuaded a sweet old lady in the opposite shack to knock up some scrambled eggs and coffee for our breakfast.

'Aah, this is the life!' he declared as we sat on a couple of up-turned buckets in her yard, surrounded by chickens and heaps of pre-industrial-age clobber.

'And it's literally downhill from now on,' I observed, ecstatic about this fact.

Sure enough, we were soon making a swift and dramatic descent towards the Pacific coast, plunging into a long-forgotten world of abundant greenery and lush valleys bursting with trees and flowers. By the time we hit the seaside town of Arica, we had dropped almost fifteen thousand feet, and to my utmost joy, the Serow was galloping along like the old days, those pesky Andes just a distant memory. Not for the first time on this journey did I feel as though I'd passed through an invisible curtain and entered another world.

Chile was a complete culture shock. Things worked. Toilets flushed, taps produced running water and restaurant menus reflected the contents of the kitchen. In the grocery shops, the goods were out on display; you could touch them, pick them up, put them in a basket and pay for them at the checkout. No more pointing through a metal grill at a dusty shelf behind the counter. But most striking of all was the return of the leisure pursuit. The Chileans had picnics, went Rollerblading and had fully embraced the concept of retail therapy. All of a sudden, life was orderly and efficient again. This was good news in many respects, it just meant that I had to be orderly and efficient too, and to be honest, I was a little bit out of practice. Rules of the road were being blatantly obeyed, which was disconcerting as I was now accustomed, and even quite partial, to a more freestyle approach to driving. Riding on the pavement appeared to be frowned upon, as was my disregard for one-way streets, red traffic lights and lane markings. But training myself to ride without the constant use of my horn and reacquainting myself with my turn signals proved to be my biggest challenge, with Robb regularly pulling alongside me, making the 'Turn your goddamn indicators off!' sign with his left hand.

However, Chile's civilised Euro vibe was restricted solely to the worlds of culture and commerce, and the elements and geography were still to be reckoned with, something we had to take seriously as we headed south on the Pan Americana towards Santiago. In this long skinny country sandwiched between the Pacific and the Andes, there was no avoiding the Atacama Desert, six hundred startling miles of nothing but sand and rock, with the thirst-inducing claim of being the 'driest place on earth.' A sign reading NEXT GAS 360 MILES saw us filling our jerry cans to the brim and Dumpster-diving for Coke bottles to carry extra fuel. With these precious emergency rations bungeed on top of our luggage, along with as much water as we could carry, we set off into the emptiness ready for some long hot days in the saddle. There was nothing in this scorched brown land, not a soul, not even a single yellow warning sign, although what hazards would there be to flag up? A plain yellow diamond? WARNING! NOTHING AHEAD.

As ever, I wallowed in the dreamy, mindless riding of a long straight desert road. After the trials and trails of the Andean countries, I had forgotten that motorcycling could be an almost soothing exercise. These days were searing, hypnotic and endless, but when the evenings turned cool we veered across the dusty land towards the ocean, where we slept on the deserted beaches and paddled in rock pools amongst Technicolor sea anemones.

Although I was no stranger to wilderness, the Atacama was in a different league. It was utterly devoid of life; not a cactus, not a lizard, not even a fly troubled this unearthly place. There were parts of the desert where rainfall had never been recorded. But despite this hostile, almost lunar environment, nitrate had been mined here in the last century and the abandoned workers' settlements still remained, preserved in the arid climes. We explored the eerie ghost town of Humberstone, creeping around its silent dusty streets and peeking into houses where the miners once lived. Ancient machinery lay redundant in the sand and even the town's bandstand and schoolhouse were still standing, both destined to a lifetime of silence.

Out on the highway, fellow road users were few and far between, so it was quite a novelty to catch up with a long line of low-loaders one morning, trucking along at a tortoise pace. They were transporting the biggest sections of concrete pipe I have ever seen, although admittedly my experience in matters of industrial drainage is limited. These monstrous loads filled both lanes of the Pan-American Highway as they crept along in front of us like giant snails, reducing our progress to a tedious crawl.

'Let's get round these guys,' called out Robb, peering down the side of the monster trucks for an escape route. We gassed it along the edge of the road, losing count of the resigned bored faces we passed in the truck cabs, but as we opened up the throttle for our final burst to the front of the line, the police escort vehicle leading this concrete caravan blocked us. The strong arm of the law was not something we had bargained on in the middle of the desert but Robb did the decent thing and drew alongside the driver's open window.

'OK to pass?' he asked in Spanish.

It didn't seem like such an unreasonable request to me, but it was all it took for the policeman's Latino fury to be unleashed. He yelled and screamed from the window, waving his white-gloved hands wildly, like a possessed Baptist preacher speaking in tongues. Robb, not understanding a word, but quite enjoying the spectacle, continued to ride along next to him, watching with amusement as he beat his fists on the steering wheel with uncontained rage, a torrent of Spanish expletives pouring forth from his mouth.

'Is that a no then?' enquired Robb.

But his continuing presence only enraged the officer further and finally he drew on his limited but highly effective knowledge of the English language to make his point perfectly clear.

'NO! FUCK YOU! NO! NO! FUCK YOU! NO!' shrieked the policeman with uncontrollable fury.

Hovering behind, I could only surmise there was a glut of American cop shows on the Chilean cable channels. We rode along obediently until a few minutes later the white-gloved hand appeared from the window and calmly waved us on.

With Chile's own Maniac Cop chewing on our dust, we left the Atacama Desert behind and entered a softer, greener land of palm trees, radiant bougainvillea and a craggy coastline identical to that of Northern California.

'It's just like being at home,' Robb commented, gazing at the rocky cliffs and ocean spray.

'We're the same latitude south from the equator as California is north,' I noticed on the map. Only now, eight months into my real-life geography lesson, was I realising how the land and climate of the northern and southern hemispheres mirrored each other.

'So that must mean it'll be getting colder and mountainous again soon, just like Canada and Alaska,' I concluded.

But we decided not to dwell too much on this thought.

Back in civilisation again, I picked up my e-mails and much to my excitement discovered a message from Rachel, my amiga of the Mexican leg, announcing her imminent arrival in Chile. She would be flying into Santiago from Panama City in a week's time and her bike was due to arrive at the port the following day. We'd kept in touch over the last few months and I knew she'd been in Central America, riding with Simon again, but there was no mention of him in her message.

'Looks like there'll be three of us for Christmas,' I said to Robb, relating the news.

'Cool, we should rent a cabin or something, down in the Lake District in southern Chile,' he said. 'I'll start checking it out, it's only a couple of weeks away.'

The festive spirit was in full swing in Santiago, a city that reminded me more of Madrid than any Latin American capital I had encountered. Although its First World European atmosphere made us feel at home on one hand, as a couple of displaced residents of the northern hemisphere, there was something peculiar about gearing up for Christmas in the roasting heat of the summer sun. Conversely, the shopping-mad Santiagans didn't appear to find anything strange in strolling around the baking streets in T-shirts, sandals and sunglasses, buying up armfuls of supposedly seasonal decorations relating to snow, frost and reindeers.

Early one morning, I was awoken by a knock at my hotel room door and a familiar voice on the other side.

'Lois, it's Rachel!'

We greeted each other excitedly and launched straight into a marathon catch-up session.

'So, what's been going on?' I said. 'I thought you were travelling with Simon again.'

'Well, after I left you in Mexico, I went back to London to work and did some supply teaching, to get some money to come out and travel again.'

'That must have been a bit of a shock to the system.'

'Yeah, it was a nightmare. East London comprehensive, the kids don't want to learn anything, especially not French, and most of the boys are bigger than me. Anyway, it's bearable if you know it's going to end.'

'Go on. . . .'

'While I was in London, Simon came back too; he had some stuff to sort out with his flat. So we got together . . .'

'You said you weren't going to!' I laughed out loud, thinking of all the times my friends and I had gone back on similarly bold statements.

'I know, I know, but, well . . . y'know . . .' she said, laughing sheepishly.

'Yes, yes, a woman has her needs. Anyway . . .'

'Simon had left his bike in Texas, so we decided to go back together and ride two-up on his bike to Mexico City, pick up my bike from Juan's and carry on through Central America together. We were getting along fine, but after a while it was the usual thing, I couldn't keep up with him, he was getting annoyed with me.'

'Well, his bike is a 650 and you're on a 250, so . . .'

'I know, but anyway, in Panama City he said he wanted to go to Colombia on his own. I didn't want to go to Colombia anyway, so I decided to ship my bike to Chile instead.'

'Yikes! So no hard feelings? Or is it all off, or what?'

'Well, no, oh, I don't know. We're still in touch.'

'He'll be lost without you!' I predicted.

Rachel looked unconvinced.

'I just cramp his style,' she said bitterly; 'y'know what blokes are like, they have this idea of travelling around the world, a lone wolf, conquering the local women and all that. Especially somewhere like South America, it all sounds so exotic.'

'Yes, all those pictures of Brazilian women wearing skimpy thongs.'

'Exactly.'

'You wait,' I said, trying to raise her spirits, 'once he's spent a few weeks riding all day in the pouring rain and reading crap paperbacks in a grotty hotel room, he'll be pining for you.'

We banged on Robb's door, made the necessary introductions and the three of us went out for breakfast.

'I've sorted out a shit-hot place for Christmas,' Robb announced animatedly, 'a cabin in the Lake District, it's got views of an active volcano and a hot tub. How fuckin' cool is that?'

We agreed that this plan was indeed a most agreeable one. I suppose it should have seemed odd, three virtual strangers planning a Christmas together, each of us thousands of miles from our homes and families. But it didn't feel particularly strange to me, and I took this as a barometer reading for how life on the road, solo or amongst strangers, had turned from novelty to normality over the last eight months. How long have I got, I wondered, before normality turns to tedium? And how long can I go on seeking novelty before the very act of seeking it becomes tedious, and there is no more novelty? The thought terrified me.

Rachel and I left Robb tinkering with his bike while we went to collect Rachel's from the port. It was a relatively straightforward experience once we'd located Fernando, the repulsively slimy shipping agent who sped us around the docks in his car, doing wheel spins and handbrake turns and showing off like a teenager who's just passed his driving test. As Rachel and I hung on for dear life, exchanging looks that suggested a mixture of pity and loathing for our testosterone-charged chauffeur, I spotted a large ornate samurai sword under the passenger seat.

'Look,' I whispered to Rachel, pointing at the weapon.

Fernando, listening in, leant round from the driver's seat with a skin-crawling leer. He picked up the sword and placed it on Rachel's lap.

'It is to keep the women in their place,' he said, winking at us in the rearview mirror before cackling a maniacal laugh and wheel-spinning off towards the loading bay, narrowly missing a pile of shipping containers.

'Here is your motorcycle,' he announced, taking us into a dark empty warehouse. But when Rachel discovered her top box had been broken into whilst in transit and emptied of everything, including her tools, Fernando's interest in us waned. He just shrugged his shoulders.

'The men on the ship, they are at sea for two weeks, they are very bored, what you think they going to do? Huh?'

Robb, Rachel and I left Santiago the next morning, heading south for the lakes and volcanoes of southern Chile, and our Christmas in the sun. After the Amalia experience I was a little bit apprehensive about the dynamics of group riding. Rachel and I had a good track record, but I wondered if three might turn out to be a crowd, and I feared the two-girls-one-boy configuration was a combination more suited to porn films than long-distance motor-cycle travel. But it seemed we were going to get along OK, despite the obvious chalk and cheesiness of my riding companions. Although Robb's Yankee confidence tended towards brashness at times, it was tempered by a laid-back side and a healthy team spirit, as well as the surprising revelation of a theology degree, which at first I took to be a joke. And Rachel, I knew, was polite enough to keep her anti-American stance to herself, although as we filled up with fuel on the outskirts of Santiago, I did see her looking scepti-cally at the sticker on Robb's gas tank depicting a horned skull and the message LIVE, RIDE, DIE.

'D'you want one for your bike?' said Robb, but she politely de-clined the offer.

'How about this one?' he said, displaying his latest acquisition, a sticker bearing the single word BOLLOX!

'Er, no thank you,' said Rachel.

It took us three long days to reach our cabin in time for Christ-mas, including one whopping day's ride of 375 miles, not a major feat for Robb on his one-litre beast, but for Rachel and me it was a gruelling slog, flat-out all day, only stopping for fuel and coffee and for Robb to make mocking comments about our slow bikes.

'That was the longest ride of my trip so far,' I observed at the end of the day as I staggered off the bike like a cripple, 'in fact, that was the longest ride of my life!'

'Yeah, me too,' groaned Rachel, performing some yoga stretches.

'Well done, girls,' said Robb, like a sadistic personal trainer after a particularly brutal workout.

But our good progress was hampered by a mysterious electrical failure on my bike, which saw me conking out halfway up a volcano and coasting back down to tarmac, praying for a miracle. The God of Motorcycling was smiling on me this time and after much fiddling by Robb and myself, it turned out to be one of those inexplicable faults that miraculously respond to a wiggling of wires. But I saw this incident as a warning sign that the Serow was feeling the strain and I feared for the little bike's well-being on the last leg of the trip. Ushuaia was less than two thousand miles away now, but the terrain and weather conditions of this final stretch across the wilds of Patagonia would be its ultimate test. The majority of the route was on unpaved roads through some extreme territory. First, over six hundred miles along the Carretera Austral, a rugged frontier highway through the most southerly and impenetrable part of Chile. And then down the infamous Ruta 40 in Argentina, another six hundred miles of gravel road cutting south across the Patagonian wilderness, renowned for its desolation, its terrible condition and the battering westerly winds with speeds of up to a hundred miles an hour.

With all this looming, we made the most of our temporary easy life in the Chilean sun. South of Santiago, the scenery was more Californian than ever; vineyards and fruit orchards spread out across the land and the air smelled sweet and warm. But as we approached the Lake District the setting made a dramatic shift towards the alpine, with waterfalls spilling through the steep wooded mountains, and snowy peaks dominating the skyline for miles around. Beautiful as it was, it signified the end of the gentle, fertile land, and from now on we knew that things could only get rougher, tougher and colder.

Christmas was spent in a time-honoured fashion: overeating and binge drinking followed by a guilty attempt at a walk on Boxing Day. But as I had feared, after three days cooped up in the cabin, Robb was showing signs of an estrogen overdose.

'Jesus Christ! Can you two talk about something interesting for once?' he spluttered in an uncharacteristic display of annoyance, following one too many references to boys and female bodily functions. There was a moment of uncomfortable silence.

'Er . . . how about bikes, what's your ultimate bike?' said Rachel hurriedly, in a diplomatic attempt to defrost the cabin.

'Ah well . . .' said Robb, already looking happier, and he proceeded to bombard us with details of his killer machine, complete with the type of shocks, exhaust and handlebars he favoured.

Maybe there was something about the cabin itself that had caused the mood to sour. Although quaint and rustic with a twee, cottagey interior, there were a few telltale new-agey trappings in sight, and it seemed there was a more sinister side to our holiday home. We had arrived laden with groceries and Christmas cheer to find the place immaculately arranged for our impending visit. The towels were folded, the beds were made, the kitchen was stocked with all the gadgets we could ever need, but lying on the glass table, displayed for maximum exposure, was the only book in the house, a weighty tome by the name of *The Urantia Book*.

'What is this?' said Rachel, leafing through the pages. 'Oh dear, this is weird. Where did you find this place, Robb?'

'On the Internet, it's owned by an American woman. I spoke to her on the phone, she seemed OK, although she did get a bit funny when she found out we were on motorcycles.'

We all agreed this made her an idiot.

A closer inspection of *The Urantia Book* revealed it to be the bible of some religious cult, written not by human hand, apparently, but by a collective of extraterrestrial entities. It also claimed that the earth was created by angels, and expressed a number of more suspect ideas as well, such as an enthusiasm for eugenics, including references to 'inferior and superior people' with the 'indigo' people falling into the former category, suffering as they did from an innate 'backwardness' and a 'slow but long-continued racial deterioration.'

'Listen to this,' quoted Rachel. ' "It is neither tenderness nor altruism to bestow futile sympathy upon degenerate human beings, unsalvable, abnormal and inferior mortals." '

'Oh dear, that's us in trouble then.'

'And there's no such word as *unsalvable*!'

Feeling slightly soiled by our foray into the creepy world of the Urantians, we hid the book in the back of a cupboard, cracked open a bottle of Chilean Merlot and speculated on the mental health of our landlady.

Two thousand four burst into view in the form of a dazzling fireworks display and boisterous street party in the nearby town of Puerto Arenas. The Chileans celebrated in style, racing each other around the town square and kissing with typical Latin passion in the middle of the road. But the rambunctious community spirit only amplified our displacement, and although we three outsiders toasted in the New Year with a plasticky clink of our disposable cups of champagne, our hearts and thoughts were elsewhere, somewhere far away in the northern hemisphere. Mine in a corner of northwest London with a twinkly eyed Austin, Rachel's somewhere on the Pan-American Highway in deepest Colombia, and Robb's? Well, he wasn't letting on, but I was guessing it was somewhere with lots of bikes, babes 'n' beer.

With the New Year came an announcement: due to technical matters our riding trio was to be disbanded. Robb's laptop had broken and getting it fixed meant a long ride back to a dealer in Santiago, leaving Rachel and me to continue south together into Patagonia.

'So, you've nearly made it, Lois, Ushuaia's just down the road,' said Rachel. She was very good about indulging my goal-orientated motorcycling, despite its silly Anglo-Saxonness.

'Well, not quite. Are you ready for a thousand miles of dirt roads, bleak, inhospitable wilderness and gale-force winds on a knackered two-fifty trail bike?'

She gave me a look that I took to mean, 'No, not really, but let's have a crack at it anyway,' and we headed out onto the highway, destination: the end of the world.

Seventeen

The prophets of doom were thundering northwards on their iron horses. Every one had a tale to tell, each more gruesome than the last. Stories of sheer human bravery, of men pitting themselves against the odds, dicing with death, or at least falling off their bikes a lot. Ruta 40 folklore abounded and the motorcyclists who had survived this fearful highway were only too happy to share their sagas, and send fear into the hearts of two hapless southbound girls. Motorcycles and their riders blown clean off the road, engines smashed to pieces, hundreds of miles with no gas stations, legs broken by flying rocks . . . They looked at our bikes and shook their heads. 'Lambs to the slaughter,' they said, 'you'll never make it on that.' They shook their heads some more, inhaling slowly with their hands on their hips, like a cowboy builder sizing up a job. And they all had the same look in their eyes, the Ruta 40 look, as if life would never be quite the same again.

'Oh, you know what it's like, people always exaggerate these things,' I assured Rachel, who was becoming less keen on our proposed route every day.

'Yes, I suppose so, they're probably just showing off.'

'Yeah, I used to listen to every story about "the road ahead" from people I met and get all worked up about things, and then, of course, you go there and it's fine—nothing to it. Anyway, it's too late now, we've got the Carretera Austral next and then Ruta 40 after that—those two roads are the only route to Ushuaia from here.'

We had just arrived on the Isle de Chiloe, a geographical anomaly in this part of South America. Where all around us the land was becoming harsher and rockier, and the weather colder and wetter, here was a warm, pretty island tacked onto the Chilean coast with a climate and scenery to suggest a chunk of northern France had floated away and somehow become lodged in the southern Pacific. The island was ablaze with flowering yellow gorse bushes, and its long straight roads ran through undulating farmland, so familiar to me that I almost expected to see Jacques Tâti careering along in front of us on his bicycle. A weather-bleached sign pointed us down a lane to a tumble-down, timber boardinghouse on the beach. Its proprietor, a lanky Irishman with the milky eyes and gentle sway of a dedicated drinker, welcomed us in with a lilting repetitious monologue, peppered with meaningless cryptic comments about himself. 'Aah, well, ladies, when you've been around like I have . . . Oh yes, you'll find out about me soon enough. . . .' he kept saying, in what he hoped was an enigmatic way, as we nodded along in time to his blathering. Fortunately, a pair of fellow guests rescued us with a homely greeting.

'Oh hello! We're from Tunbridge Wells, where are you from?'

'Aah, it's my newlyweds . . . on their honeymoon in *my* hotel,' said our landlord dreamily, before launching into a rambling story about his own honeymoon, back in the sixties.

If he hadn't revealed this nugget of info about the Tunbridge Wellians, I would have been certain that the absurdly camp male member of the couple was of the other persuasion, especially once the landlord got going on the subject of his vocation back in England. He'd spent his working life in the hotel trade and it didn't take much encouragement from me to get all the juicy details from the world of Travelodge *et al,* delivered in the style of John Inman.

'Dahling!' he gasped, leaning towards me across the communal kitchen table. 'The things I could tell you! I mean, the state people leave the bedrooms in! They're animals! We are burning sheets on a daily basis!'

'Really?' I said. 'Burning them?'

'Oh God, yes, they're beyond washing! I mean, there's only so much you can do, you know, once someone's . . . well . . .' he glanced around the room, found it empty, but still lowered his voice to a stagey whisper '. . . *defecated* on them. And blood is terribly stubborn as well, of course. Oh yes, we lose sheets all the time, we're sending hundreds, literally *hundreds*,' he screeched in excitement, 'to the laundry every day! And the laundry people steal them too.'

'Surely not,' I protested.

'Dahling,' he said firmly, fixing a beady stare on me, 'have you ever *been* to an industrial laundry?'

I had to admit a distinct lack of experience in this area and he raised his eyebrows knowingly.

'Well, let me tell you, one has to factor in a certain amount of wastage when it comes to the bed linens and of course everyone steals the bathrobes. The big corporate parties are the worst! We had a leading telecommunications company hold their staff party with us once. Never again, I tell you, never again!'

'Which company was it?' I asked, intrigued.

He looked at me, affronted.

'I'm sorry, I couldn't possibly divulge,' he said, deadly serious, as if I were about to wire the information straight to *The Sun*'s news desk.

'But there was one guest at the party, a salesman,' he spat out the word, 'we had to burn his entire bed. And when I tried to charge him for it, he threatened me! Said he was going to break my effing legs! I told him: Sir! You pay for the damage and it'll be our little se-cret. If you want to make a fuss I will charge it to the company and I'll be telling your line manager exactly why your room needs a new bed.'

'What had he done?'

'Oh, the usual. Defecation. All over the place, worst I've ever seen.' He winced theatrically at the memory. 'I said to him, You'd better pay up, or that bed will be coming straight out of your Christmas bonus, young man! Now, you don't want to work around the airports,' he continued without pausing for breath, 'and especially not the Gatwick hotels, full of Arabs and prostitutes, good tippers, though, the Arabs. Always carry a bag for an Arab or an American, the bloody Brits can carry their own bags, filthy tippers, simply dreadful! Oh, and then there was the awful woman who arrived with a bottle of bleach, bleached her entire room before she'd stay in it. Can you imagine how long it took to get rid of the smell?'

Maybe these tales evoked a bizarre nostalgia in me for a tawdry 'Carry On' brand of Englishness, but I could have listened to him for days, and it made a welcome change from the bravado-fuelled horror stories of the Ruta 40 riders. But as ever, the time came to move on and we bid farewell to the Tunbridge Wells hotelier, and boarded a ferry to the town of Chaitén on the mainland, and the start of the Carretera Austral.

In contrast to the staggering vista of mountains and fjords that greeted us on the mainland, Chaitén was truly the ugliest town I have ever seen. Laid out in a grid of unpaved streets with rows of low breeze-block housing, it was like having the run of our very own concentration camp. The boarded-up shops and a permanently closed tourist office gave the place a ghost town feel and the steady drizzle didn't do much to lift the feel-bad factor. Everything in Chaitén was grey. But just a glance upwards at the surrounding natural beauty promised a ride of Rocky Mountain–like splendour ahead.

At the first glimpse of blue sky, we sped out of town and a few miles down the road came across an elaborate monument to General Pinochet, the man behind the Carretera Austral. In a fit of paranoia about an Argentine invasion back in 1976, he had spent the next twenty years constructing the highway at enormous cost and with the loss of many lives. But in keeping with the general's well-documented disregard for the common man, the deceased ditchdiggers didn't get a mention on his monument.

'Pinochet might have his faults, but this road was one of his better ideas,' I had to admit grudgingly to Rachel as we wended our way past glaciers hanging hundreds of feet above us, waterfalls pouring down the mountains into ice blue lakes, and a continuous linear flower display, thanks to nature's roadside bouquet of daisies and pink and purple foxgloves. It was easy to see why this route had proved such a challenge to the Chilean dictator's road gangs: the terrain, varying from marshes and dense forest to jagged peaks and deep rocky rivers, was inhospitable at best, and truly impenetrable at its most severe. But with the project running way over budget, the general must have balked when the tarmac quote came in and decided to leave the road in its natural state of mud, stone and gravel. Maybe 'surface Carretera Austral' remained on his to-do list, right after 'dispose of dissenting citizens (ongoing)' and 'write thank-you card to Mrs. Thatcher,' but I hoped not. Its lack of asphalt seemed fitting in this wild country on the edge of the world and it lent the *carretera* an untamed, frontier feel reminiscent of the AlCan Highway that had launched my adventure eight months and sixteen thousand miles ago.

Perhaps it was this sense of familiarity, or that the end of my journey was in sight, or maybe I was simply enjoying myself, but despite Rachel and me deciding to tackle this road at a sensible speed, I couldn't resist the urge to go a bit faster. Not much faster—after all, my bike only did fifty-five miles an hour tops, but that felt fine, and this section was flat gravel, nothing too demanding. I opened up the throttle and looked over my shoulder, checking that Rachel was still behind me, but my view was obscured by the billow of grey dust rising in my wake. I squinted, thinking I could see the glimmer of her yellow headlight through the cloud. Craning my head round further, still unsure, I tried to make out some detail in the haze.

Just a split second too long. My front wheel hit a patch of deep gravel and the steering went wild. The inevitability of the moment hit me: Oh my God, this is it; I'm out of control! Too fast, too fast, you idiot! Too late to save it. The back wheel lost traction and my bike flipped over, hurling me hard onto the stony ground.

I lay there, dazed. Then Rachel's face floated into view through the dust cloud.

'Stay still,' she was saying, and slowly my brain registered what had happened. The bike was a few feet away on its side and my luggage lay strewn across the road. I'd landed with my right leg twisted at an angle and it hurt like hell. In a moment of heart-sinking horror, I wondered if I'd broken it. There was only one way to find out. Ignoring Rachel's instructions, I crawled to my feet and staggered around like a drunkard, clutching my right knee, but experiencing nothing more serious than a brief bout of Tourette's syndrome. I had been lucky, and I thanked the God of Motorcycling for my good fortune this time.

'Do you know how it happened?' asked Rachel. 'I couldn't see you through the dust, then suddenly your normal cloud of dust turned into a massive one, and I thought, oh dear!'

I couldn't help but laugh at this description and I looked at the deep gouge my skidding tires had left in the gravel.

'Guess I'd better keep my eyes on the road,' I said, 'and slow down a bit from now on.'

Recognising the aftermath of an accident, a couple of passing cars had stopped to help and I before I knew what was happening, I was being pleasantly mollycoddled by a jolly Brazilian woman and her family, who wiggled my limbs and inspected my grazes with an interested air. Next a middle-aged Chilean man pulled over and insisted I eat his pack lunch.

'May I take a photo please of you please?' he asked, as I tucked into the contents of his Tupperware. 'My wife will never believe me when I tell her!' And he snapped away as I sat covered in dust beside my fallen bike, chewing away and giving a thumbs-up to his wife for the cheese sandwiches.

A brief inspection revealed I had come off better than my now bent and broken luggage, and we set about collecting the detritus. The damage was nothing a few cable ties and gaffer tape couldn't cure. I'd been carrying them around for the last eight months for an occasion such as this, so there was a certain satisfaction in finally putting them to good use. We righted the bike, bungeed on the bags as best we could, and although the aches and pains were beginning to set in now, there was nothing else to do but get going again. I hadn't given much thought to the bike until now, but true to form, the Serow had survived the tumble unscathed and started right back up again as if nothing had happened.

It was with a little more caution, plus a few bruises, that I set off the following morning. The next few days turned trickier every mile with slippery, muddy hairpins taking us over the giant mountains before we descended upon a magnificent turquoise slab of water, the Lago General Carrera. Although easy on the eye, the lake was unfortunately skirted by a track of ever-deeper gravel and loose rocks, which ensured our sights were set firmly on the road and saw us moving at a painfully slow speed towards the Argentine border, aware that another six hundred miles of similar if not harsher conditions lay ahead down Ruta 40, if the rumours were to be believed.

A wooden hut and a barrier across a dirt road marked our departure from Chile. A few miles of barren no-man's land, as bleak and undesirable as a toxic waste site, lay ahead, before the cluster of buildings marking the beginning of Argentina came into view. The sky was grey and heavy, threatening a typically rainy Patagonian morning, but the team spirit rocketed sky high inside the immigration office thanks to an Argentine Marlboro Man stamping passports, whose rugged countenance, complete with twinkly blue eyes and stubbly square jaw, reminded us that there were other things to think about in life than crap road surfaces and leaky waterproof trousers. We sighed in unison.

'Next best thing—let's get something to eat,' suggested Rachel.

There was never any danger of going hungry with Rachel

around. I recalled her need to eat every few hours from our journey through Mexico, and marvelled at how she somehow managed to stay skinny despite a rampant addiction to chocolate and bread. Maybe it was the hard riding and the colder climate, but her appetite seemed keener than ever, so we set off in search of sustenance. The nearby town of Perito Moreno looked like our best bet, where we would pick up Ruta 40 and our Patagonian adventure would begin in earnest. But after riding around the town's desolate streets, peering through grimy café windows into dust-caked darkness and hopelessly rattling doors bearing faded *cerrado* signs, it was looking as if we would have to set off on empty stomachs.

Perito Moreno was how I imagined Russia. The shops were bare, the streets were windswept and empty, the grey concrete buildings were crumbling and not a single gas station had a bottle of engine oil on the shelves. With my bike's oil consumption almost equalling Rachel's caloric burn, this was a major cause for concern, considering the desolate route we were about to embark upon. Rachel was fretting in a similar fashion about the lack of food, and in desperation we turned to that bastion of civilisation and font of all knowledge, the post office.

The lady behind the counter greeted us warmly, even though we didn't want to buy any stamps.

'Is there a restaurant in town?' Rachel asked, just about keeping the urgency out of her voice.

'Yes, just one now, the pizzeria.' She gave us directions. 'It is the only one left, things are very bad now, you understand, because of the financial situation, it used to be one peso to the dollar, now it is five.'

I remembered seeing news of this economic crisis before I left England; lines of Argentines trying to get their money out of the banks, riots in Buenos Aires and stories of both the rich and poor losing all their money in a matter of days.

'It is very bad, people are very angry,' she continued, making the most of her sympathetic audience. 'The young people want to leave and go to Europe, the old people have no savings anymore, old women are working as prostitutes just to survive, it feels like wartime, but without the fighting.'

We commiserated as best we could, bought some stamps anyway and went in search of food.

'Well, that explains the lack of oil and the empty shelves, I guess,' I said to Rachel as we pushed open the door of the deserted pizza restaurant.

Inside we took a seat, examined the menu, examined the map, clocked the lack of civilisation for the next few hundred miles and ordered accordingly. There was a distinct Last Supper feeling to our extra-large margherita with extra cheese plus extra garlic bread, but there was only so much carbohydrate we could pack in and only so much procrastination we could eke out, and faced with the option of living out our days in Perito Moreno, it was Ushuaia or bust.

As our bald tires crunched onto Ruta 40, a lone armadillo appeared out of nowhere and scuttled across our path. I optimistically imagined this to be some sort of good luck symbol. It never occurred to me that it could be just the opposite. Armadillo—the creature of doom! We emerged from behind the shelter of the last hill we would see for a while and sure enough, a furious side wind immediately slammed into us, sending me flying across the road. Rachel fared a little better with her bike's lower centre of gravity but we both gasped in shock at the sheer force, and the terrible realisation—It's all true!

We fought our way onwards, struggling against the elements, using every ounce of physical strength in our upper bodies just to keep moving in a forwardly direction. It would have been bad enough on a sealed road, but on this potholed, rutted, gravel hell that stretched out in front of us, it was almost impossible to keep moving in a straight line. With the bikes leaning at a forty-five-degree angle and the engines screaming at full revs in second, we pushed on, every muscle straining; it was the only way to achieve a grip on the road.

'Oh my God!' we shouted at each other in utter disbelief. 'This is insane!'

But we could barely hear our cries over the wail of the wind.

Normally a keen map checker, I couldn't bring myself to chart our wretched progress. There was no way we would cover this section at our normal pace, but with pockets of civilisation spread few and far between, we had to keep pressing on towards the tiny black dots on the map each night—they were our only hope for food, fuel and water. Despite my long hot haul across the Atacama Desert and the desolation of the cold Andean roads, nothing had prepared me for this. Brown, pancake-flat scrubland surrounded us like an endless sea. There was not a thing on the horizon, not a hill, not a tree, just empty windswept plains and this godforsaken road cutting across it, disappearing into the distance forever. The only changeable feature in the scene was the candy-floss clouds that drifted across the giant sky like cartoon thought bubbles. My goal had been in sight a few days ago; now it felt as distant and unobtainable as the day I had first set foot in Alaska.

A black dot on the map marked Bajo Caracoles became our target for the first day, but far from being the village we were expecting, it turned out to be nothing more than a large building by the side of the road. However, it covered the basic needs of the Patagonian traveller—beds, gas, food, booze and, much to my relief, an under-the-counter supply of 10W-40. Like a Wild West outpost, the bar was full of raucous, weather-beaten men, drinking, smoking, shuffling cards and tumbling dice. I wondered where they had all come from, but I didn't want to ask. Our arrival had the typical *American Werewolf in London* effect and the room remained silent as we placed our order, broken only by a comment from the bartender that neither of us understood, but that provoked a round of Sid James–style laughter from the locals. We scuttled off to our room for an early night.

'Let's get going first thing tomorrow,' I suggested, 'the winds are worse in the afternoon.'

But at 7 A.M. they were already blowing a gale across the plains, and I dreaded to think how they would pick up in a few hours' time. We exchanged looks of dread and eased our aching bones into the saddle to do battle with Ruta 40 once again. But the winds were worse than the day before, and without warning a violent gust would regularly whisk my bike round by ninety degrees, sending me careering across the road, sliding and skidding in the gravel, banging through potholes and eventually off the road altogether. I soon devised a method to deal with these incidents by simply steering the bike in the direction the wind forced me, sending me plummeting down a steep bank or flying for yards across the scrubby plain until I could come to a controlled stop.

This survival method worked well enough until such an occasion coincided with Rachel overtaking me on my left. As a furious squall rushed in from the west, spinning my bike around, the front wheel drove slap-bang into her back wheel. I crashed. She looked around to see what had happened. She crashed. It was a comical sight: the two of us sprawled on the floor next to our supine motorcycles.

'Are you OK?' I yelled, crawling across the gravel towards her.

She called something back at me but the sound of the wind rendered our voices inaudible. We dragged ourselves towards each other on all fours, still shouting silently into the wind, and set about picking up the bikes. With them and us upright once again, we attempted to decant the contents of my jerry can into our tanks, but to no avail. The wind sprayed the gas into our faces, onto our clothes and all over the bikes. And then once more, straight off the Pacific Ocean, a howling beast of a gust slammed Rachel's bike to the dirt, the filler cap still open, precious gas disappearing into the dry earth. Gasping for breath, exhausted and aching, we lifted her bike from the ground for the second time and, sure enough, another vicious blast screamed across the plains, this time sending Rachel herself flying to the ground.

'WE'VE GOT SIX HUNDRED FUCKING MILES OF THIS!' we shouted at each other above the roaring in our ears, laughing with adrenaline-fuelled hysteria.

There was nothing else for it but to continue. Civilisation as we knew it was a long way down the road and the Patagonian land-scape remained as empty and bleak as I could imagine. The little black dots on the map became sources of fantasies but our hopes were regularly dashed when they turned out to be nonexistent or, at best, a house. Meanwhile, back on the road, the westerlies blew ever harder, the gravel piled up deeper, I was going through a litre of oil a day and ostriches were outnumbering vehicles by a ratio of fifty to one. I had never felt so aware of being in the middle of a lonely and hostile land on the edge of the world.

'Never again will I refer to the suburbs of London as being in the middle of nowhere,' I vowed to Rachel solemnly that night.

It was difficult to drum up the enthusiasm each morning. Just the thought of setting off for yet another gruelling day filled us with doom. We were now thoroughly exhausted by the relentless, slow slog and our aching, bruised bodies cried out for respite. Thankfully, at the end of a particularly punishing ride, a black dot came up trumps. Tres Lagos was a real place. This meant it had a street with more than two houses on it and its very own signpost on the highway. This was a big deal. There was even a shop, although the stock had dwindled to just a few cans of tuna and a pile of sticky cartons of Chocomilk bearing a sell-by date that evoked memories of miners' strikes and Duran Duran riding high in the charts. The man behind the counter wasn't in the business of deliv-ering good news either.

'The hotel and the restaurant closed a week ago,' he said in a matter-of-fact way.

Rachel and I exchanged our now familiar look of misery. I tried to find something positive in the idea of sitting in a tent, drinking rancid chocolate milk with a hundred-mile-an-hour gale blowing outside. But I failed. Out in the street, the light was fading fast and we began making plans to find shelter behind a building for the night. But in the house opposite a curtain was twitching and just as we were about to stake out our campsite, an elderly woman stuck her head out the door.

'Chicas?' she asked. 'Dos chicas?'

We confirmed that yes indeed, despite our unladylike form of transport, our filthy attire and distinct lack of makeup or handbags at this precise moment, we were indeed two living, breathing, real-life girls. She ventured down her garden path and inspected us a little closer, just to make sure. Once she'd got a convincing whiff of our sugar, spice and all things not very nice, she ushered us into her house, plumped up the pillows in the spare room, handed us a pile of towels and told us to get busy in the shower. She shared her tiny neat house with her daughter and grandchildren, who bombarded us with cups of coffee and a barrage of the usual questions.

'Where have you come from on your motorcycles?' enquired the grandmother.

'Well, Lois has actually come from Alaska,' said Rachel.

The old woman smiled and nodded absently.

'But we have just come down from Santiago, Chile,' continued Rachel.

Our hostess's mouth dropped open and she laid her knitting down on her lap.

'SANTIAGO! *Oh, Dios mio!*' she cried in shock. 'They have come all the way from Santiago, from SANTIAGO, CHILE!' she called out to her daughter in the kitchen, who rushed in, mouth agape at this revelation.

In the morning, an inspection of my bike revealed various missing nuts and bolts and an ominous dark patch on the ground where the rear brake fluid had leaked out from a damaged hose. The day continued in the manner to which we were now only too accustomed, although this time with the added fun of no rear brake and a nagging jangling noise. But by late afternoon we were rewarded for our toils by a welcome change in the landscape. In the distance we could see mountains sweeping upwards in surreal shades of pink and purple, and in their foothills lay sapphire lakes, calm and protected from the wind, and we knew that the worst was over.

We caught our breath in the resort town of El Calafate, where we patched up the bikes and relished every convenience and luxury item we could lay our hands on. A day later, recovered and ready for the last five hundred miles, we were heading off again into more wind, and now rain, but thankfully on glorious tarmac towards Tierra del Fuego, the island at the tip of South America with Ushuaia at its southernmost point. A half-hour ferry ride carried us across the Strait of Magellan to the island and I hung over the railing, gazing into the choppy waters, and thought about Sir Francis Drake negotiating this passage in a wild storm nearly five hundred years before. It was a humbling thought. What would he have made of this silly adventure of mine? I wondered. Maybe there was no true adventure left to be had in this shrinking global village of ours, and I longed to have been born into a time when great swathes of the earth were still wild, mysterious and unexplored, when parchment maps still warned 'Here be dragons' on the edges of uncharted territory. Adventure is just a personal thing, I decided, it means whatever you want it to. To me it just means having a go at something that might be exciting or difficult, just to see if I can. And at this moment, with a timing normally reserved for feature films, the sun came out and a school of dolphins leapt out of the water alongside the boat, flipping their tails, arcing and spinning in the air before disappearing back into the sea. I'm on my way to Tierra del Fuego, I thought jubilantly, me and my motorcycle, all the way from Alaska! I don't know about you, Sir Francis, but I think that's pretty darn exciting!

. . .

Nearly there! The end of the world is in sight.

The route to Ushuaia was dirt all the way, and the dustiest road I have ever ridden. Trucks and cars roared past us at impossible speeds, leaving a dense, gritty fog in their wake, so thick that we often had to stop and wait for it to settle. It seemed as though everyone was desperate to get to *el fin del mundo*. The green signs kept tempting us onwards: USHUAIA and an arrow pointing ever southwards, taking us through a suitably dramatic landscape of huge snowcapped mountains under a bright blue cloudless sky.

And finally there it was, the sign that I had come all this way for: BIENVENIDOS A LA CIUDAD MÁS AUSTRAL DEL MUNDO, and underneath, for those who hadn't managed to grasp the local lingo yet,

WELCOME TO THE SOUTHERNMOST CITY IN THE WORLD. I stopped and savoured the words.

This was it, I had made it. Eight and a half months, 16,798 miles. And at this moment, with a timing normally reserved for TV sitcoms, a pack of slavering, barking feral dogs appeared from nowhere and chased us down the road to the end of the world.

Eighteen

Maybe Robert Louis Stevenson had just rolled into Ushuaia when he decided 'It is better to travel hopefully than to arrive.' This town was the living embodiment of his famous maxim, but then what else could it have turned out to be? To rise to the status I had afforded it over the last year the streets would have had to be paved with gold and teeming with Robert Redford look-alikes pouring giant magnums of pink champagne into my open mouth as I whizzed past on my triumphant lap of the town square. Rachel and I settled for a beer and a pizza, and a high-spirited toast to Anglo-Saxon motorcycling tomfoolery.

'So, we'll be heading north for the first time,' said Rachel the next morning.

'Yeah, it's about two thousand miles up the east coast to Buenos Aires.' Strangely, this didn't seem like much of a big deal to either of us. 'I'd like to hang out there for a week or so before I fly home.'

'Me too. I don't even know if I do want to go home,' said Rachel. 'I might stick around and carry on up into Brazil, but I will need to go back soon and earn some more money.'

'Have you heard anything from Simon?' I asked.

'Er, yes, I got an e-mail from him last night, actually,' she said nonchalantly. 'He's heading for Buenos Aires too.'

'What did I tell you?' I said, and she allowed herself a small hint of a smile.

Argentina was enormous and those two thousand miles passed slowly. Long windswept days rolled out across the pampas, although this time the winds were battering our left side, and thankfully the main highway to the capital was sealed all the way. Long-limbed gauchos astride sleek horses cantered alongside the road, hailing us with a comradely wave like fellow motorcyclists, before galloping off into the distance across the grassy plains. Spurs, tack, rifles and animal skins adorned the walls of every roadside diner, further fuelling the romantic image of Argentina's famous horsemen.

All eyes were on Buenos Aires now and every night we planned and plotted the rampant gratification of our long-repressed urban desires. Shopping, manicures, pedicures, massages, spas, fancy restaurants; the list was exotic, endless and unaffordable, but it provided a goal that even Rachel was happy to sign up for. Maybe it was this lure of cosmopolitan life, but we were definitely slacking off, and the two-week ride to Buenos Aires turned into a catalogue of mishaps, as if every aspect of long-distance motorcycle travel was packed into one final, fraught fortnight. Chains snapped, brakes seized, oil leaked, batteries went flat, we ran out of gas (the one and only time), we slept by the side of the road and made bodged repairs that we knew would never last. Our tightly run ship had mutinied, but we didn't care. We were well and truly on the home run. And the nearer we got to the capital, the more enamoured I became of the final country on my list. Argentina was a credit to cross-pollination, where all the charms of South America and Europe had been blended, bred and rolled into one over the centuries. It was lively yet louche, the epitome of chic, but with a wild cowboy streak running through its core. And Buenos Aires was the living explosion of this rich mixture, as if Doisneau's Paris and Dodge City had been thrown together on the shores of the southern Atlantic. The city buzzed with action, impulsiveness and a tangible lust for life, helped along by the fact that everyone, male and female, was unnervingly elegant, beautiful and immaculately turned out. Then we showed up.

And a few days later, Simon showed up too. The three of us rented an apartment together and it was warming to see Rachel's increased perkiness and Simon's relief at having found an excuse to take a break from his wanderings. We entered into long discussions about travel, mainly musing on the motives behind it.

'What I've really relished is the total freedom, and the chance to just be myself all the time,' I was explaining to Simon one day, 'no one to say you're wrong, no one to tell you what to do, just an opportunity to do exactly what you want for a short period of your life. That doesn't happen very often.'

'It's funny,' he said in his thoughtful way, 'you've just listed all the things I've become utterly sick of. But I don't know what to do next, I've only got Russia and Africa left and I don't really fancy Africa.' He looked weary and downcast at the prospect of another continent.

He had been on the road for three years, and with an income from a rental property in London there was simply no real reason for him to stop travelling. As a former teacher with a Ph.D, but no professional ambition that burned brightly enough to drag him away from life on the road, he continued his journey around the world, but without any sense of real purpose.

'Sometimes you need constraints, otherwise it stops being fun.'

I could see his point. I'd had an amazing time, but I was out of cash and ready to go home. And besides, I had my own glowing embers of a grand affair that needed fanning back into life.

Our daily round of philosophising, shopping, eating and drinking was soon superseded by admin once again, and I left Rachel and Simon happily cocooned in the apartment while I ran around organising the shipping of my bike back to England. There was probably a rational argument for not bothering, but I was rather attached to the old thing now. It had served me well, considering what I'd put it through, and with a top-end rebuild and a bit of a scrub it would be back to its old tricks. I set off for my last ride on South American soil under a typically blazing midday sun, filtering through the nineteen-lane mayhem of Buenos Aires' main drag, the Avenida 9 de Julio, past grand theatres and neatly manicured parks, then east into the narrow, choked-up streets towards the port, where the glamour of the old city faded away into crumbling tower blocks and the sooty, oily grind of industry. There was a certain poignancy about rolling into the docks and leaving the Serow on the quayside, facing out to sea. It was the end. This time we weren't going to be reunited in another strange and exotic land to continue our adventures, this time we were going home, and as much as we were both ready for it, even needed it, the finality of the occasion was still tinged with a strange sadness, a nostalgia for good times gone.

Back in town I boosted my spirits by booking my flight home and phoning in my arrival time to the keeper of my glowing embers back home. When Austin picked up the phone, I felt the old familiar butterflies in my stomach. Just the sound of his voice crackling across the Atlantic sent me reeling into heart-thumping reverie and we squealed excitedly down the line at each other about our impending reunion.

The day finally rolled around, and feeling like an impostor in my new clothes, with freshly cut and dyed hair and my cleanest fingernails for nine and a half months, I hailed a cab to Buenos Aires' Ezeiza International Airport. Rachel came to see me off. We ordered some lunch and I watched the departure screen with a twitchy anticipation.

'I've got some news,' said Rachel, as she tucked ever heartily into the bread basket.

I hadn't seen much of her and Simon over the last few days, what with sorting out the bike shipment and a few last-minute shopping sprees, so I assumed they'd decided to head off together into Brazil, or ship their bikes to Russia or something.

'Oh yeah?'

'Er . . . I'm pregnant,' said Rachel.

I gaped at her.

'What!'

'Yes, I'm four months pregnant.' She smiled shyly.

'What! Four months? How! I mean, oh my God! Congratulations!' I yelped in a state of confusion, disbelief and amazement. 'I don't understand!' I spluttered.

'Well no, I was a bit surprised myself, but I've worked it out,' she said. 'It must have been when Simon and I were in Central America; I think it probably happened in Nicaragua. I'm still in shock, really,' she added with a grin.

'But how come you didn't know?'

'I haven't got a clue, everything just carried on as normal, y'know.'

I'd heard about such incidents, but they usually featured in *The National Enquirer*—'*I thought I had indigestion, then I gave birth in Wal-Mart!' says shocked new mom.* I never thought it happened in real life.

'And what about Simon?'

'He's really happy,' said Rachel, 'he was looking for an excuse to stop travelling, so I guess this is the perfect reason.'

'Great, I'm really pleased. So what are you going to do now?'

'We don't know, it's all such a shock. We'll probably go back to France or London, we haven't decided yet.'

'Hang on a minute,' I said as a realisation dawned on me, 'if you're four months gone, then you were pregnant all that time in Patagonia, when we were getting blown off the bikes and crashing in the gravel and all that!'

'I know! I know! God, I hope it's OK.'

'It'll be fine! What a great start to life, you're going to have yourself a proper little adventurer on your hands.'

Rachel laughed, but also looked a bit worried at this prediction.

'Aah, so that's why you've been eating so much!' I deduced.

'No change there,' she said, finishing off the last bread roll.

I checked the list of departures on the screen above us. My flight was boarding.

'I'd better get going,' I said.

We walked towards the gate together.

'Thanks for being a great travelling companion,' I said to her, and I meant it with all my heart. One thing I had discovered was that this was not such a common species.

'Same to you,' she said, and we hugged each other good-bye.

'Congratulations!' I shouted out after her.

Inside the gate I flashed my passport and boarding pass at a glamorous Iberian Airlines stewardess.

'There is a small problem with the seating,' she said in a thick Spanish accent, 'we are upgrading you to business class.'

'No way!' I yelped with delight. 'That's never happened to me before!'

What a day this was turning out to be! Flying home from my grand adventure to be reunited with the man of my dreams, then Rachel's news, and now my elevation to the world of luxury air travel!

I relaxed into my giant comfy seat, wiggled my feet around the infinite abyss of leg room, sifted through my selection of international newspapers and downed my complimentary glass of champagne. With a fifteen-hour flight ahead of me, and little interest in watching *Love Actually* (there were some appealing aspects about going back to England but Hugh Grant wasn't one of them) I reran the last ten months in my head, from the moment I'd left Anchorage on that cold winter morning at the Eagle River Motel, and all the miles I'd covered to get here, Argentina. It seemed too much to take in—a jumble of colour and images; it would take a while for it to settle into place. But there was one factor that had remained clear throughout—my chosen mode of transport. As I had expected, the motorcycle had proved itself to be the finest way to travel. While other travellers had whizzed past me in a bus on a rainy day, not once had I wished to change places with them. On the bike, I was always in the thick of it: smelling and tasting the air, feeling the sun and wind against my skin—and yes, the freezing cold and rain too—but them's the breaks. Of course, this was nothing new to me; it was the same anywhere in the world. But what I hadn't bargained for was how the motorcycle encouraged friendliness, curiosity from strangers that would inevitably turn into something more—an offer of hospitality, practical assistance or just some words of encouragement when I needed them most. 'You'll never want to sit on a bike again when you get back,' a few people had said before I left, and I had wondered if it might be the case. But now, sitting here on my way home, with nearly twenty thousand miles under my belt, I was thoroughly delighted to find that nothing was farther from the truth. My journey hadn't so much cured an itch, as given me an incurable disease.

Restless, I flicked through the in-flight magazine, staring absent-mindedly at a confusing map of Madrid Airport, then an article about Spanish hotels until I realised it was a thinly disguised advert. Finally I settled on an interview with some actor I'd never heard of.

'What is your favourite place?' asked the interviewer, no doubt hoping that the answer to this startlingly lame question would be an Iberian Airlines destination.

'That depends. To me, places are people,' was the actor's reply.

Yeah! I thought, y'know what, he's right! I'd been to some incredible places along my journey, and there was no denying I'd witnessed some amazing sights and had all sorts of great adventures. But more than the countries and the towns and the scenery of the last ten months, it was the people that had brought my trip to life. Some of them had passed in and out with just a wave or a kind word, with some I'd formed a lasting bond and some of them had driven me crazy! But my journey had been a whole lot richer for all of them.

The sweet clinking sound of the drinks trolley snapped me out of my contemplation.

'Here is your menu, senorita,' said the stewardess, 'would you like an aperitif?'

The trolley glittered with every variety of exotic booze you could think of. I ordered the most lurid-coloured drink I'd never heard of and perused a menu that wouldn't have looked out of place in the Savoy, thoroughly enjoying every moment of this unlikely finale to my journey. I had no idea what the future held, not tomorrow, or the next day or the next year. But I decided that my surprise upgrade was an omen for whatever lay ahead: it meant things were going to work out just fine. No, not just fine—better than ever. I was homeward bound, travelling hopefully as ever, but on this occasion I reckoned I might just prove Robert Louis Stevenson wrong.